The Notary's
3rd Edi

A guide for public notaries

Sanjay Prem Gogia LL.M.
Notary Public (England & Wales)
Former Lecturer, University of Turin, Italy (International Trade Law)
Former Tutor, University of Cambridge (Notarial Practice) and
Notarial Practice Tutor, University College London

With a foreword by

Mr. Charles George QC
Master of the Faculties

Published by Notary Training

**FOR MY FAMILY, PARTNERS,
FRIENDS, MENTORS & COLLEAGUES**

"Integrity is choosing what is right over what is convenient"

Sanjay Prem Gogia

FOREWORD

Amongst the regulatory objectives under the Legal Services Act 2007 are "protecting the public interest", "protecting and promoting the interests of consumers" and "promoting and maintaining adherence to the professional principles"; these principles include acting with independence and integrity and maintaining proper standards of work.

This edition draws attention not merely to the various statutory rules under which public notaries must order their practices, including the Code of Practice (soon to be updated), but also goes beyond this to offer advice on various practical aspects of notarial work, based on the author's now considerable professional and teaching experience. It is good also to have coverage of less familiar topics such as Remote Notarisation (chapter 11), and run off-insurance (chapter 10), and mention of the new Office for Professional Body Anti-Money Laundering Supervision (chapter 1).

It is a pleasure to commend this third edition of *The Notary's Manual*, which is a short, clear and up to date guide for public notaries and those aspiring to be admitted as such, and will help to ensure that notarial practice furthers the statutory objectives set out above.

I understand that the book is not intended for sale but for distribution to those seeking to qualify for admission as public notaries. Although the book is published by Notary Training, which also runs courses for notaries, this Foreword should not be interpreted as specific endorsement of its activities, as opposed to those of other providers.

CHARLES GEORGE QC
Master of the Faculties,
Francis Taylor Building,
Inner Temple,
London EC4Y 7BY

7 August 2018

© Sanjay Prem Gogia

Third Edition August 2018

Notary Training
www.notarytraining.co.uk

ISBN: 978-1-910693-67-4

Printed in Great Britain by Print2Demand

CONTENTS

Most Important Rules and Regulations made by the Court of Faculties

Legislation Relevant to Notaries

BIOGRAPHICAL NOTE

Sanjay pursued a bachelor's degree in Law from Government Law College, Bombay and master's degree in Law from the University of Bombay and is admitted as an Advocate at the Bar Council of Delhi in India. He has worked with Dua Associates in their New Delhi office in the areas of business & commercial laws with an emphasis on advising foreign companies to establish a presence in India. Sanjay came to England to study law at the College of Law as a recipient of the British Chevening Scholarship, followed by qualifying as a Solicitor at Allen & Overy, London. Sanjay was a founding member of the India Group at Allen & Overy and was also instrumental in forming the British – Indian Lawyers Association under the flagship of The Law Society. He was admitted as a Solicitor of the Supreme Court of England and Wales in 1998. Sanjay qualified as a Notary Public in 2004 after successfully completing his Notarial Studies at the University of Cambridge. Prior to qualifying as a Notary Public Sanjay has also worked with Eversheds. He was leading the "India Desk" at Eversheds. Sanjay is also registered as an Indian Lawyer with the legal and judicial authorities in Monaco. He was admitted as a Solicitor of Republic of Ireland in April 2010.

As a Notary Public Sanjay is involved in drawing, attesting, certifying and authenticating various kinds of deeds and documents including wills, commercial and intellectual property agreements, change of name certificates, statutory declarations and powers of attorney used in India and other parts of the world. He certifies documents for use in all jurisdictions and invariably advises clients on the wording and form of the document itself. He specialises in the preparation of notarial documents used in India and Indian consular offices in the UK. Sanjay is a former member of the "Notarial Qualification Board" and "Notarial Advisory Board" of the Faculty Office of the Archbishop of Canterbury which deals with regulation of notaries in England & Wales.

Sanjay is a former tutor at the Post Graduate course in Notarial Practice, University of Cambridge and a former lecturer to the University of Turin, Italy at LL.M in International Trade Law. He has been a tutor in notarial practice at the University College London since September 2013. He is one of the founding members and partner of Notary Training. Sanjay has lectured extensively on notarial issues and have also authored numerous articles published by the Notaries Society of England and Wales.

PREFACE & ACKNOWLEDGEMENTS

Every notary is required to be professional. Notaries are usually held in high accountability and are relied upon by the public because of the high degree of responsibility which they exercise. For this reason, among others, each notary public needs a reliable manual at hand which he or she may turn for answers to the questions, problems and dilemma which from time to time present themselves. With such a need in mind it was the publisher's goal to prepare at best the various practice rules, relevant legislation and the code of practice.

The text covers various topics which a Notary Public is likely to be concerned such as legalisation requirements of various countries and rules and regulations made by the Court of Faculties. I am grateful to the Faculty Office for permitting to publish the practice rules and code of practice in this manual. I am thankful to the Foreign & Commonwealth Office, Legal Ombudsman and The National Archives for permitting to publish various texts. Finally, my thanks to The Notaries Society for all their help, support and guidance.

Not a single book would ever be written without the help of friends & colleagues who have encouraged me to produce this manual. I am grateful to Martin Jinks, Robert Bond, Anne McMahon, Dipty Raja and above all, my mentor, Michael Pulvermacher. I am grateful to Amanda Cooper and her team at the Foreign & Commonwealth Office. I would also like to thank Dale Burgess for printing this manual and James Beard and his team at CDN for updates on legalisation requirements. I am thankful to Mr. Charles George QC, Master of the Faculties for writing the foreword to this edition.

Suggestions from readers for further improvement of this manual in the subsequent editions will be most gratefully acknowledged.

Sanjay Prem Gogia
August 2018

INTRODUCTION

A Notary Public ranks among the most distinct and ancient professions in England & Wales. Public Notaries are officers of the law and their primary responsibility is the preparation and authentication of legal documentation usually used overseas or at various foreign consulates in England and Wales. A notary's principal duty is to authenticate under seal and signature various documents executed in England and Wales. This is a function which is and has been from time immemorial well recognised by international law and custom among all countries. Notarised documents often form a vital part of international trade.

Apart from a few specialised duties, such as the issue of ship protests, protests of bills of exchange, and the certification of copies and translations, the English and Welsh notary is dependent for his/her status and livelihood on the fact that his/her intervention is required in order to authenticate and render effective legal documents executed here for use overseas. In other words, the execution of a notarial act by a notary in England and Wales involves, in the vast majority of cases, a document which is intended to take effect abroad.

There are currently around 800 practising notaries in England and Wales including the 38 Scrivener notaries. The majority are also solicitors or barristers but there are a good number who practise as notaries only. Scrivener notaries also deal with legal translation and the preparation of legal documents in other languages. All notaries admitted in England and Wales (General and Scrivener notaries) receive an identical notarial faculty. The acts of all notaries should be regarded as having identical validity and force as all notaries in England and Wales are regulated identically, have a notarial faculty and hold identical annual notarial practising certificate.

The Faculty Office has been exercising regulatory functions since its creation by The Ecclesiastical Licences Act 1533. The Master of the Faculties, the judicial officer in charge of the Faculty Office, is the approved regulator and appointing authority as set out in the Legal Services Act 2007. There are two members' associations, one for Scrivener notaries and one for General notaries. Scrivener notaries are full members of the International Union of Latin Notariat (UINL) whereas The Notaries' Society has observer status at UINL.

The Faculty Office has been working to maintain the independence and training of the notarial profession in order that the reputation of the profession is enhanced not only in England & Wales but throughout the world. In recent years this has seen the introduction of a two-year post-graduate level notarial practice course run by the Faculty of Laws at University College London. The character of the notary as an international legal officer is paramount in both civil and common law traditions.

The notarial profession is an independent one and the majority of the notaries are sole practitioners. Some work in partnership and others through a limited company but not as Alternative Business Structures ("ABS"). For notaries the ABS model will not be in the client's best interests and undermines professional independence because neutrality and independence are vital elements of the notary's role and function.

Chapter 1

ETHICS AND RULES OF PROFESSIONAL CONDUCT

As far as ethics and the rules of professional conduct in the notarial profession are concerned it seems to me that there are professional standards which come into play in our practising lives in three respects:

- the first is in the Faculty issued by the Faculty Office at the time of admission as a public notary;
- the second is the practising rules (principally The Notaries Practice Rules 2014 as amended in 2017);
- the third is the Code of Practice approved by the Master of the Faculties pursuant to The Notaries Practice Rules 2014 as amended in 2017.

1. **The Notarial Faculty**
   A Notarial Faculty requires that a notary should "faithfully exercise the office of a public notary". A notary should make contracts or instruments for or between any party or parties requiring the same and s/he should not add or diminish anything without the knowledge and consent of such party or parties that may alter the substance of the fact. S/he should not make or attest any act, contract or instrument in which s/he knows there is violence or fraud and in all such things s/he should act uprightly and justly in the business of public notary according to the best of her/his skill and ability. The Code of Practice makes it clear that the oath of a notary taken prior to the grant of the Notarial Faculty is the basis of the whole of notary's practice.

2. **The Notaries Practice Rules 2014 as amended in 2017 ("the Rules")**
   Under Rule 4 of the Rules a notary shall:
   - uphold the rule of law and the proper administration of justice;
   - act with integrity;
   - maintain his/her independence and impartiality;
   - provide a prompt and proper standard of service for all clients;
   - act in a way that maintains public trust in the office of notary
   - comply with all legal and regulatory obligations and cooperate with the Master and any persons or body appointed

by him/her in the exercise of the Masters regulatory functions;

- operate his/her notarial practice in accordance with proper governance and sound financial and risk management principles; and
- operate his/her notarial practice in such a way as to provide equality of opportunity and respect for diversity.

Rule 5 provides that a notary shall at all times have regard to any code or codes of practice approved by the Master of the Faculties.

Under Rule 6 a notary who is bankrupt may not practice as a notary on his/her own behalf or as the sole member of a professional partnership until he is discharged from bankruptcy. However, there is no restriction from practising as an employee of another notary.

Under Rule 7 of the Rules, a notary should not directly or indirectly obtain or attempt to obtain instructions for professional work or permit another person to do so on his/her behalf. Neither must s/he do anything in the course of practising as a notary, in any manner which compromises or impairs;

- the principles (rule 4);
- a person's freedom to instruct a notary of his/her choice;
- the notary's ability to act in the best interests of the client;
- the good repute of the notary or of the notarial profession;
- the notary's proper standard of work; or
- the notary's duty of care to persons in all jurisdictions who may place legitimate reliance on his/her notarial acts.

Rule 8 imposes a duty on the notary to inform the client, at the time of accepting instructions, of the right to make a complaint under the Conduct and Discipline Rules 2015 and/or the Legal Services Act 2007 as well as how to make such a complaint. Any person following the proper procedure can make conduct complaints. The current procedure for all notaries who are members of The Notaries' Society is that such notary should first seek to address the complaint promptly on his own. However, if the matter cannot be resolved, then the complainant should write to the Secretary of the Notaries' Society. If the matter is still not resolved to the satisfaction of the complainant, the complainant can complain direct to the Legal Ombudsman.

Under Rule 9, a notary shall not favour the interests of one client over those of another and shall not favour his own interests or those of any other person over those of his clients. Generally, a notary conducting a conveyancing transaction as a notary rather than as a solicitor, must not act for both seller and buyer in a transaction relating to property situated in England and Wales. A notary may exceptionally be permitted to act for both parties in situations specified in Rule 6A of the Rules.

Under Rule 10, a notary must act impartially and, in particular, must not perform any notarial act which involves or may affect:
- his/her own affairs;
- the affairs of his/her spouse or partner or a person to whom the notary is engaged to be married;
- the affairs of a person to whom s/he is directly and closely related;
- the affairs of a person with whom s/he is in a professional partnership or by whom s/he is employed or from whom s/he receives a benefit by being provided with office accommodation or other facilities for his/her notarial practice;
- the affairs of a person who has appointed the notary to be his/her attorney which concern a matter within the scope of the power of attorney granted;
- the affairs of a trust of which s/he is a trustee or of an estate where s/he is a personal representative of the deceased;
- the affairs of a body corporate of whose board of directors or governing body s/he is a member;
- the affairs of an employee of the notary;
- the affairs of a partnership of which s/he is a member or of a company in which the notary holds shares either exceeding 5% of the issued share capital or having a market value exceeding such figure as the Master may from time to time specify.

Under Rule 11 a notary who is an employee of a non- notary shall take all proper and reasonable steps in the exercise of his notarial practice to maintain his/her independence.

Under Rule 12 notarial acts shall normally be drawn in English language. A notary may prepare notarial act in a language other than English if he/she has sufficient knowledge of the language concerned. However, a notary can authenticate the execution of signatures of document in any language provided the signatory understands the document and the notary's authentication is in English unless he/she is competent to do so in the foreign language.

Rule 13 makes it clear that any notary giving an undertaking, whether oral or in writing shall be personally liable for that undertaking.

Under Rule 14 a notary may advertise his/her practice provided that
- the principles (Rule 4) are upheld;
- the client's freedom to instruct is not unduly restricted;
- the notaries good reputation for integrity and professional standard of work is not thereby damaged;
- he/she complies with any relevant non-statutory code of advertising standards.

A notary will be required to comply with the Advertising Standards Authority (ASA) which is a self-regulatory organisation of the advertising industry in the United Kingdom. The ASA is a non-statutory organisation and so cannot interpret or enforce legislation. However, its code of advertising practice broadly reflects legislation in many respects. The ASA is not funded by the British Government, but by a levy on the advertising industry. Its role is to "regulate the content of advertisements, sales promotions and direct marketing in the UK" by investigating "complaints made about ads, sales promotions or direct marketing", and deciding whether such advertising complies with its advertising standards.

Under rule 16 even if a client has been introduced to the notary by a third-party he/she must be able to advice the client independently regardless of his/her own interests.

Under Rule 18.1 a notary may charge a professional fee for all notarial work undertaken by him/her and the basis upon which that fee will be calculated or the fee to be charged for the work done, shall be made known in advance to any new instructing person. Unless otherwise permitted under rule 18.3 a notary is not permitted to share his/her professional fees with any person not entitled to act as a notary. Rule 18.4 introduced in 2017 states that a notary who practices within or on behalf of a limited company limited liability partnership may share his/her professional fees provided that the equity of the company or partnership is wholly-owned by the notary or notaries who are directors or partners of the company or partnership.

Rule 19 was amended in 2017. Under this rule a notary may not practise under a name which is likely to mislead (intentionally or unintentionally) or bring the profession into disrepute.

Under rule 21 a notary shall ensure that the office is open during normal working hours and is properly supervised. Where the operation or supervision is prevented by illness, accident or other unforeseen cause for a prolonged period, suitable alternative arrangements shall be made to ensure compliance with this rule. Rule 21.5 been introduced in 2017 states that a notary shall not employ a member of the specified profession without express written permission of the registrar where that person has had a finding of professional misconduct.

'Specified Profession' means a profession specified in the Schedule of Conduct & Discipline Rules 2015 which includes Solicitor, Barrister, Chartered Legal Executive, Licensed Conveyancer in England & Wales and Avocat or other legal practitioner in a country outside England and Wales. Finally any other authorised person as defined by Section 18 of the Legal Services Act 2007 authorised to carry out reserved legal services. The Master may by order add to or amend the Schedule. It shall be the duty of any notary who is also a member of a Specified Profession and against whom a complaint has been made to the relevant body of that profession , and where such complaint has been found by that body to be substantiated (whether in part or in whole), to report such finding forthwith to the Registrar (whether or not a penalty is imposed by such relevant body of that profession and without regard to the nature of such penalty).

Rule 22 imposes the obligation for notaries to complete continuing professional education during each practice year. This rule was first introduced in the year 2010.

Under rule 23 notaries are required to maintain records of notarial acts both in private and public form. A notary shall maintain and preserve records for up to 12 years for private form notarial acts. Public form notarial acts are required to be maintained permanently. All these records may be maintained electronically.

Under rule 24 notaries premises, records may be inspected from time to time on behalf of the Master of the Faculties. The records which may be inspected in accordance with rule 24.1 shall include all documents in the notary's possession relating in any way to his/her practice as a notary, whether or not they also relate to non-notarial matters, and shall include documents stored by means of a digital or other electronic system.

Under rule 25 Notaries ceasing their practice may deposit their records at County or Metropolitan archives in England and Wales. However, it does depend on each particular record office being willing to accept the particular records. The Master passed an order pursuant to rule 25.1.3 on 13 July 2017 that before depositing the records the notary shall first enter into an agreement with the said County or Metropolitan archives. The order confirms that no other person other than the notary or the registrar of the faculty office may have access to such records for a period of at least 30 years from the date of deposit or such longer period as may be appropriate, such as public form notarial acts.

3.   The Code of Practice

Rule 5 of the Notaries Practice Rules 2014 provides that
5.1   A notary shall at all times have regard to any Code or Codes of Practice approved by the Master from time to time.
5.2   Failure to comply with this Rule may amount to "Notarial Misconduct" as defined by Rule 2 of the Notaries (Conduct & Discipline) Rules 2011.

The Code of Practice deals with core areas of reserved legal activities and notarial services. Guidance and statements of best practice contained in the Code are not obligatory but a notary must be aware of the Code and consider the statements of best practice contained in it when providing notarial services. The Code of Practice is designed to help notaries to comply with their professional obligations, to safeguard the interests of their clients and the interests of all persons placing legitimate reliance on notarial acts, and to enhance professional standards. The Code of Practice is to assist notaries in their day to day practice. It also provides the public with an accessible document explaining the level of service to be provided by notaries. The Code of Practice is not new rules but is intended as a resource for the profession.

Chapter 1: A notary shall uphold the rule of law and the proper administration of justice

"A notary is required, in common with all other lawyers, to uphold the rule of law and the proper administration of justice. This is the foremost and overriding professional duty of any lawyer. It involves the protection of human rights at a basic level, ensuring that no one is above the law, and also includes specific tasks such as acting as a gatekeeper in the battle against terrorist funding and money laundering, questions of privacy, privilege, and data protection that pervade the practice of any lawyer. These particular considerations are dealt with later in this Code".

Chapter 2: A notary shall act with integrity

"Integrity is central to the notarial profession and the office of a notary. Notaries are appointed by a Faculty issued in the name of the Archbishop of Canterbury and under the seal of the Archbishop's Faculty Office. The Faculty states that *"full faith ought to be given as well in Judgment as thereout to the instruments to be from this time made by you"*, which means that courts, other authorities, and all recipients of notarial acts should be able to trust those acts without further enquiry".

Chapter 3: A notary shall maintain his independence and impartiality

"Notaries are entrusted with matters of considerable importance for clients, whether private clients or business clients, and the independence and impartiality of notaries is of paramount importance for the safeguarding of clients' interests. Independence means your independence and if you practise jointly with other notaries it means in addition the independence of your notarial firm. Independence also encompasses your ability and the ability of your notarial practice to give independent advice to a client and to provide notarial services independently".

Chapter 4: A notary shall provide a prompt and proper standard of service for all clients

"You should provide a prompt and proper standard of service for all clients. A notary's clients may, for example, be private individuals, small businesses, charities, government agencies, and multinational corporations. Different clients have different needs, but all are entitled to the same prompt and proper standard of service. Providing a prompt service includes responding to enquiries without undue delay. If you are unable to respond to a client's enquiry promptly, the client should be directed to the next nearest notary or another notary in the same vicinity who may be able to respond promptly. Providing a prompt service also means that, before accepting a client's instructions, you ensure that you are able to act on them properly and promptly".

Chapter 5: A notary shall act in a way that maintains the trust in the office of notary which the public may reasonably expect
"Members of the public should be able to place their trust in you. Any behaviour that undermines this trust damages not only you, but also the ability of the notarial profession and the legal profession as a whole to serve society. Conduct that might maintain trust in the office of notary is a broad area, and trust can be undermined by a failure to consider or implement other Principles. Consequently, this section of the Code should not be considered as comprehensive or discrete but as covering aspects of conduct specifically related to trust in the office of notary not covered elsewhere, in particular under the headings of Chapter 1, Chapter 2 and Chapter 3. When you act as a notary, whether in dealings with clients and their advisers, the Master of the Faculties, other notaries, or in a public or semi-public forum, your behaviour should reflect the high standards and integrity of the notarial profession".

Chapter 6: A notary shall comply with all legal and regulatory obligations and cooperate with the Master and any persons or body appointed by him in exercise of the Master's regulatory functions
"Notaries have legal obligations under the general law, especially as service providers, traders, data controllers, and as gatekeepers under anti-money-laundering and prevention-of-terrorism legislation. A notary may only carry out notarial activities, oaths administration, reserved instrument activities and probate activities, and provide services as a notary in general, if in possession of a valid practising certificate. An unrestricted practising certificate authorises a notary to provide services generally, including the Reserved Legal Activities mentioned above, but subject to supervision and continuing professional education requirements".

Chapter 7: A notary shall operate his notarial practice in accordance with proper governance and sound financial and risk management principles
"The financial good standing of a notary's practice is of key importance for a notary's clients and for the reputation of the notarial profession as a whole. The financial good standing of a notary's practice is of key importance for a notary's clients and

for the reputation of the notarial profession as a whole. The financial good standing of a notary's practice is dependent on proper governance and properly applied risk-management principles so that the practice is not left open to uninsured claims or claims that may exceed the insurance held by the notary or notarial firm. A claim of this nature could have a detrimental effect for the client, and may result in financial difficulties, even the bankruptcy of a notary or the insolvency of a notarial firm".

Chapter 8: A notary shall operate his notarial practice in such a way as to provide equality of opportunity and respect for diversity

"As a matter of general rule of law notaries must comply with equality legislation. Equality legislation is relevant in a number of ways to the carrying out of notarial activities and in particular a notary should ensure in particular that notarial services are available to clients with disabilities, and that persons with a protected characteristic are not discriminated against, actively or passively".

Chapter 9: Accounts

"Notaries are required to comply with the Accounts Rules, the Accounts (Deposit Interest) Rules and the Trust Accounts Rules. There are further rules relating to accounts in the Practice Rules and the Inspections Regulations. Chapter 9 goes through the main points a notary needs to be aware of in order to comply with the various accounts rules that may apply to the notary's practice".

Chapter 10: Anti Money Laundering

"Notaries must be familiar with and comply with all anti-money-laundering and anti-terrorism legislation as it applies to notaries. The application of this legislation to notaries is explained and illustrated in an Official AML Guidance document approved by the Treasury. The Official AML Guidance is provided in hard copy to all newly qualified notaries by the Faculty Office and is freely available to download from the website of the Faculty Office". A new oversight supervisory body, the Office for Professional Body Anti-Money Laundering Supervision (OPBAS) has been created which sits within the Financial Conduct Authority and notaries will be required to comply with rules and regulations of OPBAS.

Chapter 11: Complaints

"A notary's clients and persons who have been refused notarial services have the right to make a complaint about the notary who provided (or refused to provide) those services, and to have that complaint resolved. Notaries are required to inform clients of their right to make a complaint and the procedure for doing so [Practice Rule 8].

A notary must provide clients with a signposting notice in the regulatory format that explains the right to complain and "how a complaint may be made when accepting instructions for professional work or changing the terms on which he or she is acting [Practice Rule 8.1]. Practice Rule 8.2 clarifies that the signposting notice may be provided by e-mail. A reference to the notary's complaints procedure being available on the notary's website or otherwise on request is not sufficient to comply with Practice Rule 8".

Chapter 12: Conflicts of Interest

Practice Rule 9.1 sets out the general principle that in the conduct of his or her practice a notary shall not favour the interests of one client over those of another and shall not favour his or her own interests or those of any other person over those of his clients.

Practice Rule 9.4 relates to conflicts of interest in the context of notarial services that are not conveyancing transactions.

Practice Rule 9.4.2 is clear – "a notary does not act for both parties to a transaction merely by preparing or authenticating a notarial act in his capacity as a public certifying officer even though that act may concern two or more parties". A notary may therefore authenticate an instrument transferring title of an asset signed by both buyer and seller. For a syndicated loan transaction, a notary may act for more than one lender without the need to obtain consent in writing from each party involved. Practice Rule 9.4.2 covers the majority of the day-to-day notarial work a notary will deal with, but not conveyancing matters.

Where the notary does act for two or more parties to a transaction, for example by advising both purchaser and seller of a ship, then in all cases save for conveyancing matters the notary may act for both parties to the transaction if:

- each party has consented in writing to the notary so acting; and
- the notary is satisfied that there is no conflict of interest between the parties".

Chapter 13: Continuing Professional Education

"Continuing professional education for notaries is intended to ensure that notaries are kept up to date with developments in relevant law and practice and to enhance the provision of notarial services to the public. All notaries are required to acquire six CPE credit points during each Continuing Professional Education period. One CPE credit point equates to one hour of educational activity".

Chapter 14: Data Protection
"Notaries are data controllers and must comply with the obligations of a data controller under data protection legislation, particularly with regard to the collection and retention of sensitive personal data. Notaries must also comply with the obligation under data protection legislation to register with the Information Commissioner's Office and to provide accurate information with regard to the nature of their notarial practice. A notary's clients have the right to know what personal data is being collected and retained".

Chapter 15: Inspections
"The Notaries (Inspections) Regulations 2014 were made by the Master of the Faculties which introduced a system of inspections for all notaries in England and Wales.

Each year the practices of randomly selected notaries [Inspections Regulations 1] are inspected by one or more inspectors selected by the Registrar from a panel appointed for the purpose by the Master of the Faculties [Inspections Regulations 2].

Notaries are given at least seven days' notice of an inspection [Inspections Regulations 4] and as far as is reasonably possible the inspector is not a notary practising in the same geographical area as the notary being inspected, is not known personally to that notary, and not a person with whom a professional or commercial conflict of interest might arise [Inspections Regulations 3]".

Chapter 16: Insurance
"Notaries are required to hold professional indemnity insurance and fidelity insurance cover. The detailed requirements for the maintenance of insurance by a notary are contained in the Practising Certificates Rules. A practising certificate will only be issued to a notary if the application is accompanied by a current certificate of insurance against civil liability covering the notary in connection with his or her practice as a notary (professional indemnity insurance) and a current certificate of insurance against financial loss suffered by a third party in consequence of any dishonest or fraudulent act or omission in connection with his or her practice as a notary (fidelity insurance)".

Chapter 17: Record Keeping and File Storage

"There are clear rules for the recording, retention and preservation of notarial acts [Practice Rule 23]. The general rule is set out in Practice Rule 23 which is that a notary must keep "proper records" in accordance with the requirements set out in the rest of Practice Rule 23".

Chapter 18: Supervision

"The Post-Admission Rules provide for newly qualified notaries to be supervised during the first two years of practice. The supervision of newly qualified notaries is designed to provide notaries with the support and encouragement of an experienced notary during their first two years of providing notarial services, and to facilitate the monitoring of the newly qualified notary's work".

Chapter 19: Undertakings

"You are personally liable for any undertaking given as a notary whether oral or in writing [Practice Rule 13]. Undertakings are most likely to be given by notary-conveyancers in the course of providing conveyancing services, but all notaries should be aware of the strict rules governing undertakings and not inadvertently or recklessly give an undertaking that subsequently cannot be honoured".

Chapter 20: Conveyancing

"The Principles contained in Practice Rule 4 are the basis for the conduct of all notary-conveyancers and underpin the expectations of your Regulator and the public with regard to the conveyancing services that you provide as a notary".

Chapter 21: Probate

"The Principles contained in Practice Rule 4 underpin the conduct and expectations of all notaries carrying out probate activities as a notary".

The complete code of practice can be found at the Faculty Office website. **http://www.facultyoffice.org.uk/notary**

We are fast reaching a stage where the expectations of clients are increasing day by day. It is extremely important as a profession that we become stronger by adhering to the current practice rules and code of practice and continue providing a prompt, efficient and cost effective professional service.

Chapter 2

RECORD KEEPING

Record-keeping is one of the most important functions of a notary. If there is any doubt as to whether or not s/he did a particular act, the notary must be able to give a clear answer.

A previous Master the late Sir John Owen introduced The Notaries (Records) Rules 1991 which provided that every public notary shall keep a permanent record of all notarial acts 'in accordance with good notarial practice'. At the time this was deemed to be, for provincial notaries in respect of public form documents, a record of the original or a complete copy of such documents. In the case of a private document, it meant that either a description of the document or an extract from such a document should be kept. For scrivener notaries, the rule was subsequently confirmed that public form documents should be issued in duplicate with one original to be kept in the protocol (and in exceptional cases a complete photocopy of the document could be kept instead). The protocol was to be preserved permanently. With regard to other documents, a record was to be kept in the protocol of the names of the parties and the nature of the document attested. This record was to be kept for six years.

Subsequent amendments to record-keeping rules (see the Notaries Practice Rules 2009 & 2014) have removed the differences between the record keeping requirements of scrivener notaries and general notaries, although many notaries (scriveners and general notaries) prefer to retain a duplicate original of a public form document rather than a photocopy, thereby replicating the practice of Civil Law notaries.

Guidance as to how records should be maintained by a Notary Public is given in the first edition of "The General Notary". Whilst a tutor on the Notarial Practice course at the University of Cambridge and now at University College London, I have always directed students to the form of register given in "The General Notary" as I consider it absolutely imperative for notaries to keep proper records in a proper format. I give below the format for ease of reference.

Chapter 17 of the Code of Practice reiterate the rules for the recording, retention and presentation of notarial acts. It provides that "notaries records are as a general principle are confidential, but a person who has a proper interest in the notarial act, such as the notary's client, a personal representative of a deceased client, or an agent authorised by the notary's client in a notarial may apply for a copy of the file record of that act and if the notarial act was prepared in the public form, a copy of the act from the notary's protocol [practice rule 23.6]. If there is any doubt as a person's proper interest in a particular notarial act, the Master of the Faculties has the authority to decide the question [practice rule 23.7]. A notary may charge a reasonable fee for providing this copy".

Rule 23.1 of the 2014 Rules states that a notary shall keep proper records of his/her notarial acts. Rule 23.2 states that the records so kept shall be sufficient to identify:
- the date of the act;
- the person at whose request the act was performed;
- the person or persons, if any, intervening in the act and, in the case of a person who intervened in a representative capacity, the name of his principal;
- the method of identification of the party or parties intervening in the notarial act, and in the case of a party intervening in a representative capacity, any evidence produced to the notary of that party's entitlement so to intervene;
- the nature of the act and the fee charged.

I think the nature of the act should be slightly elaborated in addition to the above. For eg: brief particulars of the nature of the document "Power of Attorney by AB empowering CD to sell plot no.99 Main Street, Whitetown, Yellow County, Utopia" especially in cases where a copy of the document is not kept in private form.

Under Rule 23.3, where the notarial act is in the public form, the notary shall place an original of the act or a complete photographic copy of the same in a protocol, which shall be preserved permanently by the notary.

A digital or electronic storage system is now permitted provided that documents are stored in indelible or unalterable form. It is the duty of the notary to inform the Faculty Office of any passwords for such electronic filing.

Rule 23.4 states that records of acts not in public form, (kept in accordance with Rule 23.2), shall be preserved for a minimum period of twelve years and, for the avoidance of doubt, such preservation may also be by means of a suitable digital or other electronic system, which enables the storage of documents in an indelible and unalterable format. (Note: it is clear that strictly speaking the requirement is for the *record* of the act to be maintained for 12 years, but not necessarily a *copy* of the notarial act). However, Rule 23.3 does require a copy of a public form notarial act to be stored, in the form stated above. It is not sufficient for the purposes of Rule 23.3 to keep a mere record of a public form notarial act.

Currently Rule 25 states that when a notary ceases to practise as such then he shall arrange for his records to be transferred to notary in practice appointed by the retiring notary or his continuing notarial partners or alternatively another notary in practice approved by the Master and appointed by the persons having custody of the records (eg. personal representatives, or to an archive designated for the purpose under regulations made by the Master from time to time. The persons making such transfer shall give written particulars to the Registrar of the date of transfer and the person or archive to which the records were transferred. Records in electronic format will now be much easier to be so transferred and maintained.

It is pertinent to remember that records should always be kept up to date, as the Master or any person authorised by the Master may inspect such records at any time. This power is reserved to the Master under Rule 24 of the Rules. A reduction in the period of time during which records must be maintained, currently permanently, and ability for all records to be maintained in an indelible and unalterable electronic format would, in my opinion, make record-keeping more appropriate to the twenty-first century.

The files produced by notary when providing conveyancing and probate services are not subject to the record-keeping rules for notarial acts. The Code of Practice provides "any records whether paper-based or electronic, must be stored safely and securely, and in a manner that will provide for them to be readily accessed as needed at any point in what may be a lengthy (and in some cases indefinite) period of storage. Proper records must therefore carefully catalogued and stored in an environment that will not bring about rapid deterioration (excess moisture and heat). If records are being stored electronically consideration must be given to file redundancy on a regular basis and if necessary, the file type or format updated, or the file storage device replaced, so that access to the electronic records may be assured as time passes and technology changes".

The Master of the Faculties approved on 25th April 2018 the use of NotarySAFE for storing records. NotarySAFE allows notaries to encrypt, upload and store notarial documents in a secure data centre, keeping sensitive data safe from hackers and other potential threats. NotarySAFE is managed by the Notaries Society.

Protocol No.	Full name and address of person(s) or company requesting the act	Name and address of appearer(s) (if different)	Proof of identity and evidence of representative capacity (copied?[✓])	✓	Nature of act (copied? [✓]) and any matter to record	✓	Country: Legalisation Required?	Fee and Disburse-ments (paid? [✓])

Chapter 3

LEGAL OMBUDSMAN & SIGN POSTING

The 2007 Legal Services Act (the Act) has its genesis in a report written by Sir David Clementi in 2004. Clementi in turn responded to three issues:

- a report on competition in the professions by the OFT in 2001 which saw restrictions on external ownership of legal businesses as a barrier to entry;
- a significant collapse in public confidence in the Solicitors' disciplinary scheme as a result of scandal about access to Government funding in mining compensation cases; and, finally,
- persistent problems in the handling of service complaints in relation to the legal profession, at its worst, saw routine cases taking more than two years to resolve as a matter of course.

Clementi concluded that a pure self-regulatory system was no longer operating in the public or consumer interest, as opposed to that of the profession.

In legal services, that response was to leave the primary responsibility for regulation of individuals and entities with the self-regulatory bodies – The Faculty Office, The Law Society, The Bar Council and five others. But they were compelled to make a clear separation between their professional/lobbying/ "trade union" activities on the one hand and their regulatory functions on the other. Thus the 'arms' length' (and, it was hoped, independent) regulators were born.

A new statutory body, the Legal Services Board, was created to oversee that settlement. Alongside that, an independent Office for Legal Complaints was established to run a Legal Ombudsman scheme to ensure faster redress for individual consumers.

The LSB is a non-departmental public body of the Ministry of Justice (MoJ), but one over which the MoJ has no material powers of direction. The LSB has to have a lay Chair and a lay majority and is funded from a levy which it places on the regulatory bodies which it oversees. The Lord Chancellor gives formal consent to the budget as a check to make sure that the LSB does not engage in gratuitous empire building.

The statutory regulation of notaries is the oldest of the professions that the LSB has responsibility for. The Ecclesiastical Licences Act 1533 (passed in 1534) was one of the products of King Henry VIII's marital troubles. Under the guidance of Thomas Cromwell, as Chancellor of the Exchequer, the third session of the English Reformation Parliament passed (amongst other things) the legislation necessary for the Archbishop of Canterbury to regulate Notaries. It is fair to say then that the statutory regulation of Notaries was born at a time of change and change has been fairly constant in the nearly 500 years since.

Concerns about new entrants are nothing new. In 1749 the scriveners in the City of London were highlighting the rigour of the training and the value of the qualification of scriveners over and above that of mere notaries and solicitors. Well times change and now nearly 80% of notaries are also practising solicitors.

Since 2007 there has been significant change in the regulatory requirements facing notaries. Notaries now have:
- Complaints handling rules
- Ombudsman scheme
- Continuing professional development requirements
- New supervisory arrangements; and
- Code of practice

These changes are not without cost and the practicing certificate fee has increased. It is worth pointing out in this context that poor notarial conduct can cost people a lot of money (as shown by a disciplinary decision by the Court of Faculties in recent cases of Ella Imison, Ricardo Lado and Robert Ward).

The Faculty Office is making in delivering more risk based regulation by focusing on practitioners that provide services with higher risks such as probate and conveyancing. There is now a level of transparency of its new website, its moves towards making data openly available and its efforts to modernise its approach and seek to deliver the outcomes consumers and providers need.

Change is not an easy process and with change comes costs. The LSB has imposed too many restrictions and obligations that the cost of regulation has increased dramatically. The cost of regulation is something which affects everyone in the legal profession. But not just practitioners – consumers as well, as higher costs of regulation ultimately get passed on to consumers in higher fees charged for services.

In the rapidly changing and competitive world of legal services, one of the best ways to ensure long-term success is through client satisfaction. A recent survey into the use of legal services by the Legal Ombudsman found that 82% of consumers would choose a lawyer based on personal experience or recommendations from friends, relatives and work colleagues. Satisfied customers will be loyal; they will use your services again. Satisfied customers spread the word; they'll tell other people how much they like your business and value the service you offer. You won't have to invest as much time and energy (or money) bringing new people through your door.

Research done by the Legal Ombudsman shows that a good complaints process – one that is well explained and easy to follow – can increase customer confidence in a business, particularly if any problems that arise are addressed speedily and effectively. It demonstrates that the business has confidence in the service offered and a commitment to delivering those services to the highest standards.

According to the Legal Ombudsman using an internal complaints procedure, will help notaries and lawyers to improve their levels of customer service overall, to reduce the number of complaints finding their way to the Legal Ombudsman and to increase service standards across the profession. As well as reinforcing some of the practical and common sense approaches to good complaint handling, this chapter highlights some of the steps that can be taken to ensure the process works towards a positive outcome for all.

Before you receive a complaint
Having a clear complaints process in place will mean you are ready to deal with a complaint when the time comes. Some things to consider are:

- Appointing someone to act as a point of contact, to whom complaints should be sent in the first instance: this will avoid the possibility of complaints going unanswered due to a lack of ownership. Give their details on your correspondence and your website. Usually sole practitioners are themselves the first point of contact.

- Sometimes involving someone else early in the process may help. This will allow the complaint to be moderated and gives you the benefit of a more objective viewpoint. In addition, complainants often appreciate having an objective opinion.

- The complaints process should be accessible to all, including vulnerable customers and those with special needs or requirements. You should be contactable by email, phone and letter. Complaints do not need to be made in writing. Be alert to any customer contact that looks like a complaint.

- If you are unable to resolve the complaint, you should inform your customer that they can take it to the Legal Ombudsman. This will usually happen after the option of the informal complaints procedure managed by the Notaries Society has been exhausted.

Ten simple steps recommended by the Legal Ombudsman under the headings:

Listen, Inform, Respond

Listen
1. **Identify when a complaint is being made.** When a customer is unhappy with the service they receive, there are factors that could prevent them from making a formal complaint. They might feel intimidated or concerned that a complaint will affect their matter, or they may have special needs or requirements, which need accommodating in order to make your complaints process accessible and fair.

2. **Understand the reason for the complaint.** Good practice takes into consideration the type of complaint that's being made. Try to spot the signs and 'softer' cues to establish early on what type of complaint is being made. For instance, although they may not mention the word 'complaint', a customer may indicate they're unhappy with the costs or that they're confused about the length of time a case is taking to proceed.

   It may also be helpful to think about any underlying reasons for the complaint. Perhaps a customer is anxious about the progress of their case, hasn't fully understood the legal process or is working to a limited budget. Take these things into account as the complaint progresses.

Inform
3. **Acknowledge the complaint within two working days of receipt.** Good practice requires a timely acknowledgement of a complaint. The experience of consumers in other sectors shows that a response within two working days increases their confidence in a complaint handling process.

4. **Provide a map of options.** Rather than just asking the customer what they want to do next, provide options. For example, you could offer formal and informal routes to resolving their complaint. For instance, if the issue relates to greater clarity over costs, you might simply need to provide the customer with a more detailed breakdown of their bill. In this way, the complaint could be dealt with quickly and informally. On the other hand, if the complaint is about whether you have followed their instructions regarding the work it may require a more formal route in which both parties provide written evidence to support their arguments.

5. **Spell out implications.** Reassure the customer that they won't be charged for complaining. Be clear and upfront about how long it will take to investigate the complaint and that you have eight weeks within which to resolve it. Additionally, some customers may be concerned that raising a formal complaint will prejudice or disrupt their matter. You should explain what, if any, impact the complaint will have on the work being done as early as possible.

6. **Use clear, comprehensible language and neutral tone.** Clarity in any communication is vital to a considered and effective complaints procedure. Avoid jargon and emotive or provocative language.

Respond
7. **Share your findings.** Once you have conducted a thorough investigation and have established all the facts required to make a decision, share the findings and your conclusion with your customer. Include as much detail as is necessary for the customer to understand how and why you have reached a decision.

8. **If you find that you provided poor service** acknowledge what went wrong and offer the customer a suitable remedy, along with a full explanation of what happened. The remedy should be proportionate to the level of poor service. For example, if there was a small administrative error that didn't adversely impact their matter but which caused minor inconvenience, an apology might be more appropriate. If, on the other hand, they've been overcharged, it would be sensible to apologise, refund the amount and perhaps pay a small amount of compensation.

9. **If you decide you offered a reasonable service** provide a full and clear explanation about how you reached that decision and show evidence where possible.

10.   **Signpost the customer to the Legal Ombudsman.** If you can't agree on a resolution to the complaint you must signpost your customer to us.

Chapter 6 of the code of practice provides that notaries must provide clients with a signposting notice that explains the right to complain and how the complaint may be made.

Mandatory Information for General Notaries to be given to all Notarial Clients under Section 8 of The Notaries Practice Rules 2014

My notarial practice is regulated by the Faculty Office of the Archbishop of Canterbury:

The Faculty Office
1, The Sanctuary
Westminster
London, SW1P 3JT
Tel: 020 7222 5381
Email: faculty.office@1thesanctuary.com
Website: www.facultyoffice.org.uk

If you are dissatisfied about the service you have received, please do not hesitate to contact me. If I am unable to resolve the matter you may then complain to the Notaries Society of which I am a member, who have a Complaints Procedure which is approved by the Faculty Office. This procedure is free to use and is designed to provide a quick resolution to any dispute.

In that case please write (but do not enclose any original documents) with full details of your complaint to:-

Secretary of The Notaries Society
Old Church Chambers
23 Sandhill Road
St James
Northampton, NN5 5LH
Email secretary@thenotariessociety.org.uk
Tel: 01604 758908

If you have any difficulty in making a complaint in writing, please do not hesitate to call the Notaries Society/the Faculty Office for assistance.

Finally, even if you have your complaint considered under the Notaries Society Approved Complaints Procedure, you may at the end of that procedure, or after a period of eight weeks from the date you first notified me that you were dissatisfied, make your complaint to the Legal Ombudsman*, if you are not happy with the result:

Legal Ombudsman
PO Box 6806
Wolverhampton, WV1 9WJ
Tel: 0300 555 0333
Email: enquiries@legalombudsman.org.uk
Website: www.legalombudsman.org.uk

If you decide to make a complaint to the Legal Ombudsman you must refer your matter to the Legal Ombudsman within six months from the conclusion of the complaint process.

*certain kinds of commercial entities are not eligible to make a complaint to the Legal Ombudsman – please refer to the Legal Ombudsman Scheme Rules or consult the Faculty office.

Mandatory Information for Scrivener Notaries to be given to all Notarial Clients under Section 8 of The Notaries Practice Rules 2014

This notarial practice is regulated by the Master of the Faculties through the Faculty Office of the Archbishop of Canterbury:

The Faculty Office
1, The Sanctuary
Westminster
London, SW1P 3JT
Tel: 020 7222 5381

If you are dissatisfied about the service you have received from myself please do not hesitate to contact me with your instructions.

If I am unable to resolve the matter you may then complain to The Scriveners Company, which has a role in the regulation of scrivener notaries. Please write (but do not enclose any original documents) with full details of your complaint to the following address:

The Clerk
The Scriveners Company
HQS Wellington
Temple Stairs
Victoria Embankment
London, WC2R 2PN
Email: clerk@scriveners.org.uk

The Company will arrange for your complaint to be considered by a panel of 3 individuals who will be independent of the Scrivener Notary against whom the complaint has been made. The procedure is free to use and is designed to provide a quick resolution to any dispute. If you have any difficulty making a complaint in writing, please do not hesitate to telephone the Clerk of the Company for assistance on:

Tel: 020 7240 0529

If you remain dissatisfied you may make a complaint to the Legal Ombudsman at the end of the Scriveners Company's Complaints Procedure or after eight weeks have elapsed from the date on which you made your complaint to me:

Legal Ombudsman
PO Box 6806
Wolverhampton, WV1 9WJ
Tel: 0300 555 0333
Email: enquiries@legalombudsman.org.uk
Website: www.legalombudsman.org.uk

Where there is no approved procedure then under Rule 3.5 of the Conduct and Discipline Rules 2015 the Registrar may refer the matter to a panel of notaries. The notary carrying out these functions shall be entitled to a fixed fee to be specified by the Master which shall be payable by the notary complained against. The current fee approved by the Master which shall be payable by the notary complained against. Such a notary as a member of the panel will not be appointed a Nominated Notary under Rule 4 of the C&D Rules. A panel of notaries shall not consist of not less than 4 notaries.

An act of a notary may be construed as notarial misconduct where a notary prevents someone from providing information to the Master of the Faculties or Legal Ombudsman. A notary may also be held liable where a notary enters into an agreement to the effect that the Master of the Faculties and/or the legal ombudsman are precluded from investigating any actual or potential complaint or allegation of notarial misconduct.

Chapter 4

TERMS & CONDITIONS OF PRACTICE

Terms and conditions of the client agreement should be carefully drafted by Notaries to ensure that the instructions received and work to be carried out are clear. It is usually helpful to have pre-drafted terms and conditions which can provide notaries with a secure, legal foundation to protect their rights in dealing with clients. If disputes or problems arise, these will be readily resolved if clients can make reference to clearly written terms and conditions. Chapter 7 of the Code of Practice provides that risk management principles should be applied by notaries in order to identify events and circumstances that may imperil the continuing provision of services to the public.

So, what else are terms and conditions good for? How should one go about drawing them up? It is important to limit the risk, not the business. Terms and Conditions should be an essential part of a notary's practice. Not only are they a good risk management tool, they protect the notary's interests in the event of a dispute with a client by clarifying key elements of the business relationship in which the notary is engaged. It forms the basis of the contract which should be in writing. If you have an oral agreement, you may forget to include some elements and there could be disagreement or misunderstanding about some matters e.g. the parameters of the notary's involvement, release of documents or payment of fees. With a written agreement, all the terms and conditions should be crystal clear at any point in time.

One should not take it for granted that the threads of a business relationship are strong enough to withstand any crisis. The fact is that disagreements can, and do, arise especially if a close personal relationship is intertwined with a business one. If a notary agrees everything verbally, s/he may not always mention the things that seem to be obvious or apparently familiar. It is these issues that usually create trouble in the future if and when you need to enforce any agreement made. Written contracts are of course much better evidence and therefore much easier to enforce should you end up in court.

Written terms and conditions can help a notary in three important ways:

1. They clarify key issues which helps to settle disputes and so reduce the possibility of a formal claim being made against you.

2.   They can help keep the cost of your Professional Indemnity insurance down. Insurance companies look to insure businesses that carry out good risk management which includes issuing written Terms and Conditions. Poor risk management leads to claims, and more expensive Professional Indemnity cover.

3.   They enhance your professional image. A client meeting which includes written Terms and Conditions shows that you take your business seriously.

Terms and Conditions don't have to be lengthy or complex. One page on the back of a quote can often suffice and, as long as you can prove that you've presented the client with your terms of business, you don't necessarily need them to return a signed copy although this would be preferable. The client is then less able to argue that they were not accepted. Terms and Conditions should be drawn up by a professional with knowledge and sufficient experience about notarial business and the relevant notarial practice rules.

If you are a sole practitioner notary, it is very important that you get into the habit of always using written terms and conditions. This is because you probably don't have deep pockets should you be sued. If you use written terms and conditions, it is also far less likely that you will end up in court - your clients will be much more inclined to work with you to find a solution and try to work things out.

Under Rule 8 of the Notarial Practice Rules 2014 as amended in 2017 a Notary must inform a client in writing how to complain in a form prescribed by the Master "from time to time". Also, under Rule 15.1 a notary must make the basis of his/her charges known in advance. The Rule does not say that this should be communicated in writing but without any doubt this would be sensible as it provides a clear point of reference should there be any query about costs.

Whilst the basis of charge may not be the only provision in terms and conditions, most clients might think it the most important one. For the notary, surely a key reason for ensuring clients agree to terms and conditions is to ensure that the notary's liability is limited (to the extent permitted by law and by using a well-drafted limitation of liability clause) to a figure that matches the Master's requirement for a minimum level of PI cover (currently £1,000,000). Even though there is no history of litigation against notaries in England & Wales, and only a few cases of disciplinary proceedings, there is no reason to be complacent and it is very sensible to have written terms and conditions.

I set out below some sample standard terms and conditions which may be used. Advice can always be sought from a commercial specialist well versed in such documents.

Draft Terms & Conditions

1. HOURS OF BUSINESS: My office hours are 09:30 to 17:30 from Monday to Friday. In appropriate cases I can arrange to see you outside my usual office hours, or away from the office. In such cases I would charge a reasonable fee for travelling time plus the cost of my travel.

2. RESPONSIBILITY: A Notary's first duty is to the transaction as a whole. Notarial acts are relied upon by clients, third parties and foreign governments and officials worldwide. Unless otherwise agreed in writing, a Notary's responsibility is limited to the Notarial formalities and does not extend to advice on or drafting of documentation or in relation to substantive legal input on the matter under consideration. I do not give foreign law advice.

3. FEES: My present hourly rate is £180 and my minimum fee is £60. I reserve the right to vary these rates in respect of extremely urgent work or work done outside ordinary office hours or at the weekend.

4. PAYMENT: My charges are normally payable on presentation of my invoice (usually at the meeting) by cash, cheque or by immediate BACS transfer. Notarised documents will not normally be released until all fees and disbursements have been paid in full.

5. DISBURSEMENTS: You are responsible for all payments which I make on your behalf. Typical examples are legalisation fees paid to the Foreign and Commonwealth Office and/or an Embassy, legalisation agents' fees, Companies Registry fees, courier fees and special delivery postage charges. However, I shall not incur these expenses without first obtaining your consent to do so.

6. DOCUMENTATION TO BE PREPARED: I may need more than one appointment to finalise the matter, particularly if it is necessary for me to prepare all or some of the documentation.

7. PROOF OF IDENTITY: Identification of individuals and proof of residential address is required. This is usually by way of a current passport, photo card driving licence or national identity card and a

recent gas, electricity or other bill or bank statement. Exceptionally, other proof may be acceptable.

If you act on behalf of a company, I will need to establish that it exists and that the signatory has authority to represent it. I generally conduct my own checks at the Companies House. In some cases, I may ask you to produce a certificate of incorporation, good standing certificate or other similar evidence.

8.   WRITTEN TRANSLATION: In cases where I do not have knowledge of the language in which the document is written, official translations may be required.

9.   LIABILITY: I carry professional indemnity liability cover of £1,000,000 which is the minimum level of cover specified by the Master of the Faculties. I therefore limit the level of my liability to you to £1,000,000 unless you are injured or die as a result of my negligence, in which case my liability is without limit.

10.   COMPLAINTS: I aim to provide all clients with an efficient and high standard of service. However, in the unlikely event that you should wish to complain, then you should follow the complaints procedure set out below. Notaries are regulated by the Faculty Office of the Archbishop of Canterbury: The Faculty Office, 1, The Sanctuary, Westminster, London SW1 3JT, Telephone: 020 7222 5381, Email: faculty.office@1thesanctuary.com, Website: www.facultyoffice.org.uk

If you are dissatisfied about the service you have received, please do not hesitate to contact me. If I am unable to resolve the matter then you may complain to the Notaries Society of which I am a member, who have a Complaints Procedure which is approved by the Faculty Office. This procedure is free to use and is designed to provide a quick resolution to any dispute.

In that case please write (but do not enclose any original documents) with full details of your complaint to: The Secretary of The Notaries Society, Old Church Chambers, 23 Sandhill Road, St James, Northampton NN5 5LH, Email: secretary@thenotariessociety.org.uk, Tel: 01604 758908

If you have any difficulty making a complaint in writing, please do not hesitate to call the Notaries Society/the Faculty Office for assistance.

Finally, even if you have your complaint considered under the Notaries Society Approved Complaints Procedure, you may at the end of that procedure, or after a period of eight weeks from the date you first notified me that you were dissatisfied, make your complaint to the Legal Ombudsman*, if you are not happy with the result:

Legal Ombudsman, P.O. Box 6806, Wolverhampton, WV1 9WJ,

Tel: 0300 555 0333, Email: enquiries@legalombudsman.org.uk, Website: www.legalombudsman.org.uk

If you decide to make a complaint to the Legal Ombudsman you must refer your matter to the Legal Ombudsman within six months from the conclusion of the complaint process.

*certain kinds of commercial entities are not eligible to make a complaint to the Legal Ombudsman – please refer to the Legal Ombudsman Scheme Rules or consult the Faculty office.

11. RECORDS: At the end of the matter, a formal entry of the main details of your transaction and frequently copies of the notarised document must be kept. In particular, when I am requested to certify some documents such as public deeds, the above details will also be kept in my notarial protocols.

12. EMAIL COMMUNICATIONS: In performing my services I may wish to send messages and documents to you by electronic mail (email). Like other means of communication, email is not entirely risk-free and carries with it the possibility (among other things) of corruption, inadvertent misdirection, non-delivery of confidential material, inadvertent deletion is or unauthorised access.

Nevertheless, I believe that the use of email can sometimes deliver worthwhile benefits in terms of speed, accuracy and efficiency of communications, and I recommend that where applicable it should be used in relation to the provision of my services in your matter. Accordingly, I shall unless you notify me to the contrary in writing, regard your acceptance of my terms of engagement as including your agreement to the use of email.

13. DATA PROTECTION: Except as explained below, I will maintain my professional and legal obligations of confidentiality in relation to the work I undertake for you and in relation to information which comes into my possession in the course of undertaking that work.

However, provided that any such disclosures are limited to need-to-know basis, I may make disclosure of information which is confidential to you.

a. For the purposes of acting for you including without limitation disclosures to your other advisers or third parties involved in the work I am undertaking for you, such as FCO, Foreign Embassies and legalisation agents;

b. to my staff, accountant and auditor for the purpose of my accounts;

c. to my professional indemnity insurers in relation to your matter if it becomes necessary under the terms of my professional indemnity insurance to notify communications which would ordinarily be protected by legal professional privilege;

d. as required by law or by any regulatory authority to which I am subject;

e. for the purposes of complying with my obligations under anti-money laundering or counter terrorist financing legislation for the time being in force;

f. for the purpose of applying my risk management policies.

g. for my legitimate interests (or those of a third party) and your interests; and

h. for any public interest.

14. ANTI-MONEY LAUNDERING: Notaries are obliged under the Anti-Money Laundering Legislation to take measures to protect against fraud and forgery. To ensure that I comply with this you acknowledge and agree that. I may make all such enquiries as I deem necessary or appropriate in order to comply with my duty, and you will provide me with such documents and information as I may request. Your failure to do so will entitle me to terminate my engagement and cease acting for you forthwith.

15. EQUALITY AND DIVERSITY: I am committed to promoting equality and diversity in all of my dealings with clients and third parties.

16. THE RELEVANT LAW: The law which governs my contract with you is English Law and it is agreed that any dispute relating to my services shall be resolved by the English courts.

Signature: ……………………………………………………

For and on behalf of: ………………………………………..

Date: ……………………………………………………………

Chapter 5

GENERAL PRINCIPLES

Practice Rule 4 sets out eight Principles. The Principles are all-pervasive and must be observed by notaries in all aspects of their practice. A notary's practice encompasses all services provided by the notary in that capacity and so may extend beyond the production of notarial acts, in particular to the administration of oaths, conveyancing and probate services if those services are provided by a notary in that capacity.

1. **Uphold the rule of law**

   A notary has obligations, not only to clients, but also to any court, land registry and to third parties who may place legitimate reliance on his/her notarial act and should not attempt to deceive or knowingly or recklessly mislead others or mislead the court in any manner. Chapter 1 of the Code of Practice makes it clear that notaries are required to uphold the rule of law and proper administration of justice. Notaries duty of care is to all persons in all jurisdictions who place legitimate reliance on his/her notarial acts. Notaries duty to act as an independent, impartial and expert public certifying officer when carrying out notarial activities. A notary should not take unfair advantage of any of his/her clients and should only act in a manner which promotes the proper operation of legal systems throughout the world.

   This includes conduct in relation to undertakings given by a notary. A notary is personally liable on such undertakings. Performance within an agreed timescale or within a reasonable amount of time of all undertakings given by a notary is extremely important. A notary should never act in his/her professional capacity to advance his/her personal interests. Neither should a notary take unfair advantage of third parties in either the notary's professional or personal capacity.

2. **Act with integrity**

   Personal integrity is central to the role of a notary and should characterise all professional dealings with clients, other lawyers and the public. A notary must not, in private life or professional practice, engage in dishonourable or questionable conduct that casts doubt on the notary's integrity or competence, or which reflects adversely on the integrity of the notarial profession. The main principles regarding integrity include independence, confidentiality, avoiding conflicts of interest and maintaining professional standards. Factors that create integrity risks can include pressure of work and financial pressures. However, there are a variety of ethical and integrity safeguards, both voluntary and compulsory, that can guide notaries through these risks. These include confidentiality, the notaries' code of practice, practice rules, conflict of interest guidelines and training.

Chapter 2 of the Code of Practice mentions that notaries are authorised to carry out reserve legal activities. The fact that notaries are authorised persons shows that notaries are trusted to conduct themselves with integrity in relation to the provisions of legal services generally. The acts of a notary authenticated in England and Wales are accepted and relied throughout the world as full and final proof of the matters authenticated.

3. **Maintain independence and impartiality**
"Independence" means the notary's independence, and not merely the ability to deal independently with a client. A notary should avoid situations which might put independence at risk - e.g. giving control of the notary's practice to a third party which is beyond the regulatory reach of the Faculty Office.

Every notary should subordinate his/her personal interests, within which he carries on professional activities or in which he has an interest, to those of his client and should safeguard his professional independence at all times. No notary shall conclude an agreement that could jeopardize the independence, impartiality, objectivity, or integrity required to practise the notarial profession.

A notary shall avoid all situations where he/she could have a conflict of interest and the notary's judgment or loyalty may be unfavourably affected. Chapter 3 of the Code of Practice points out that independence also encompasses the ability of a notary to give independent advice to clients and provide notarial services independently. Every notary should inform his client in writing of the fees and disbursements paid to a third party or paid by a third party on behalf of the client.

4. **Proper standard of service**
Notaries should provide a proper standard of client care and of work. This includes exercising competence, skill and diligence and taking into account the individual needs and circumstances of each client. For a notary, being competent and efficient is an integral part of the requirement to provide a proper standard of service.

A notary is expected to provide services to clients in a manner which protects their interests in the matter, complies with the proper administration of justice (particularly when deciding whether to accept or terminate any instructions) and the notary must comply with the Practice Rules 2014. Services provided by notaries to their clients should be delivered in a timely manner and notaries should take account of clients' needs and circumstances.

Clients should be informed as to how the services are being provided and regulated. Clients should be informed in writing at the outset of their matter of their right to complain and how complaints are dealt by the regulator and legal ombudsman. Clients should receive the best possible information at the time of engagement about the likely overall cost of their matter and of complaints procedure.

Chapter 4 of the Code of Practice points that providing a prompt service also means that, before accepting the client's instructions, the notary ensures that he/she is able to act on them properly and promptly. Providing a proper standard of service means exercising competence, skill and diligence. The particular needs and circumstances of each client should be taken into consideration. Notarial misconduct includes following below the standard of service reasonably expected of a notary.

5. **Maintain trust in the office of a notary's**
Members of the public should be able to place their trust in the office of a notary. Any behaviour either within or outside the professional practice which undermines this trust, damages not only the notary, but also the ability of the notarial profession as a whole to serve society.

According to the results of a survey commissioned by consumer watchdog, the Legal Services Consumer Panel, in 2011, less than half of the general public trust the legal profession. Lawyers ran third in the table of 'trustworthy' professions, after doctors, who were trusted by 85%, and teachers, trusted by 71%.

As a special type of lawyer, living in a world where people generally do not always trust the legal profession, notaries have an opportunity to stand out from the crowd. Notaries can show why notaries can be trusted and should do all in their power to accomplish this. Notaries need to show clients that notaries know what we are doing, are not going to overcharge them and will do all they can to help the client.

Chapter 5 of the Code of Practice mentions that whilst acting as a notary the behaviour should be such which reflects the high standards and integrity of the notarial profession. One meaning of the trust in the office of notary is that clients confidential information is protected once it has been entrusted to a notary. Trust in the office of notary is that trust may be placed in the notarial act prepared by a notary. The notarial act shall be tamperproof as much as possible particularly if it extends to more than a sheet of paper. The security of notarial act should be backed by notarial records.

6. **Comply with legal and regulatory obligations**
A notary should ensure that he/she complies with all the profession's reporting and notification requirements and respond promptly and substantively to professional communications. A notary needs to ensure that he/she complies with all the reporting and notification requirements in the Practice Rules 2014 and the Code of Practice. A notary should provide the Faculty Office with correct and proper information to enable the Faculty Office to decide upon any application for a practising certificate or registration.

A notary needs to notify the Faculty Office promptly of any material changes to relevant information about himself/herself, including serious financial difficulty, action taken against the notary by another regulator and any serious failure to comply with General Principles. A notary should co-operate fully with the Faculty Office and the Legal Ombudsman at all times including in relation to any inspection and investigation about a claim for redress against such notary.

Pursuant to a notice under Rule 24 of the Practice Rules 2014, a notary should produce, for inspection to the inspector appointed by the Faculty Office, documents held by such notary. Notaries need to provide all information and explanations requested and to comply with all requests from the Faculty Office as to the form in which notarial documents are held electronically including any passwords.

According to chapter 6 of the Code of Practice an unrestricted practising certificate authorises a notary to provide services generally, including reserved legal activities. Any restriction placed on the notaries practising certificate must be complied with. Notaries must provide clients with a signposting notice that explains the right to complain and how the complaint may be made.

7. Sound management principles

Responsibility for the management of his/her business rests with the notary. The notary should determine what arrangements are appropriate to meet the professional outcomes. Factors to be taken into account will include the size and complexity of work, experience and qualifications of colleagues; the number of offices and the nature of the work undertaken.

Where the notary is using a third party to provide services (often described as "outsourcing", such as legalisation of notarial acts) it is extremely important to have a clear time scale and ensuring consent has been obtained to use such a third party.

Effective systems and controls should be in place to achieve and comply with all these 'Principles'. The notary needs to identify, monitor and manage risks to comply with all the Principles.

The notary needs to maintain systems and controls for monitoring the financial stability of the practice and risks to money and documents entrusted by clients and others. The notary needs to comply with legislation applicable to the practice, including anti-money laundering and data protection legislation. The notary should purchase the level of professional indemnity insurance cover that is appropriate for practice, taking into account potential levels of claim by clients. Also, the necessary fidelity insurance should be in place as required by the Faculty Office by joining The Notaries Guarantee Limited. The current fidelity and professional indemnity insurance is required for at least one million pounds.

Protection of confidential information is a fundamental feature of a notary's relationship with clients. It exists as a concept both as a matter of law and as a matter of conduct. This duty continues despite the end of the matter and even after the death of the client.

Sound management principles according to chapter 7 of the Code of Practice means managing the notarial practice effectively and conscientiously. Notaries are obliged to maintain proper premises at which clients may be seen safely and in comfort, the availability of suitable equipment for the issuance of notarial acts, including computer hardware and printing facilities.

8. **Provide equal opportunity and respect for diversity**

This Principle goes to the heart of the duty of a public notary – to be available to any member of the public. It is important to encourage equality of opportunity and respect for diversity, and preventing unlawful discrimination, in relationship with any clients. The requirements apply in relation to age, disability, gender reassignment, marriage and civil partnership, pregnancy and maternity, race, religion or belief, sex and sexual orientation.

Everyone needs to contribute to compliance with these requirements, for example by treating each other and clients fairly and with respect, by embedding such values in the workplace and by challenging inappropriate behaviour and processes.

As a matter of general law everyone must comply with requirements set out in legislation - including the Equality Act 2010. A notary must not discriminate unlawfully, or victimise or harass anyone, in the course of his/her professional dealings. A notary should make reasonable adjustments to ensure that disabled clients are not placed at a substantial disadvantage compared to those who are not disabled and must not pass on the costs of these adjustments to these disabled clients. Any complaints of discrimination should be dealt with promptly, fairly, openly, and effectively by the notary.

Under chapter 8 of the Code of Practice Equality is also relevant with notarial firms. When advertising and accessing applications, all applicants must be given equal opportunity. The principle also relates to protection that must be given to vulnerable clients. Vulnerability may be derived from literacy, disability, mental health issues, illness, divorce or loss of employment.

Chapter 6

SUPERVISION

NOTARIES (POST-ADMISSION) RULES 2009 ("2009 Rules"), which came into force during the year 2009, require that during the period of practice under supervision the notary to whom these rules apply ("the supervised notary") shall practise as a notary only under the supervision of another notary ("the supervisor"). The supervisor shall hold a current practising certificate entered in or issued from the Court of Faculties and must have been engaged in actual practice as a notary for a minimum period of five years from the date of admission.

Under the 2009 Rules, a notary acting as supervisor shall be located within a reasonable distance, unlike previous rules where there was a restriction to be located within a radius of 50 miles (or within a distance which s/he is able to travel in two hours in normal conditions, if shorter) from the office of the supervised notary.

Under the 2009 Rules the following aspects of a notary's practice shall be excluded from the general requirement of supervision:

(a)   conveyancing and probate, in the case of a notary who is also a solicitor and who would be entitled to carry out conveyancing and probate as a solicitor without supervision, or who does in fact receive such supervision in relation to his practice as a solicitor as is required by the Solicitors Act 1974 and the rules made thereunder;

(b)   conveyancing, in the case of a notary who is also a licensed conveyancer and who would be entitled to carry out conveyancing as such without supervision, or who does in fact receive such supervision in relation to his practice as a licensed conveyancer as is required by the statutes and rules governing that profession.

Under the Old Rules the supervisor was required to visit the office of the supervised notary at least once in every period of four months and was required to inspect the records and accounts of the supervised notary relating to that period.

Under the 2009 Rules a new obligation has been imposed on the supervised notary with regard to visiting the supervisor. The supervised notary shall visit the office of the supervisor (a) no later than six months after the supervisor's first visit, and (b) for a second time no later than six months after the supervisor's second visit. The supervised notary shall produce to the supervisor for inspection the records and accounts of the supervised notary. The two years of supervised practice should be continuous. Breaking the supervised period for any reason will require an explanation and the supervisor will invariably require the period to be extended, which will be supported by the Faculty Office.

The supervisor is required to make himself/herself available at all reasonable times to offer advice and guidance to the supervised notary on matters covered by the supervision and shall make enquiries of the supervised notary at least once in every three month period by e-mail or other means of communication as to the notary's progress and any matter of concern to the supervised notary. The supervised notary shall within one week of receipt of the supervisor's communication provide the supervisor by e-mail or other means of communication a short report about his/her progress and shall include any request for advice and guidance as necessary, and both the supervisor and the supervised notary shall keep a record of these communications. The supervisor must contact the supervised notary at least every three months raising any matters of concern to which the supervised notary must respond within one week.

The supervisor notary is entitled to charge the supervised notary a fee. An Order made by the Master, entitled the Notaries (Supervision & Fees) Regulations 2010 under Rule 8 of the Notaries (Post-Admission) Rules 2009, increased the maximum fee which may be charged by a supervisor from £100 to £250 together with reasonable expenses, travel and (where necessary) accommodation plus the amount of any VAT due thereon.

The underlying ethos of supervision is to build a practical relationship between the supervisor and the supervised notary. Rule 4 of 2009 Rules deals with the choice of supervisor. It is always sensible to have the supervisor in a different location so that there are no conflicts in terms of business competition between supervisor and supervisee.

The supervisee is required to comply with 2009 Rules and the Practice Rules 2014 as amended in 2017. The compliance issue is stipulated in Rule 5 of the 2009 Rules and puts an obligation on the supervisor to ensure that the supervisee conducts himself/herself "in a manner calculated to maintain the reputation of the office and profession of public notary".

A large number of senior notaries are sometimes not willing to act as supervisors as they are not clear about what is expected of them. Having conducted research on Notary Talk in relation to supervision it was clear from the responses of younger notaries that some supervisors are very diligent and they look at records, accounts etc. very seriously and spend around 2 to 3 hours in every meeting, whereas some supervisors just have lunch with their supervisees and discuss matters briefly. Some new notaries feel that more meetings are needed in the first year as compared to the second year. A few feel that four meetings are not enough.

At the end of the supervision period a formal report will be required from the supervisor. There is no prescribed form but it should include:

- An indication of the courses and seminars attended by the supervised notary under rule 6.
- The opinion of the supervisor as to whether the supervised notary should be permitted to practise without supervision.

Both the supervisor and the supervised notary shall respond in writing to any questions put by the Master in relation to the supervision and produce to the Faculty Office such documents as the Master may require.

It appears to me that there are varying standards in notarial work. In order to be consistent throughout the profession it is important to have a supervision agreement in writing whereby it is clear from day one what is expected from both the supervisor and the supervised notary. This is the standard practice for training barristers and solicitors. The Bar Standards Board, which regulates barristers, recommends a "pupillage contract" and the SRA recommends a "training contract" for trainee solicitors. It is also important to have a supervision agreement where a supervisor is supervising only notarial matters excluding probate and conveyancing.

The supervisor should meet the notary at his/her office, as soon as possible after s/he has received his faculty, so that s/he can check that the notary is ready to practise. The meeting must not be more than one month after the notary has been issued with his/her first practising certificate.

The supervisor should ensure that the supervised notary has all the basic equipment, insurance and practising certificate in order to enable him/her to commence notarial practice and discuss the following:

1.   The notary needs to be familiar with the Notaries Practice Rules 2014 and especially rules relating to record-keeping, fees, inspection, publicity and impartiality.

2.   The supervised notary needs to be familiar with Notaries Post-Admission Rules 2009;

3.   The supervised notary needs to be aware of money laundering guidance and rules relating to this area;

4.   If the supervised notary is involved with probate and conveyancing it is very likely that a client account would need to be maintained. However, if he/she is only undertaking notarial practice, a separate account should be sufficient. It is certainly not recommended to mix professional income with a personal bank account.

5.   Where the supervised notary is working in a firm of solicitors, the firm's letterhead should not be used for notarial practice. The majority of notaries have their own separate letterheads;

6.   Notarial stationery is a prerequisite before commencing practice. There are various colours of wafers and ribbons which the supervised notary can use. However, it is important to be consistent and not change the colours frequently. A good quality seal always helps. Both manual and electronic riveters are available. Eyelets are available in three different sizes, 3.2 mm, 4.2 mm and 5.5 mm.

7.   Notarial inspectors are keen that the notarial seal should be locked overnight. It is therefore important to have a secure place for this purpose.

8.   Notarytalk is a discussion forum for notaries in England and Wales. Membership is recommended and there is no membership fee. The supervised notary may either contact Avril McDowell direct at avril.mcdowell@btclick.com or Laura Delacroix-Humphreys at notary@delacroix-humphreys.com.

9.   There is a lot of information which the supervised notary may find useful on the Notaries Society and Notary Training websites. It is recommended to get familiar with these websites. (www.thenotariessociety.org.uk & www.notarytraining.co.uk)

10. Books relating to notarial issues are certainly a great help. These include "Brooke's Notary", Dunford's "The Notary: a practical guide for England and Wales" and "The Notary's Clerk", Butler's "Solemn Acts in Foreign Languages" (scanned version available) and Sanjay Gogia's "Notarial Practice in India" and "The Notary's Manual".

11. Notarial records are required to be maintained for both private and public form documents. The supervised notary should maintain a protocol for public form notarial acts and a notarial register for private

form notarial acts. Compliance with rule 23 is of utmost importance for a practising notary. Such records should be kept in a place which is secure and accessible as and when required.

12. The majority of notarised documents require an Apostille from the Foreign and Commonwealth office (FCO) or an Apostille and legalisation by the Consulate/Embassy. The supervised notary needs to know a good consular agent.

13. All notaries are required to provide their specimen signatures to the FCO together with an impression of their notarial seal. Some embassies/consulates may also require specimen signatures and seals.

14. It is compulsory to hold professional indemnity and fidelity insurance before commencement of notarial practice. The current requirements for both professional indemnity insurance and fidelity insurance are £1 million.

15. Registration with the Information Commissioner's office is advisable. The current fee is £35 per annum.

16. Terms and conditions of practice should be provided to clients at the time of any new instructions. There is a helpful precedent in chapter 4 of this manual. These also include signposting in relation to complaints.

17. Every newly qualified notary is required to attend one education day in each of the first two years. The Notaries Society provides these courses, which are accredited by the Faculty Office.

The Master of the Faculties is undertaking a full overhaul of the Post-Admission Rules and after consultation with both the societies it is likely that the new rules will be in place later this year or early next year.

SUPERVISION AGREEMENT

I certainly recommend that the supervised notary draws up an agreement before the commencement of supervision between the supervisor and the supervised notary, laying out in detail the arrangements and ambit of supervision as well as the grounds on which supervision might be terminated. This could include the following:

This contract is made on

Between   (name of Supervisor) and
                                                   (name of the Supervised notary)

1.   The purpose of this agreement is to set out the principle duties and responsibilities of the Supervisor and the Supervised notary in accordance with the Notaries (Post Admission) Rules 2009 and guidance issued from time to time by The Faculty Office.

2.   The Supervisor agrees to provide training to the Supervisee in accordance with the requirements of the Faculty Office.

3.   The Supervised notary agrees to be trained by the Supervisor.

4.   Supervisor has appointed (Insert name of supervisor) to be the Supervisor who will ensure that training is given in accordance with the requirements of the Faculty Office.

Date of commencement and fixed term

5.   This contract commenced on ………… and shall continue for 2 years or until the Supervision is completed if longer, subject to the provisions for earlier termination.

Undertakings of Supervisee

6.   The supervisee will:
     a.   Make a payment of £250 plus VAT (if applicable) for each supervision meeting or any other fee prescribed by the Faculty Office from time to time.
     b.   Reimburse the supervisor for reasonable expenses incurred by the Supervisor for the purposes of the supervision.

7. The Supervisor shall not delegate any of his/her responsibilities under this agreement to any other person without the prior written consent of the supervisee. If applicable, the Supervisor will inform the supervisee of the name or names of those to whom responsibility has been delegated.

8. The Supervisor will:
    a. ensure that adequate arrangements are made for the supervision and guidance of the supervisee;
    b. make suitable arrangements to monitor the supervisee's progress and provide feedback on progress;
    c. ensure that there are adequate arrangements for helping the Supervised notary;
    d. comply with the requirements of the Faculty Office.

Undertakings of the Supervised notary

9. The Supervised notary will:
    a. Carry out faithfully and diligently any task of an educational nature or reasonable instructions given by the supervisor.
    b. Keep a proper record of training received and work done;
    c. Comply with the requirements of the Faculty Office;
    d. Attend both education days as required by the Supervisor and the Faculty Office.
    e. Treat all information about the clients of the supervisor as wholly confidential;

Disputes

10. Any dispute about this contract or the conduct of either party in relation to it may be referred to the Faculty Office (or any delegated person) who must deal with it within two weeks of referral.

Applicable law

11. This contract shall be subject to English Law.

Notice

12. Any notice in respect of matters in this contract must be in writing and given either personally or by email addressed to either party.

Termination

13. This contract may be terminated by:
  a. Agreement between the Supervisor and Supervisee.
  b. The Supervisor in the event of:
   i. Serious notarial misconduct by the Supervisee;
   ii. Poor performance by the Supervisee provided that at least one formal written warning about performance has been given prior to the termination.
  c. One month's notice in writing given by the Supervised notary giving reasons for such termination.

Signed by the Supervisor
Date

Signed by the Supervised notary
Date

Chapter 7

COMPLAINTS

There are six reserved legal activities – the exercise of a right of audience in court, the conduct of litigation, reserved instrument activities, probate activities, notarial activities and the administration of oaths. These activities can only be carried out by authorised persons or exempt persons as defined by the Legal Services Act 2007. Authorised persons are those persons authorised to carry on the activity by a relevant approved regulator. Our relevant approved regulator is the Faculty Office. However, the LSB is the overarching regulator. It is a criminal offence to carry out a reserved legal activity without appropriate authorisation and the offence attracts a 12 months maximum sentence on summary conviction or a 2 year sentence on indictment.

To complain about the work of a notary, a client needs to first ascertain that the individual was providing legal services in the capacity of a notary (and not as a Solicitor or other legal professional). Every client of a notary shall be supplied with information about the complaints procedure when the notary is first instructed.

If the complainant wishes to make a formal complaint about the service received from a Notary he should first endeavour to raise the issue with the Notary directly. If this does not resolve the matter he should follow the complaints procedure.

STEP 1 - First Tier Complaints Procedure
If the Notary is a Scrivener Notary, contact the Society of Scrivener Notaries for the 1st-stage complaints procedure. For all other Notaries, contact the Secretary of the Notaries Society for the 1st-stage complaints procedure. The relevant Society will be able to inform the Complainant if a Notary is a member. If the Notary is not a member of either of the membership bodies, the Faculty Office will handle the matter directly, and will refer the complaint to be considered by one of a panel of independent Notaries. The 1st-stage procedure is free to use and is designed to provide a quick resolution to any dispute. The Complainant should write (but not enclosing any original documents) with full details of the complaint to the relevant Society (or, if applicable, to The Faculty Office). If the Complainant has any difficulty making a complaint in writing, the Complainant may call the relevant Society or The Faculty Office for assistance. Under this step the matter is considered by two senior notaries

usually the President and Vice President who make a decision, in many cases as to what the fair charge should be for the work done.

STEP 2 - Formal Investigation

If a complaint is made against a Notary and is not resolved under the 1st-stage procedure, the matter is then referred by the Registrar of the Faculty Office to an experienced independent Notary (a 'Nominated Notary') for investigation. Allegations about the conduct or practice of a Scrivener Notary are referred to the Society of Scrivener Notaries. Whilst the matter is being investigated or proceedings are in progress the Registrar may issue an Interim Order to suspend the Notary from practice or limit the Notary's practice if it is required for the protection of the public.

STEP 3 - Disciplinary Proceedings in the Court of Faculties

If the Nominated Notary considers there may be a case that the Notary has committed Notarial Misconduct the Nominated Notary will prepare and prosecute disciplinary proceedings in the Court of Faculties. In such a scenario the Nominated Notary becomes the Competent Complainant. Disciplinary cases in the Court of Faculties are presided over by an independent judge (the 'Commissary' or his Deputy) sitting with two Assessors; not the Master of the Faculties. The details of the timetable for Proceedings in the Court are set out in the Notaries (Conduct and Discipline) Rules 2015, subject to any case-specific directions by the Registrar or Commissary.

The disciplinary sanctions against a Notary who is proved to have committed Notarial Misconduct are:
- Striking off the Roll of Notaries
- Suspension from practice as a Notary (indefinitely, or for a period of time, or until certain conditions have been met)
- Imposing conditions on the Notarial practice of the Notary
- Requiring further training of the Notary
- Ordering that the Notary is reprimanded

A Notary may, in time, apply to the Court for a review of the sanction(s) imposed. The Court of Faculties has power to require compensation payments to be made by the Notary to the client who has suffered loss as a result of the Notary's Misconduct. The Court can further order that if indemnity or other monetary payments are not made by the Notary to the client or other person/body then the Notary shall be struck off the Roll of Notaries.

It is pertinent that such a client can only be indemnified where the client can prove that "actual loss" as a result of notarial misconduct has been suffered. The Court of Faculties shall not direct any payment exceeding £10,000 or such higher sum as the Master may from time to time specify for the purpose of the Conduct and Discipline Rules. The Court of Faculties has discretion in relation to payment of costs and it may be any of the following:

1. The costs of either party to the complaint to be paid by the other party;
2. The costs of the court be paid by either party or by both parties, whether in equal or unequal shares;
3. The cost of either party or of the court to be paid from the contingency fund; or
4. A party against whom an order for costs is made shall instead of paying those costs to the other party or the court pay them into the contingency fund.

STEP 4 – Dissatisfaction with Complaints Procedures

If the Complainant decides to make a complaint to the Legal Ombudsman, the Complainant must refer the matter to the Legal Ombudsman within six months from the conclusion of the complaints process. The details of Legal Ombudsman are:
Legal Ombudsman
PO Box 6806
Wolverhampton, WV1 9WJ
Tel: 0300 555 0333
Email: enquiries@legalombudsman.org.uk
Website: www.legalombudsman.org.uk

The Legal Ombudsman deals with complaints about poor service. Poor service includes failure to keep the client properly informed about their legal matter. The Faculty Office deals with failures to comply with professional obligations as provided in Notaries Practice Rules 2014. The Legal Ombudsman's website will help identify how a Client can best receive help. If a Client reports poor service to the Legal Services Ombudsman and they consider this amounts to a failure to comply with professional obligations they will also pass the matter to the Faculty Office to consider. The Legal Ombudsman may direct a firm or individual to pay compensation for poor service.

A notary might have to refer a complainant to the Faculty Office rather than the Legal Ombudsman if it is an allegation of misconduct.

Regulation

Complaints has been a vexed and unhappy question for much of the legal profession other than notaries for years, probably caused by being self regulated. The statutory powers given to the Ombudsman - the ability to command the co-operation of lawyers and impose remedies including compensation have proved key to avoiding the sorts of impasse which bedevilled the previous arrangements relating to solicitors. But whereas in other areas of professional life the introduction of a genuinely independent Ombudsman scheme led to a significant rise in the number of customers complaining, there has been no such increase with notaries.

However, YouGov research carried out a few years ago showed that the biggest brake on complaints was customer fear. In some cases, this was merely fear of looking a fool. Law is a mysterious business with its own language and traditions, not easily accessible to the layperson but many complainants feared that the response from the lawyer would be less than helpful. What notaries need to remember is that good complaints handling is good for business. In notarial practice, it remains the case that most clients come via personal recommendation and keeping customers happy is essential to future income.

The Notaries Conduct and Discipline Rules 2015 have been revised due to a number of recent disciplinary cases. It is important to limit the costs of disciplinary cases especially as costs were high and depleted the contingency fund. Under the 2015 Rules, scrivener notaries will be able to investigate a complaint against a general notary and a general notary will be able to investigate a complaint against a scrivener notary. Now there is no distinction between scrivener and general notaries for the purposes of these rules except for first tier complaints. Complaints against general notaries are to be referred to The Notaries Society and in case of scriveners the complaint will be referred to The Scriveners Company.

Under the 2015 rules, a "notarial act" means any act that has validity by virtue only of its preparation, performance, authentication, attestation or verification by a notary and includes any such act carried out by electronic means. "Notarial misconduct" under the 2015 rules means any the following:
1.   Fraudulent conduct;
2.   Practising as a notary without a valid notarial practising certificate or in breach of a condition or limitation imposed on a notarial practising certificate.
3.   Serious misconduct which may include failure to observe the requirements of these rules or of the Notaries Practice Rules 2014

or falling seriously below the standard of service reasonably to be expected of a notary or persistent failure to provide the standard of service reasonably expected of a notary.

As provided in STEP 2 above, where a complaint is made against a notary and is not resolved under the first tier procedure, the registrar of the Faculty Office then appoints a nominated notary who must have held a notarial practising certificate for not less than five years. A nominated notary shall be independent of and not personally be acquainted with the notary who is the subject of the allegation of the notarial misconduct being investigated. If the Registrar is unable to identify a nominated notary who fulfils the requirement under the 2015 rules the Master may appoint an independent person who need not be a notary to act in place of a nominated notary and that person shall carry out all functions conferred on the nominated notary by the 2015 Rules.

A power is also given to nominated notaries to inspect documents in the possession of a notary in the course of an investigation into possible notarial misconduct subject to a duty not to disclose the document(s) or information without leave of the court except in the detection, investigation or prosecution of a crime, to the law enforcement and prosecution authorities. The principal duties of the nominated notary have been set out for the first time:

1.   to diligently and expeditiously investigate evidence of or an allegation of notarial misconduct;
2.   report in writing to the registrar;
3.   to make a complaint and prepare and prosecute disciplinary proceedings against a notary in the court of faculties if after investigation, the nominated notary reasonably believes that there is a prime facie case of notarial misconduct to be answered.

It is now the practice in the Court of Faculties to give written evidence in the form of a witness statement containing a statement of truth rather than in an affidavit form. The advantage is that a statement of truth need not be sworn or affirmed before a solicitor, notary or other commissioner for oaths. It is provided that hearings should be in public unless this would cause exceptional hardship or exceptional prejudice to party, witness etc or would prejudicial to the interests of justice. The Court of Faculties shall make finding of facts on the balance of probabilities. However, if the allegation made against the notary involves directly or by implication a finding of fraud, dishonesty or criminal activity on the part of the notary, the court must be satisfied on the evidence beyond reasonable doubt.

Cases at the Court of Faculties.

In the matter of Simon Dickson Meadows Craven
This is a case of September 1996. In this case the Nominated Notary investigated allegations of Notarial Misconduct by Mr Craven. The allegations were:
- That between June 1992 and April 1996 Mr Craven practised as a Notary in such a manner as compromised and/or impaired the good repute of the notary or the Notary's profession and/or the Notary's proper standard of work as required under the Notaries Practice Rules 1998 and
- In the same period, he failed to ensure that his office was properly supervised as required by Notaries Practice Rules 1998.

The Court of Faculties concluded that the office where he practised was not properly adequately supervised and was harmful to the repute of notaries generally. The other issue arose as to whether a letter dated the 6th January 1995 was an undertaking that subject to production of satisfactory receipts he would reimburse the client the cost of installing an alarm system and locks at the former matrimonial home but thereafter he failed to honour that undertaking.

Mr Craven's denied that he was practising notary and claimed even if he were he had not given any undertaking to pay for the cost of the locks. The Court of Faculties found that he had been practising as a notary, that the letter of 16 January 1995 was an undertaking that he had received an invoice for the work for which he had taken no steps to verify or disprove despite his suspicions about it.

The Court held that Mr Craven was in breach of his undertaking. In the light of these findings it was held that he should be suspended from practice until further order. Mr Craven was ordered to pay the costs of the Nominated Notary and the expenses to the Court.

In the matter of John Anthony Orchard
This is also an unreported case of December 2007 and the following are relevant extracts from the court's judgement. The complaint is put on the basis of an affidavit from the Nominated Notary dated 3rd April 2007 which stated that:
(i) On or about 5th August 2005 John Anthony Orchard informed his client that the fees payable for certifying a copy of his passport for use in the United States of America would be approximately or about £50.

(ii)   On 12th August 2005, John Anthony Orchard sent a bill for £70 for his fees for certifying a copy of such a passport and £19 for a legalisation fee payable to the Foreign & Commonwealth Office.

(iii)   Either such fee exceeded by £20 the fee made known in advance by John Anthony Orchard pursuant to Rule 15.1 of the Notaries Practice Rules 2001 or alternatively Mr Orchard did not make known in advance to his client the basis on which his fee for providing a certified copy of a passport would be calculated or the fee to be charged for such service as required by the same rule.

Nominated Notary's affidavit was supported by Mr. Perry's witness statement of which Mr Orchard had notice. Nominated Notary's affidavit did not include the letter which Mr Orchard wrote to the client dated 14th September 2005 which ended with the threat. "If I do not receive settlement within the next seven days I will notify the IRS that you are not willing to pay for the certificate to be legalised at the Foreign Office and I wish to cancel the same". The Court of Faculties said the following:

"We considered this case on the basis on which it was put before us namely a breach of Rule 15.1 of the Notaries Practice Rules 2001 which it is said amounted to conduct unbefitting of a notary. A Notary may charge a professional fee for all notarial work undertaken by him and the basis upon which such fee will be calculated or the fee to be charged for the work done should be made known in advance to any new client. We find a charge of approximately or about £50 quoted by Mr Orchard, or in the words of the Rules was made known to Mr Parry. This having been done the fee should have been £50 and not £70. Mr Parry was entirely within his rights to insist on the fee of £50. The Court of Faculties said this rule is one of the most important rules for the protection on the public and must be strictly adhered to. The client is entitled to know precisely the basis of the charges he will have to pay. Mr Orchard not only did not observe this basic rule of conduct but failed to correct the fee when the discrepancy was pointed out to him. We considered that this was conduct unbefitting a notary."

The Court of Faculties held that "It is not entirely clear to the court whether or not Mr. Parry has paid Mr Orchard's fee (as opposed to disbursements). If he has paid more than £50 we order Mr Orchard indemnifies Mr. Parry in respect of any sum which his client has paid over £50 (plus the £19 disbursements which it is agreed should have been paid). In addition, Mr Orchard should pay Mr. Parry a penalty of £100 in respect of the time and trouble which he has caused his client and Mr Orchard must also pay the costs of the Nominated Notary amounting to

£1,045, 00. However, he must pay the court costs amounting to £350 and the expenses of the assessor members of the panel amounting to £720."

In the matter of Gurrinder Singh Matharu

This is also an unreported case of December 2007. Gurrinder Singh Matharu was a notary in Birmingham. He was involved in the sale of property in West Midlands. In the same matter he was acting for the mortgagee (which was his father's company and he was the secretary of that company). There was a clear conflict of interest and the practice rules were very clear where there was conflict of interest in a conveyancing transaction. Mr. Matharu practising certificate was endorsed by the Faculty Office that he shall not act as notary in a conveyancing matter and he was required to pay £3,500 Nominated Notary's fee and pay £1,370 court fees and expenses.

In the matter of Robert JH Ward

This is a reported matter of April 2015. A complaint was made against Mr Ward by the Nominated Notary under Conduct and Discipline Rules 2011. As a result of his investigation into the conduct of Mr Ward the Nominated Notary made the following allegations:-

(a)   He had represented both parties to a Declaration of Trust without obtaining written consent to act for both sides.
(b)   Flawed drafting of the Declaration of Trust.
(c)   He failed to notify the mortgage company, which he represented, as required of material facts relating to the status of the purchaser and the property.
(d)   Failure to advise that an unsigned Will was invalid.
(e)   Failure to list the assets on the Will.
(f)   Failure to advise on the inclusion of a property within the Will.
(g)   Failure to advise on the consequences of leaving one of their children out of the Will.
(h)   Ambiguous drafting of the Will.
(i)   A failure to identify for whom he was acting in respect of the administration of the estate.
(j)   Acting for parties when there was a conflict.
(k)   Misleading a party from whom he had accepted instructions as to his entitlement.

As there were number of complaints set out by the Nominated Notary, the Court decided that these could be divided into four parts and addressed this complaint accordingly.

1. The declaration of trust

The Court of Faculties considered that, whatever the parties to the Declaration wanted him to do, Mr Ward should have advised them to seek separate advice. The Court believed that, had that happened, the subsequent difficulties may never have occurred. The Court was aware of the benefit of hindsight in these matters and did not make any adverse finding against him in this regard. On its own this does not amount to serious misconduct but is indicative of a less than careful approach to his work as a Notary.

The Court was of the view that the drafting of the Declaration was seriously flawed. The court held that the drafting of the Declaration did not follow the express instructions of the parties to it.

2. The Mortgage offer

The client applied for a mortgage. Mr Ward was under a duty to inform the mortgagee of certain material facts. The duty was on him to provide his client with that material information. The court held that in respect of his client, he nevertheless fell seriously below the standard of service reasonably to be expected of a Public Notary in such a way as to amount to serious misconduct.

3. The Will

The court was of the view an ambiguity in drafting each of the Wills would have resulted in the beneficiary receiving £5,000 on the death of the client to the detriment of the other beneficiaries under the Will. The Court of Faculties considered this to be a fundamental and basic error in drafting and the Court was very surprised that a Notary with over 30 years' experience and a person who was for many years a qualified solicitor should make such an error. The Court concluded that he fell seriously below the standard of service reasonably to be expected of a Public Notary in such a way as to amount to serious misconduct.

4. Administration of Estate

The allegation made by the Nominated Notary was that Mr. Ward continued to accept instructions from both parties in relation to the administration of the estate. The court rejected Mr Ward's submission that he was motivated to act as he did to save the family costs and held he should not have done so. A failure to recognise the conflict amounted to serious misconduct. The Court decided that the appropriate penalty was to order that Mr Ward be admonished. "Mr Ward will have to pay the costs of the Nominated Notary. Unless and until the Rules are amended the Court was constrained not to award the costs of the investigation of this Complaint against Mr Ward. The Court calculated that the costs incurred in preparing for and presenting this case were £10,961.16. In addition, Mr

Ward had to pay the court costs (not quantified). The Court ordered that the costs of investigation, being £5,000 plus VAT, making a total of £6,000, are to be borne by the Contingency Fund."

A full decision on this matter is on the Faculty Office website.

In the matter of Ricardo Antonio Lado

This is a reported matter of April 2015. There were two Complaints made by the Nominated Notary under the Notaries (Conduct and Discipline) Rules 2011 ("the 2011 Rules") against Ricardo Antonio Lado ("Mr Lado"). The Nominated Notary presented the complaints and Mr Lado was represented by Mr Daniel Follon of Counsel. The first Complaint was under the following heads and it was alleged that Mr Lado:

(1) failed to carry out the instructions of his clients within a reasonable time or, in some cases, at all;

(2) failed to keep his clients informed of progress or lack of progress in their respective matters;

(3) charged clients fees for work he did for them which were unreasonably high;

(4) charged clients for work which he had not done;

(5) failed to supply clients with the information required by rules 5A and 15 of the Notaries Practice Rules 2009 either at all or else at an unreasonably long time after accepting instructions; and

(6) issued notarial documents which were untrue or in the alternative misleading.

The second Complaint with another client it was alleged Notarial Misconduct by Mr Lado in that he:

(1) failed to carry out instruction of his client within a reasonable time or, in some cases, at all;

(2) failed to keep his client informed of progress or lack of progress in the matter in which he was instructed; and

(3) failed to do what he said he would do and in relation to the Nominated Notary investigations giving rise to the complaint.

As regards the allegation that Mr Lado failed to carry out instructions the Court of Faculties was of the view that although Mr Lado's conduct of their affairs was open to serious criticism the Court did not find Notarial Misconduct in this respect. However, the court found Notarial Misconduct proved in respect of Lado's failure to keep the client is informed of progress.

The allegation that the clients were charged unreasonably high fees was withdrawn during the hearing as was the allegation that they were not supplied with the information required by the 2009 Rules in respect of some of them. The remaining allegation was that Mr Lado charged for work which he had not done, namely the legalisation of the document. The document was not in fact legalised and at the time when Mr Lado first sent his bill he knew that it had not been. The court found Notarial Misconduct proved in this respect. As regards the Second Complaint which related to delay in carrying out the clients' instructions was inordinate and inexcusable. The court found Mr Lado's failure to keep the client of progress constituted Notarial Misconduct.

In relation to the remaining issue namely Mr Lado's failure to do what he said he would do and his failure to do what he said he would do in relation to the investigations of the Nominated Notary. The Court found Notarial Misconduct proved in this respect. The fact that the Nominated Notary asked Mr Lado for delivery of the file by May 2014 and the papers were only delivered to his client on 23 January 2015 spoke for itself. It was submitted to the court that the reason why Mr Lado did not accede to the Nominated Notary's request was that he considered him not to be independent. That may well have been the reason but it does not provide any measure of justification for a failure to comply with a reasonable requirement of an appointed Nominated Notary.

The Court accepted that from June 2014 Mr Lado was seriously unwell but this could provide no sort of explanation of the failure to deliver the papers for about 8 months. The file was not voluminous. Mr Lado said in evidence that he did a little light work whilst he was away ill and it is to be borne in mind that rule 21.3 of the 2014 Rules requires suitable alternative arrangements to be made without delay where the operation of a notary's office is prevented by illness.

The Court of Faculties felt that Mr Lado had a casual attitude to the carrying out of his instructions and keeping clients informed of progress and a reluctance to accept his failures in this respect. The Court felt that it may be that a major cause of his problems was that he accepted more work than he was able with his limited resources to undertake efficiently. The Court of Faculties penalised him with 2 years supervision and half day approved courses. He was also required to pay £6,500 part Nominated Notary's costs plus £9,839 which was 66% of court costs.
A full decision on this matter is on the Faculty Office website.

In the matter of Ella Elizabeth Imison
This is a reported matter of May 2014. There was a preliminary issue in this case which was required by the court to be considered in relation to standard of proof which the Court had to reach before finding misconduct. The Notaries (Conduct and Discipline) Rules 2011 is silent on the issue.

However, the then correct Paragraph 26 of the "Guidance for Nominated Notaries issued by the Master of the Faculties" states that:- "The Court applies the criminal standard of proof when adjudicating on a complaint."

The Court noted that the Solicitor's Regulatory Authority applies the civil standard of proof when it makes a disciplinary decision without referring it on to the Solicitor's Disciplinary Tribunal ("SDT"). The rules governing the SDT are silent as to the standard of proof to be adopted but seem to adopt the higher standard. The Bar maintains the criminal standard of proof. The Court decided on the balance of authority to apply the civil standard of proof in respect of the first two allegations, but in respect of the third allegation we have decided that the higher criminal standard of proof should be adopted.

In this case Ella Imison, Scrivener Notary accepted instructions from The Insight Companies in respect of public investment which they sought in a crop growing scheme in Mozambique known as the "Moringa Miracle Tree Project". It offered quick and attractive returns on the investment and attracted, amongst others, a number of retired people to invest. Over the period which was substantially in 2010 and 2011 approximately 100 investors invested a total of $3 million. All the money had been lost. There was no evidence of any crop growing having taken place or that the money was invested in any way in the scheme and it was concluded that this was a fraudulent scheme.

Firstly, the Court considered that it was not a normal notarial transaction. She was not asked to notarise any documents for use abroad. She was being used as little more than a post box for investors in this country to invest in the scheme in Mozambique. Ella Imison claimed that she was providing conveyancing services to her client but there was nothing to convey.

As a result of these and other issues The Court found that Ella Imison provided services on behalf of Insight group of companies in connection with purported agreements with the public for the alleged sale and purchase of rights in the Moringa Miracle Tree Project in circumstances which led to the public trust reposed in the office of notary being undermined.

The second allegation was on the requirements of the Notaries Accounts Rules 1989 ("NAR"). Ella Imison's client account designated "Imison & Co. Insight Client Account" received monies transferred to it by individual Investors. At the point of receipt, the Respondent's firm although not acting for an Investor was holding such money as agent or in some other capacity for an Investor and as such for the purposes of the NAR the money was therefore Client Money at that point.

The court was of the view that there was no evidence that the Respondent operated a client account in a manner that fell seriously below the standard of service reasonably to be expected of a public notary. The client account appears to have been operated with reasonable efficiency and therefore find Allegation 2 not proved.

The third Allegation contains reference to three alleged actions or inactions, namely,

(a) Failing to take adequate due diligence and/or ongoing monitoring measures and/or

(b) Failing to take adequate steps to record such measures as she had taken to satisfy herself that it was appropriate or prudent by reference to The Guidance to accept instructions, and/or

(c) Failing to take adequate steps to satisfy herself that she was not in breach of the Notaries (Prevention of Money Laundering) Rules 2008 by acting in a manner which fell seriously below the standard of service reasonably to be expected of public notary and/or in a manner likely to compromise and/or impair the good reputation of the notarial profession.

It was alleged that during May 2010 information came to Ella Imison in the course of business giving reasonable grounds for knowing or suspecting that a person was engaged in money laundering or terrorist financing as a result of which Ella Imison as the Nominated Officer should have lodged a report as required by Part 7 of the Proceeds of Crime Act 2002 and obtained the clearance referred to. The court was of the view that the complainant had not proved the allegation beyond reasonable doubt.

The second and third allegations were failures and in breach of Rule 3.2 of the Notaries (Prevention of Money Laundering) Rules 2008. The Court found that such failures are likely to compromise or impair the good repute of the notary or of the notarial profession and are therefore contrary to Rule 5.4 of the Notaries Practice Rules 2009. The court was of the view that the complainant had proved the allegation beyond reasonable doubt.

The court ordered that Ella Imison be suspended from practice as a Notary for a period of 4 months from 29th May 2014. From the end of that period and for five years thereafter Ella Imison may only act as a

Notary either in partnership with another qualified Notary or as an employee within another notarial firm.

The net costs payable by Ella Imison to the Complainant was £94,581.12, which had to be paid within six weeks. The balance of the costs payable to the Complainant were met from the Contingency fund in the amount of £65,418.88, comprising (1) £19,363-55 which the Complainant cannot recover from Ella Imison, (2) £19,020-83 of the Respondent's costs which is to be set off from the costs recoverable from the Respondent by the Complainant for work undertaken in respect of an allegation which was not pursued, an abandoned application to suspend Ella Imison and in respect of those parts of the allegations which were not proved, and (3) £27,034-50 being the costs of investigation. Ella Imison had to pay 75% of the Court costs and the balance of 25% is to be paid from the Contingency Fund.

A full decision on this matter is on the Faculty Office website.

Chapter 8

NOTARIAL INSPECTIONS

The first sort of inspection was a pilot study carried out by The Notaries Society in 1995 to try and find out how notaries were keeping their notarial records. Eleven notaries were inspected in the West Country, the twelfth notary who was asked to join in the study had kept no records. The study revealed a fairly reasonable standard of record keeping but several of the notaries who took part commented that they did not know what they should be keeping because 1991 Records rules simply stated:

3(1) It shall be the duty of every notary......to maintain and keep in accordance with good notarial practice a permanent record of all notarial acts.."

There was provision for clarification of what was god notarial practice in regulations and approved publications of which there was some guidance in The General Notary.

Following on from this The Notaries Society invited notaries to bring their records to the Annual conferences and Further Education Days in 1995 to 1999 for comments. A further 26 records were seen in this manner, ranging from some which were badly written that they were almost indecipherable to some keeping complete notarial records. I suspect that the Master could always have inspected a notary's records if he felt it necessary but the first specific rule providing for inspections seems to be rule 4 Notaries Record Rules 1991.That rule has continued in subsequent practice rules including Notaries Practice Rules 2014.

The LSB has been urging the Faculty Office that more has to be done in putting clients first in its report namely "Developing Regulatory Standards" published in December 2012. The Master then decided to conduct regular inspections and interventions to reassure the LSB that the Faculty Office was being more proactive. Sadly, in recent years public trust in traditional institutions – e.g. in the medical, legal, banking and political sectors has been seriously eroded.

In 2014 the Master made Notaries (Inspections) Regulations which sets out a scheme providing for an annual selection by the Registrar of notaries' records, practices for inspection and appointment of inspectors who have practised continuously for at least 10 years. The Faculty Office avoids any conflicts of interest between the inspector and the notary being inspected. The inspector's fees are paid by the Faculty Office which is currently £420 per inspection plus expenses. Inspectors are required to complete a pro forma questionnaire and make a short report summarising the inspection within 14 days. It is of paramount importance the preservation of confidentiality is maintained of the inspected records.

It is intended that the records and practices of around 20 notaries are inspected every year. The inspections are conducted by practising notaries who have more than 10 years' standing. The Faculty Office gives at least 7 days' notice to the notaries to be inspected. The inspecting notary will also provide a written summary of his findings in a report to the Master. So far 102 notaries have been selected for inspection including the ones in 2018 but not yet inspected. One notary refused to meet with the inspector and is no longer in practice. One was on a lengthy absence from his office. Two could not be inspected because of their ill health and substitutes were made for them. One notary was inspected twice because the standards of his practice was considered unsatisfactory on the first inspection. Until 2018 there was a division of inspections between the South and North of England and Wales. However, because there are many more notaries in the South-East of England this division has been abandoned and the previous 'North Inspector' is now being sent in to London.

The Master shall give such directions as he thinks fit which may include ordering a further inspection or inspections or the carrying out of training or supervision of the notary's practice, or aspects of it, and for such period or periods, as he may direct. Where the inspecting notary's report discloses matters which may amount to an allegation of notarial misconduct, as defined by rule 2.1 of the Notaries' (Conduct and Discipline) Rules 2015, then the Registrar of the Faculty Office shall proceed to appoint a Nominated Notary to investigate the allegation pursuant to rule 5 of those Rules. Where an inspection of a notary's accounts is ordered pursuant to Rule 12 of the Notaries' Accounts Rules 1989 (as amended) the provisions of that Rule shall apply together with such directions as may be given by the Master or Registrar in the particular case and the procedure set out in Regulations 6-9 shall be followed. The Master has approved the following questionnaire for inspections during April 2018:

1. *What is your assessment of the notary's general availability to see clients and the suitability of the premises used for such purposes? Please comment with reference to issues such as location, accessibility (for the disabled), proximity to public transport, privacy and records, etc.)*

2. *What is your assessment of the means by which the notary's practice is publicised other than the websites of the Faculty Office*

and *The Notaries Society? Please check any website for ease of usage, and for clarity and accuracy of information, including information about regulation.*

3. *To what extent do the notary's records comply with the requirements of Rule 23 of the Notaries Practice Rules 2014? You may require the production of a document from the protocol at random. Was a record made of proof of identity supplied by the client?*

4. *How does the notary provide regulatory information to clients, such as details at the outset on how a complaint may be made and how fees will be calculated? Does the notary have set terms of business and are these given to the client at a suitable time? (If the notary undertakes conveyancing or probate as a notary, please answer question 4, separately with regard to these types of work.)*

5. *Are the clients charged a fee which accords with the information given to the clients under r.18.1 Notaries Practice Rules 2014? If the fee was calculated on a time basis was the time spent properly recorded? If the notary undertakes conveyancing or probate as a notary, please answer question 5 separately with regard to these types of work.*

6. *Is there evidence that the notarial acts have been completed in a timely manner and correspondence and other communications answered promptly? If the notary undertakes conveyancing or probate as a notary, please answer question 6 separately with regard to these types of work.*

7. *Is there evidence that the notary has properly identified appearors and do the names and addresses and identification document details (if any) on the document match with the proof or proofs of identity provided? Have corporate bodies been properly identified by number and jurisdiction of incorporation? This may necessitate checking the document itself and enquiring how issues of non-matching are dealt with.*

8. *If the notary did not personally deal with legalisation, is there evidence that the notary gave the client advice as to the possible need for legalisation and whether the country concerned would normally require legalisation of the notary's signature and seal?*

9. *With reference to the work in reserved legal activities being undertaken by the notary, do you consider the notary's skills and knowledge are adequate, having regard in particular to the principles in Rule 14 of the Notaries Practice Rules 2014? Please consider in particular the correct form applicable to documents and the procedure for execution, the notary's linguistic ability, the special needs of particular clients (arising from disability, dependency etc.) If the notary undertakes conveyancing or probate as a notary, please answer question 9 separately with regard to these types of work.*

10. *Does the notary undertake work which is not a reserved legal activity under s.12 Legal Services Act 2007? Do you consider the notary's skills and knowledge are adequate to do this? (Examples of this might be advising on the law and procedures in foreign jurisdictions, drafting documents for use in foreign jurisdictions, advising on matters of English law.)*

11. *What is your assessment of the notary's approach to continuing professional education and ensuring that requisite skills are up to date? In particular, has the notary maintained an up to date CPE record showing points obtained up to the inspection date of the last and current practice years? The certificates of completion of approved CPE should be inspected for the same period.*

    If the notary undertakes conveyancing or probate as a notary, please answer question 11 separately with regard to these types of work.

12. *Is there any record of complaints received and action taken in respect of them? It is not part of your function to investigate the adequacy of any action taken.*

13. *Does the notary seek feedback from clients as to how they have experienced his services? Does this feedback or anything else show whether or not the clients are satisfied with the service provided?*

14. *Does the notary maintain a Notarial Office Bank Account (and a Clients Bank Account if required)? If so who is able to authorise transactions on any notarial practice bank account(s)? Are these people adequately trained to do so? (Please consider the need for knowledge of the Notarial Accounts Rules1989, money laundering and proceeds of crime regulation and internet fraud). If there is no*

Notarial Office Bank Account, how are notarial fees banked and disbursements and expenses paid?

15.   15.1. Has the notary accessed the current guide to Anti- Money Laundering, if not, is the notary aware of it and knows how to access it?

        15.2 How many reports of suspicious transactions has the notary made to the National Crime Agency in the last three years?

        15.3 Have you found on inspection any transactions which seem suspicious and ought to have been considered for reporting but have not been?

16.   Please inspect the information disclosed by the notary to his professional indemnity insurers and his policy to ensure that all the activities undertaken by the notary in the notarial practice are covered?

17.   17.1. Please inspect the certificate of the notary's registration with the Information Commissioner's Office.

        17.2. Please inspect evidence that the notary has the necessary policies in place to meet all the principles of the General Data Protection Directive; including (but not limited to) supply to clients of information about retention of personal data and the legal compliance by third-party suppliers whose services are used by the notary to assist the fulfilment of notarial functions.

        17.3. What action has the notary taken to ensure that the confidentiality of notarial records is preserved, including against hacking?

18.   Does the notary have stationery including bills/invoices, which relate solely to the notarial practice?

19.   Is there anything in the register, protocol or other records which appears to disclose a breach of the Notaries Practice Rules 2014 or the Notaries Practice Rules 2009? If the notary undertakes conveyancing or probate as a notary, please answer question 19 separately with regard to these types of work.

20.   Is there any other aspect of the notary's practice or records which appears to give cause for concern?
        If the notary undertakes conveyancing or probate as a notary, please answer question 20 separately with regard to these types of work.

Please specify any concerns you may have which could be satisfied by production of evidence of change by the notary and what would be a reasonable time for this to be done. (Directions for such evidence will not normally be given in relation to matters of serious misconduct)

21. *Is there any other aspect of the notary's practice that you consider to be instructive or otherwise commendable? If the notary undertakes conveyancing or probate as a notary, please answer question 21 separately with regard to these types of work. Is there any aspect of the notary's practice that you consider to be instructive to other practitioners or otherwise commendable?*

Notarial Inspections can be a daunting prospect; however, with an understanding of the practice rules, coupled with proper procedures and processes in place to ensure compliance, they should not be seen as daunting but instead a positive experience. The inspection regime also provides assurance to both the wider profession and the public that the Faculty Office is protecting their interests by reducing risk through inspection and intervention and ensuring the advice and guidance issued to the profession is up to date.

The Inspectors want to help promote high standards and are happy to give advice where procedures merely need to be tightened up. Accordingly, the preparation for an inspection should not have to start when you receive the notification of an Inspection but is an ongoing process to ensure that you are up to date with your knowledge of the Practice Rules and that your systems and processes are compliant.

The Questionnaire approved by the Master is also an information gathering exercise to understand how the profession is practising. One should ensure that the notarial records are up to date. This helps the inspection run more smoothly and prevents any delay at the outset. Most of the records are those routinely prepared by notaries during their day to day work as required under Rule 23 of the Notaries Practice Rules 2014 (as amended).

Procedure of Inspections
At the beginning of each year the Faculty Office selects twenty notaries whose practices are to be inspected, 10 by each inspector and the Inspectors are sent the list and asked to make sure there are no problems, for example, because they know the notary. The Inspectors then sort out how and when they are going to do each inspection. As it is desirable and saves expense if two inspections can be made on the same day this

involves sorting out the geographical spread and then train or car journey times.

The Inspector then asks the Faculty Office to write to the Notary about to be inspected giving them at least 7 days warning that they have been selected for inspection during a close fortnight period and that the inspector will be in touch to arrange an appointment for the inspection.

When the Faculty Office letter has been sent out the Inspector will check with the notary to see what her or his availability is over the phone. As this usually involves 2 or 3 notaries usually more than one phone call is needed. Quite frequently it is not possible to fit suggested dates into the diaries of all the notaries going to be inspected over the same time.

The Inspector then writes to the notary and a specimen of the sort of letter which is given below. The Inspector after reaching the notary's office looks at the district it is in and the access to the office, parking and public transport. At the end of the session the Inspector briefly goes through the questionnaire with the notary and outline what he thinks answers to the questions are likely to be. Frequently at this stage the notary asks what he can do to improve the practice and the Inspector is happy to make suggestions.

The Inspector normally takes between 2 ½ hrs to 3hrs excluding travelling time for each inspection. A practice which does probate and or/conveyancing needs a whole day. The Inspector then prepares draft answers to the questionnaire which are required to be submitted within 14 days together with a short report to the Faculty Office. This usually takes about another 3 hours. As soon as possible ie within a couple of days the inspector sends the draft answers and a short report to the notary for comment on whether the notary thinks the inspector has got things wrong or been unfair. Before the end of the 14 days the inspector answers to the questionnaire and the short report are sent to the Faculty Office. The Faculty Office then pays the inspector fees which since 2015 has been £420 for each inspection plus expenses, chiefly train fares and may include overnight accommodation.

At the end of each year the three inspectors prepare a general report for the Master on the inspections for that year. There is then a meeting between the inspectors, the Master and officials of the Faculty Office to discuss the reports on the individuals and the general report. These discussions have resulted in such things as: In one case that the inspected notary should be re-inspected because of the low standards of some of the work. Amendments to the questionnaire, for instance this year it has been extended on money laundering and information protection. Encouraging the inspector to require proof of changes in practice eg. letterheads, notarial acts, identification procedures.

Letter from the inspector

To,
Notary public,

Notarial Inspection Regulations 2014

Dear Notary,

I am writing to confirm our telephone conversation this afternoon when we arranged that I will carry out my inspection of your notarial practice on the afternoon of Tuesday the.... 2018 starting at about 2.15pm. There is no set way for the inspection to be carried out but probably the sort of programme is likely to be:

- *For an hour and a half or maybe more we discuss your practice and the records you keep.*

- *For the next hour or more I inspect the notarial records you have kept under the Notaries Practice Rules 2014 also any other relevant files and documents we identify in our initial discussion. My experience of previous inspections suggests that I may need your help for this at least to start with.*

I believe that as a notary you only do notarial work ie authentication but if you do any other work as a notary, eg. commercial advice, will writing, conveyancing or probate, I will need to inspect any relevant files. The length of time this takes depends on what I need to look at. Usually for these other types of work I look at two or three files from each category and it is only if I am not content with what I see on these files that I will need to look at other files. I choose the files so we will need to have a list of matters that have been current in about the last two years or so.

Final 45-60 mins. We deal with any queries I have and I discuss with you my proposed answers to the questionnaire of which you should have a copy. I will also discuss with you what I am proposing to write in my short report so that you can put me right on anything I may have misunderstood.

It would be helpful if you could have the following records and files available and anything else you may think I should see:- Notarial register or equivalent covering at least the last 12 months. Protocol or equivalent file covering at least the last 12 months Current Appointments diary. Information sheet (if any) given to clients and/or any terms of business. Bills/Invoices for last 12 months. Any office bank account paying in book and bank statements for the last year.

Files for matters you have dealt with in the last two years – don't get them all out in advance just have them reasonably accessible. All Continuing Education records and certificates of courses attended for last two years. Current certificate of registration with Information Commissioner and your data protection policy.

Reports of matters suspected of money laundering reported to the National Crime Agency. If any of your records are kept electronically I will need your help in finding the relevant information.

It would only be if I am concerned about anything in your current practices that I would need to refer to any earlier records, but it would a good idea for these to be available just in case.

I have been asked to check that when you renewed your professional indemnity insurance you disclosed to your insurers all the types of work that you do. I suspect that this is probably shown in your renewal papers and I should be grateful if you could have these available. The reason for this is that the Faculty Office is concerned that some notaries are giving advice on foreign legal matters eg. Spanish property law without having any qualification except perhaps some years of experience and I am asked to check that insurers have been informed of all work that is being undertaken.

When I have drafted my answers to the Faculty Office questionnaire and my short report to the Master I should be able to send them to you so that you can tell me if there is anything I have misunderstood or been unfair about before I send them to the Faculty Office. Usually I can only allow a few days for comments as I am obliged by the regulations to send the final answers and report to the Faculty Office within 14 days of the inspection. My fees are paid by the Faculty Office.

If you have any queries please do not hesitate to contact me. I should be travelling up from London on the morning of the …………but if you need to contact me after I have left London please try my mobile 07777 111 222 but it will not be switched on all the time. Thank you for giving me your mobile number.

Yours sincerely,

Inspectors' Observations: Amongst the matters the Inspectors have commented on are as follows.

To do with the office:

- All inspected notaries say they are willing to act outside office hours and at places convenient to clients when necessary eg. nursing and residential homes, seeing clients in their cars when they cannot easily get out of them.
- Only one matter found where the notarial act had taken too long most dealt with in 24 hours plus legalisation time.
- Sensible dealing with 'moans' eg fees too high, or unexpected expenses (translation fees above translator's quote) on the basis the 'customer is always right'.
- A wide variety of electronic storage systems, many devised by the notary, only one or two of which have the inspectors been able to use without help. Records are supposed to be accessible by any notary appointed by the Faculty Office.
- Failure to notify passwords to the Faculty Office.
- Using stationery of the solicitors' practice with which the notary is associated.
- Failure to supply clients with the regulatory information about complaints as soon as possible or at all.
- Failure to record fee quotes.
- Almost all notarial work is done on a fixed fee basis.
- Several notaries pay their notarial fees into the clients account of a solicitors practice (this is legitimate) but not easy to trace fees on inspections.
- Confusion about who the regulator of the practice was because some of activities were under Solicitors Regulation Authority regulation and other under the Faculty Office and the information on websites and/or stationery was not clear.

To do with notarial acts;

- Failing to identify companies and there directors sufficiently eg. no company search, no company number and jurisdiction.
- Authenticating signatures of parties when they do not sign or acknowledge in the notary's presence, should only be done when signature well known and after checking by phone with signatory.
- Insecure acts ie using staples and not sewing or signing and sealing each page and stating how many pages there are.

- Indecipherable signatures so that it is not obvious which signature is the notaries, also causes problems for the legalisation office.
- Insecure seals – glue may not be adequate and need extra.
- Insufficient acts eg. not identifying what the notary is authenticating, no date or place of acts,
- Delays in probate matters.
- Terms of business too complicated and not provided in time for clients to understand before appearing before the notary, should be supplied at first contact or as soon as possible thereafter.

An inspector must investigate whether the notary has complied with Rule 22 of the Notaries Practice Rules 2014 in relation to Continuing Professional Education. The current requirement is that each notary must obtain 6 points in each practice year of which at least 3 points must be through an accredited activity but the balance can be earned at the rate of 1 point per hour spent on an unaccredited activity eg. reading a relevant publication such as The Notary. However, a notary does not require CPE in the first two years. Instead, a newly qualified notary is required to attend an Education day in each of the first two years – these are approved by the Master.

Under Rule 23.3, where the notarial act is in the public form, the notary shall place an original of the act or a complete photographic copy of the same in a protocol, which shall be preserved permanently by the notary. A digital or electronic storage system is now permitted provided that documents are stored in indelible or unalterable form. Rule 23.4 states that records of acts not in public form, kept in accordance with Rule 23.2, shall be preserved for a minimum period of twelve years and, for the avoidance of doubt, such preservation may be by means of a suitable digital or other electronic system, providing for the storage of documents in an indelible and unalterable format. An inspector may enquire as to where the records are archived especially if there is any risk of fire, theft, flood or hacking. As regards to the electronic passwords the inspector would be keen to know whether the password is provided to the Faculty Office.

One of the best ways to inform the client about various regulatory information is by way of an information sheet incorporating terms and conditions discussed in the previous chapter which may include fees, client identification, complaints, liability, professional indemnity insurance, legalisation and any other issues which arise from time to time.

The inspector may also ask about the security of seals and physical possession of CPE Certificates. How does the notary handle complaints and how quickly does a client get an appointment may also be relevant. Inspectors are conducted at short notice and therefore it is important to conduct internal audit. Notaries should look at treating internal audit the same way as external audit by inspectors. This should include review of records, risk management and financial audit relating to income and expenditure.

Inspections provide a useful independent and objective source of assessment of a notarial practice. It is extremely important that necessary steps should be taken by each notary in preparing and managing a good notarial practice. A great statesman once said "If you fail to prepare, be prepared to fail". Benjamin Franklin.

Chapter 9

LEGALISATION OF DOCUMENTS BY FCO

Legalisation means an act of making the document lawful. The traditional rule *acta probant sese ipsa* does not seem to hold good on the international level; although this rule seems to be easy to accept within a particular country, where the institutions are familiar with the official language. For this reason, the receiving jurisdiction needs to know that the notary is actually an appointed notary in that jurisdiction. The Hague Convention reduces all of the formalities of legalisation to the simple delivery of a certificate in a prescribed form, entitled "Apostille", by the authorities of the State where the document originates. This certificate is usually provided after the document is sealed and signed by a Notary Public.

In the United Kingdom Legalisation is done by the Foreign and Commonwealth Office. On 5 October 1961 at the 9th session of The Hague Conference on private international law the Convention was drawn up, designed to make provision for the abolition of legalisation between the several countries concerned. The Hague Convention abolishes the requirement of diplomatic and consular legalisation for public documents originating in one Convention country and intended for use in another.

The Hague Convention has been ratified by a number of countries and the procedure under the same is known as the grant of an Apostille. An Apostille (French word meaning notation) is a standard certification provided under The Hague Convention. The procedure means that once the document has been notarised by the Notary then the Apostille has to be affixed by the FCO. The apostille issued by the FCO is tri-lingual (English-French-Spanish). The Hague Convention came into force for the UK on 14 January 1965.

Requirements of the FCO in relation to the Certification of Documents

When a notary public signs the document, he/she must:
- note the type of certification he/she has done (e.g. the document is a true copy of the original)
- use his/her personal signature, not a company signature
- include the date of certification
- include his/her business address

If a notarial certificate is added, it must be attached to the document. The certificate must also contain a specific reference to the document that has been certified. If a notary public from England, Wales or Northern Ireland signs a document for legalisation, he/she must also stamp or emboss the document with his/her notarial seal.

ACRO Police Certificate
An ACRO Police Certificate can only be legalised if it has been either:
- signed by an official from the issuing authority
- certified by a notary

A photocopy of the document will not be accepted by the FCO.

Affidavit
An affidavit can only be legalised if it has been certified by a notary.
The FCO will also legalise a certified photocopy of the Affidavit.

Articles of Association
Articles of association can only be legalised if they have been either:
- signed by an official from the issuing authority
- certified by a notary

The FCO will also legalise a certified photocopy of the Articles of Association.

Bank Statement
A bank statement can only be legalised if it has been certified by a notary.
The FCO will also legalise a certified photocopy of the Bank Statement.

Baptism Certificate
A baptism certificate can only be legalised if it has been certified by a notary.
The FCO will also legalise a certified photocopy of the Baptism Certificate.

Birth Certificate

A birth certificate can be legalised if it is either:

- an official certified copy issued by the General Register Office (GRO) with the original seal
- an original certificate (or original certified copy) issued by a local register office, member of the Clergy or an authorised person, bearing the original signature of the official who issued the certificate

It can take longer to legalise a signature on an original certificate, especially if it was issued more than 25 years ago.

A photocopy of the document will not be accepted by the FCO.

Certificate of Incorporation

A certificate of incorporation can only be legalised if it has been either:

- signed by an official from the issuing authority
- certified by a notary

The FCO will also legalise a certified photocopy of the certificate of incorporation.

Certificate of Free Sale

A certificate of free sale can only be legalised if either:

- it has been signed by an official from the issuing authority
- it says 'signature valid' next to a tick and has been certified by a notary.

The FCO will also legalise a certified photocopy of the certificate of free sale.

Certificate of Memorandum

A certificate of memorandum can only be legalised if it has been either:

- signed by an official from the issuing authority
- certified by a notary

The FCO will also legalise a certified photocopy of the certificate of memorandum.
.

Certificate of Naturalisation

A certificate of naturalisation can only be legalised if it has been either:

- signed by an official from the issuing authority
- certified by a notary

The FCO will also legalise a certified photocopy of the certificate of naturalisation. It can take longer to legalise a signature on an original certificate, and it will probably be easier to certify it.

Certificate of No Impediment
A certificate of no impediment can be legalised if it:
- is an original certificate issued by a local register office
- has the original signature of the official who issued the certificate

A photocopy of the certificate of no impediment will not be accepted by the FCO.

Chamber of Commerce Document
A Chamber of Commerce document can only be legalised if it relates to a commercial or trade matter and has been either:
- signed by an official from the issuing authority
- certified by a notary

Change of Name Deed
A change of name deed can only be legalised if it has been certified by a notary.

The FCO will also legalise a certified photocopy of the change of name deed.

Civil Partnership Certificate
A civil partnership certificate can be legalised if it is either:
- an official certified copy of the certificate issued by the General Register Office (GRO) with the original seal
- an original certificate (or original certified copy) issued by a local register office, with the original signature of the official who issued the certificate

It can take longer to legalise a signature on an original certificate, especially if it was issued before 1991.

It might be quicker to order a certified copy of the certificate from the GRO. A photocopy of the document will not be accepted by the FCO.

Criminal Records Bureau (CRB) document
A CRB document can only be legalised if it has been either:
- signed by an official from the issuing authority
- certified by a notary

A photocopy of the document will not be accepted by the FCO.

Companies House Document
A Companies House document can only be legalised if it has been either:
- signed by an official from the issuing authority
- certified by a notary

The FCO will also legalise a certified photocopy of a Companies House document.

Court Document

A court document must have been issued by either the:
- County Court
- Court of Bankruptcy
- Family Division of the High Court of Justice
- High Court of Justice
- Sheriff Court
- HM Courts and Tribunal Service (HMCTS)

Documents can include Decree Nisi, Decree Absolute, Grant of Probate.

It can only be legalised if it has either:
- the original seal or ink stamp of the court
- the signature of a court official
- been certified by a notary

Since April 2015 courts in England and Wales started to issue documents as PDF only, without any ink signature or seal and these digitally produced documents must be certified by a notary before they can be legalised

Death Certificate

A death certificate can be legalised if it is either:
- an official certified copy issued by the General Register Office (GRO) with the original seal
- an original certificate (or original certified copy) issued by a local register office, with the original signature of the official who issued the certificate

It can take longer to legalise a signature on an original certificate, especially if it was issued before 1991.

It might be quicker to order a certified copy of the certificate from the GRO. A photocopy of the document will not be accepted by the FCO.

Degree Certificate (UK)

A degree certificate must be awarded by a UK recognised body.

It must also be certified by:
- a notary public in the UK

It may be possible to get an original certificate certified by an official of the British Council overseas.

The FCO will also legalise a certified photocopy of the degree certificate.

Document from the Department of Business, Innovation and Skills (BIS)

A BIS document can only be legalised if it has been either:
- signed by an official from the issuing authority
- certified

The FCO will also legalise a certified photocopy of a BIS document.

Department of Health Document

A Department of Health document can only be legalised if it has been either:
- signed by an official from the issuing authority
- certified

The FCO will also legalise a certified photocopy of a Department of Health document.

Diploma (Level 4 or above as on UK qualification framework)

A diploma must be accredited by either:
- Scottish Qualifications Authority
- OfQual
- The Council for Curriculum, Examinations & Assessment (CCEA) (in Northern Ireland)
- Qualifications Wales

It must also be certified, signed and dated by either:
- a notary public in the UK

It may be possible to get an original certificate certified by an official of the British Council overseas.

A photocopy of the diploma can be legalised, but it must be certified by a notary.

Diploma (level 3 or below on UK qualification frame work or vocational)

A diploma must be awarded by a recognised UK awarding body.

It must also be certified, signed and dated by either:
- a notary public in the UK

It may be possible to get an original certificate certified by an official of the British Council overseas.

A photocopy of the diploma can be legalised, but it must be certified by a notary.

Disclosure Scotland Document

A Disclosure Scotland document can only be legalised if it has been either:
- signed by an official from the issuing authority
- certified by a notary

A photocopy of a Disclosure Scotland document will not be accepted by the FCO.

Driving Licence (Copy)
A driving licence can only be legalised if it has been certified by a notary.

Educational Certificate (UK)
An educational certificate must be issued by an institution that is recognised as an education provider in the UK by:
- The Accreditation Body for Language Services (ABLS)
- British Accreditation Council (BAC)
- Home Office – Register of Sponsors
- Open and Distance Learning Quality Council
- UKAS

It must also be certified, signed and dated by either:
- a notary public in the UK
- an official of the British Council (only original certificates)

It may be possible to get an original certificate certified by an official of the British Council overseas.

The FCO will also legalise a certified photocopy of an educational certificate.

Export Certificate
An export certificate can be legalised if it has been certified by a Chamber of Commerce or a notary.

Fingerprints Document
A fingerprints document can only be legalised if it has been either:
- signed by an official from the issuing authority
- certified by a notary

A photocopy of the fingerprints document will not be accepted by the FCO.

HM Revenue and Customs Document
Your HM Revenue and Customs document can only be legalised if it has been either:
- signed by an official from the issuing authority
- certified by a notary

The FCO will also legalise a certified photocopy of HM Revenue and Customs document.

Home Office Document
A Home Office document can only be legalised if it has been either:
- signed by an official from the issuing authority

- certified by a notary

The FCO will also legalise a certified photocopy of a Home Office document.

Last Will and Testament

A last will and testament must have been issued by either the
- County Court
- Court of Bankruptcy
- Family Division of the High Court of Justice
- High Court of Justice
- Sheriff Court

It can only be legalised if it has either:
- the original seal or ink stamp of the court
- the signature of a court official
- been certified by a notary

It can take the Legalisation Office longer to legalise a court document that only has a signature. A document certified by a notary might make the process quicker.

Letter from an Employer

A letter from an employer can only be legalised if it has been certified by a notary.

The FCO will also legalise a certified photocopy of a letter from an employer.

Letter of Enrolment

A letter of enrolment can only be legalised if it has been certified and makes no mention of having obtained a qualification.

The FCO will also legalise a certified photocopy of a letter of enrolment.

Letter of Invitation

A letter of invitation can only be legalised if it has been certified.

The FCO will also legalise a certified photocopy of the letter of invitation.

Letter of No Trace

A letter of no trace can be legalised if it is either:
- an official certified copy of the certificate issued by the General Register Office (GRO) with the original seal
- an original certificate (or original certified copy) issued by a local register office, with the original signature of the official who issued the certificate

It can take longer to legalise a signature on an original certificate, especially if it was issued before 1991.

It might be quicker to order a certified copy of the certificate from the GRO.

A photocopy of the document will not be accepted by the FCO.

Medical Documents
A medical document must be signed by either:
- a doctor registered with the General Medical Council.
- A nurse or midwife registered with the Nursing & Midwifery Council
- A dentist registered with the General Dental Council
- Been certified by a notary

A document cannot be legalised if it has been signed on behalf of one doctor by another doctor or a non-registered member of staff.

Marriage Certificate
A marriage certificate can be legalised if it is either:
- an official certified copy issued by the General Register Office (GRO) with the original seal
- an original certificate (or original certified copy) issued by a church, religious establishment or local register office, with the original signature of the official who issued the certificate

It can take longer to legalise a signature on an original certificate, especially if it was issued before 1991.

It might be quicker to order a certified copy of the certificate from the GRO. Non-GRO marriage certificates (e.g. Islamic marriage certificates) cannot be legalised unless they are certified. A photocopy of the document will not be accepted by the FCO.

Passport (copy only)
A copy of the passport can only be legalised if it has
- been certified by a notary.
- contains the signature of the holder

The FCO requires a photocopy - the actual passport will not be accepted.

Pet Export Document from DEFRA
A pet export document can only be legalised if it has been signed and stamped by a veterinary surgeon registered with the Department of Food and Rural Affairs.

Police Disclosure Document
A police disclosure document can only be legalised if it has been either:
- signed by an official from the issuing authority
- certified

A photocopy of the document will not be accepted by the FCO.

Power of Attorney

A power of attorney can only be legalised

- been certified by a notary.
- A Lasting Power of Attorney (LPA) issued by the Office of public Guardian in England and Wales must be validated by the OPG. The original will bear a perforated 'validated' seal.

The FCO will also legalise a certified photocopy of the power of attorney or LPA.

Religious Document

A religious document can only be legalised if it has been certified by a notary. The FCO will also legalise a certified photocopy of the religious document.

Statutory Declaration

A statutory declaration can only be legalised if it has been certified by a notary. The FCO will also legalise a certified photocopy of the statutory declaration.

TEFL/TESOL certificates

Teaching English as a Foreign Language and Teaching English to Speakers of other language certificate can be legalised if:

- the provider has both a UK address and telephone number in the UK which is visible and active on their website
- If the certificate implies it is a qualification (ie Diploma/Master) this must be verified on Ofqual
- Been certified by a notary

TEFL certificates are unregulated and there is no recognised body that oversees them globally. Claims by overseas providers that they have UK accreditation, means they have been assessed to meet UK training standards and does not mean they are recognised UK certificates.

Translation

- A translation from a foreign language into English can only be legalised if it has been certified by a notary
- A translation from English into a Foreign language can be certified by a notary. The legalisation office does not require to see the original document (but this is helpful); if not available a brief description in the certification as to the type of document is (ie Power of Attorney, employment letter etc). If the certification is not in English please ensure that it can be identified by the Legalisation office.

The FCO will also legalise a certified photocopy of the translation.

Utility Bill

A utility bill can only be legalised if it has been certified by a notary. The FCO will also legalise a certified photocopy of the utility bill.

Sending of documents to the Legalisation Office, Foreign and Commonwealth Office

If you are sending your documents by post from the UK:

Legalisation Office
Foreign and Commonwealth Office
PO Box 6255
Milton Keynes
MK10 1XX

If you are sending your documents from abroad or by courier from the UK:

Legalisation Office
Foreign and Commonwealth Office
Hanslope Park
Hanslope
Milton Keynes
MK19 7BH

You cannot deliver documents to these addresses in person - only by post or courier.

If you are a member of the DX Exchange courier service you can also send your application to:

The Legalisation Office
Foreign and Commonwealth Office
DX 310701
Milton Keynes 26

Premium Business Service (Central London)

Customers with business-related documents or customers acting on behalf of a company or its clients may use the same-day Premium Service in central London. Business customers must pre-register before using this service. The Premium business fee is £75 per signature we confirm and payment will only be accepted online.

Premium Service Legalisation Office
Ground Floor, Department for Education
Sanctuary Buildings
Great Smith Street
London SW1P 3BT

Chapter 10

INSURANCE

Rule 6.1 of the NOTARIES (PRACTISING CERTIFICATES) RULES 2012 states that all Notaries in practice as such within England and Wales shall at all times hold insurance covering their notarial practice for the following:

6.1.1 insurance against civil liability for professional negligence incurred by the Notary in connection with his or her practice as a Notary; and

6.1.2 insurance against financial loss suffered by a third party in consequence of any dishonest or fraudulent act or any omission by the Notary in connection with his or her practice as a Notary.

Practice rule 3.1 of the practice rules 2014 as amended in 2017 states that notaries are required to provide "appropriate notarial services to any person lawfully and reasonably requiring the same". A notary is therefore required to ensure that insurance cover is sufficient to meet the requirements and contains no restrictions that would affect the ability of a notary to provide appropriate notarial services. Chapter 16 of the code of practice requires notaries to hold professional indemnity insurance and Fidelity cover.

Professional Indemnity Insurance
Practising notaries in England and Wales are required to obtain professional indemnity insurance (PII). PII is insurance that covers civil liability claims arising from work in notarial practice. These claims most commonly involve professional negligence. PII also increases financial security and serves an important public interest function by covering civil liability claims, including certain related defence costs, and certain regulatory awards made against a notary by the Legal Services Ombudsman and the Office for Legal Complaints.

It ensures that the public does not suffer loss, which might otherwise be uncompensated. This is important in maintaining public confidence in the integrity and standing of notaries. A notary needs to demonstrate to the Faculty Office that the notary has a policy of insurance in place as part of the practising certificate renewal process. Notaries must hold cover at all times while practising.

Where a notary is relying on professional Indemnity Insurance cover held by his/her firm, it must be clear that this policy extends cover to their

Notarial practice. If Notarial work is undertaken in conjunction with his/her firm and is covered by the firm's policy on that basis, the notary will be required to provide confirmation that this is the case. Alternatively, if notarial work is undertaken in a personal capacity a notary will be required to provide a copy of an endorsement, or equivalent confirmation, from an insurance company confirming that independent work as a notary is covered by the policy.

As evidence of PII cover, a notary is required to provide the relevant extracts from the policy schedule confirming the dates of the policy and the limit of cover (the minimum limit of cover is £1,000,000 by Order of the Master dated 17th April 2012). A notary who provides conveyancing and probate services must declare those activities to his or her insurance provider and ensure the policy provides adequate cover for those activities.

Fidelity Cover
Fidelity cover is not about negligence insurance, it is about dishonesty. It is to cover the risk of the notary misappropriating the client's money. If a notary's Solicitor PI Insurer does not offer Fidelity Insurance then the notary will be required to join The Notaries Guarantee Limited. The Notaries Guarantee Insurance year runs from 1 January to 31 December. The current contribution is around £300 per annum and is provided by RK Harrison, Insurance brokers. Where a notary is relying on professional Indemnity Insurance and/or Fidelity Insurance cover held by the notary's firm it must be clear that this policy extends cover to the notarial practice.

The Faculty Office does not believe, as a matter of legal interpretation, that the cover afforded by the SRA Compensation Fund could extend to losses in respect of notarial business, since the SRA Compensation Fund Rules 2011 indicate that the fund only covers losses arising "in the course of an activity of a kind which is part of the usual business of [a solicitor]". Therefore, cover under the SRA Compensation Fund will not be accepted by the Faculty Office as evidence of Fidelity Insurance.

As evidence of Fidelity Insurance cover, a notary is required to provide the relevant extracts from the policy schedule confirming the dates of the policy and the limit of cover, or evidence of membership of the Notaries Guarantee Limited. If a notary is a sole principal and/or seeking to rely on Fidelity Insurance cover held in own name, in addition to the evidence requested above, the Faculty Office must receive a copy of the terms and conditions of the policy and express confirmation from the insurers that the policy would cover your dishonest and/or fraudulent acts, or those of any employee, with respect to your notarial work. The Faculty Office currently requires a minimum limit of cover is £1,000,000 (£ 1 million).

Run-off insurance

Run-off insurance is seen by many professionals as being very different to the "normal" professional indemnity insurance. However, the key to understanding the basics of run-off cover is to look at the "claims made" nature of PII.

PII is arranged on a "claims made" basis and provides cover to notaries, whether they are sole traders or limited companies, or partnerships including LLPs. This means that it is the insurer which is providing cover at the time the claim is made, that picks up the defence (and ultimately awards) of the claim, rather than the insurer at the time that the work or negligent act took place. Run-off cover is necessary because after the cessation of the business (usually because of retirement), there remains the possibility that claims may be notified to the retired notary.

So who needs run-off cover? For Notaries, whilst there is a requirement to carry a minimum limit of indemnity of £1m whilst in practice, there is no such mandate or guidance when it comes to retirement. However, a number of other professions are directed by their regulating bodies to take out and maintain run-off cover for a specific period of time, e.g. the Solicitors Regulatory Authority (SRA) stipulates a 6 year minimum period for cover because beyond that time the majority of claims would be time barred. This 6 year period is also matched by the Royal Institution of Chartered Surveyors (RICS).

A professional retiring is the typical reason for purchasing run-off insurance and it is particularly important for sole practitioners, of which the majority of notaries are. With larger firms the business is often sold or taken on by a younger principal who maintains the PI cover and therefore provides the run-off under that policy. However, this is not always the case, as the new owner may not wish to have the responsibility of the legacy liabilities. On the other hand, the outgoing incumbent may not want the responsibility of his liabilities being trusted to someone else. With both situations it is necessary to keep a run-off policy in force after retirement, to cover any claims that may arise in the future.

For the notarial profession, which does not have a minimum period laid down by the Faculty Office, the maintenance of a run-off policy is more an act of prudence or sound risk management and a number of notaries will simply do it because it helps them sleep better knowing that there is a safety net in place.

Other forms of insurance

The code of practice provides that "notaries who see clients at their place of business should be aware of the need to have those premises adequately insured not only in terms of safeguarding equipment, client files, records and work in progress, but also to cover the necessary public liability insurance to safeguard employees and visitors to the premises".

Chapter 11

REMOTE NOTARISATION

In modern times one of the ways a document may be executed as by interactive videoconferencing. It has been seen that lawyers in other parts of the world may witness documents by live interactive videoconferencing link, instead of being physically present in the offices. However, for notaries in England and Wales I think that the minimum obligations of a notary is to:

- to verify the identity of the client in accordance with rule 23 of the Notaries Practice Rules 2014; and
- to keep records; 12 years for private form notarial acts and forever in case of public form notarial acts;

In considering the issue of a notary witnessing a signature via live videoconferencing, I think witnessing requirements could not be met:

- A notary cannot know what document the signer is signatory and cannot know for certain that the paper the lawyer must sign was the paper signed by the person who executed the document;
- Off-screen influences and the lack of proximity may detract from the notary's ability to verify the identity of the person who signed the document.

Under English law the words "appeared before" require an actual physical appearance before the public officer, and not an appearance by means of videoconferencing technology.

I also think that permitting documents to be executed at one location and sent to another location for completion by a witness would provide increased opportunities for fraud and would therefore increase the exposure to claims. There has been a bit of discussion on the appropriateness of attesting an affidavit (or declaration or affirmation) by Skype (which is just another form of video).

The first question which comes to mind are the worlds "in the presence of a witness" the notary is sufficient if the notary can see and hear the affiant/deponent by video link or by videophone link as with Skype video?

Affidavits taken by telephone alone (i.e. voice connection) have been held in a New York court not to have been properly done.

The second question is: If you believe that a video appearance is not sufficient to support commissioning, should it be? Are there safeguards required, and do we want to start fine tuning a well-known requirement to adapt it to the electronic age?

The Implementation question: How well would the notary be able to see the document signed by the affiant in order to know that what he/she later got on his/her desk for commissioning was the same document?

Finally, what difference would or should it make if the affiant and the notary were in different jurisdictions? Would it matter in which jurisdiction the affidavit was to be used?

The law in England and Wales on allowing videoconferencing for witness testimony in a trial appears to be well-settled and the courts generally tend to favour allowing it. The landmark case on this issue is the decision from *Polanski v Conde Nast Publications Ltd* [2005] UKHL 10 (HL). In this case the Claimant brought libel proceedings against *Vanity Fair* over an article that alleged he had shamelessly attempted to seduce a lady in a New York restaurant whilst en route to his wife's funeral following her brutal murder. He obtained permission from Eady J before trial to give evidence by video link (VCF) from France under CPR Part 32.3, on the ground that if he came to this country he would be extradited to the USA, from where he had fled in the 1970s whilst awaiting sentence for a criminal conviction. The Court of Appeal discharged the order on the basis that the general policy of the courts should be to discourage litigants from escaping the normal processes of the law rather than to facilitate this. They also held that the assumption on which the Judge's order had been made, namely that if VCF evidence were refused the Claimant's witness statement could have gone in anyway as hearsay evidence, was wrong. The Claimant appealed to the House of Lords where the issue was "whether the Claimant should be allowed to give his evidence by VCF and whether allowing the Judge's order to stand would bring the administration of justice into disrepute". The House of Lords allowing the Appeal (by a 3-2 majority) As between the parties the order was correctly made and the respondent would suffer no prejudice from the evidence being given by VCF. (Rule 32.3 of the Civil Procedure Rules (the rules governing allowance of videoconference testimony). Almost all the case law following Polanski has proceeded on the basis that, as a matter of public policy, giving evidence by videoconferencing is preferable to giving no evidence at all. Although these guiding principles were applied in respect of giving witness testimony, and not necessarily witnessing a signature, it is possible that the same principles may guide the courts here.

In fact, the High Court of Justice in the case of *Re ML (Use of Skype Technology)* [2013] EWHC 2091 (Fam) allowed the signing of adoption consent forms to be witnessed via Skype. This involved an adoption order in relation to an 11-year-old girl of Tibetan Mongolian origin who had been brought to the UK from Nepal by a British couple.

The child's parents, who have a number of other children and are now separated, live in poverty. They were unable to care for their daughter, who went to live with her grandparents at the age of three, where she was mistreated. The adopters, who have business in Nepal, found her on the street in 2007 in a pitiful state. They arranged for her to be looked after and educated, but difficulties continued and in January 2011, they brought her to England on an education visa. Since arriving here she has thrived and in due course an adoption application was issued. All the appropriate procedural steps were taken, including notification of the Home Office.

The adopters stated that they had brought the child to England with the blessing of her parents, with whom they had had some contact over the years. Mindful of cases in which enquiries have shown that children have been brought to this country with false histories, the court directed that the parents should be contacted and offered the opportunity to give their consent. In these circumstances it is not possible for a Children's Guardian to make these enquiries abroad. The parties' efforts to advance matters through international social services or via the British Embassy in Kathmandu came to nothing.

The solution in this case was that the Guardian's solicitor engaged a local lawyer who speaks the parents' language. Arrangements were made for the English court documents to be translated and sent to the lawyer. The parents separately attended at the lawyer's office, where interviews took place. These were viewed from England by the Guardian and the child's solicitor on Skype. They were able to witness in real time the parents signing the consent forms by thumbprint, and photographs of the event were taken. Had questions by the Guardian to the parents been necessary, they could have been asked.

"This process satisfied me that the parents had freely and unconditionally consented to the adoption, and also that they had received no financial inducement. It has also provided a record for the child of her parents' participation and support for an adoption that she very much wants."
The process satisfied the court that the parents had freely and unconditionally consented to the adoption, and also that they had received no financial inducement. However, it has to be noted that *Re ML* was a

very unusual and fact-specific case, and that further support for signing documents over Skype has not been expressed by the courts.

In another decision by the same judge (*R v C and S* [2013] EWHC 1295 (Fam)), the court refused an application for taking evidence by Skype, rather than traditional videoconferencing (indeed, the judge noted that it will more often be the case that Skype will not be allowed). This is because Skype's technical limitations (including problems in everyone seeing and hearing the picture) make it inappropriate for the court environment. It was also noted that the judge would not be willing to use Skype if there was any alternative.

In an opinion of the Council of the Law Society of 26 January 2017 it offered guidance to the members of the society. The Notaries Society stated in an opinion that "a notary must in all instances identify the party appearing before him or her, confirmed that he or she has expressed their free will to be bound by the terms of the instrument (absence of violence fraud or undue influence). The Council was of the view that the notary's professional duties as expressed in the foregoing are best achieved by insisting on the party's physical personal appearance."

In light of the above it is clear that remote notarisation is not a valid form of execution of documents in England and Wales.

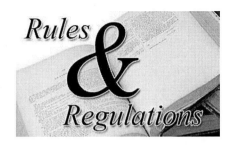

MOST IMPORTANT RULES AND REGULATIONS MADE BY THE COURT OF FACULTIES

Notaries (Qualification) Rules 2017

Notaries Practice Rules 2014 (As Amended)

Notaries (Conduct and Discipline) Rules 2015 (As Amended)

Notaries (Conduct and Discipline) Fees & Costs Order 2015

Notaries (Inspections) Regulations 2014

Notaries (Practising Certificates) Rules 2012

Notaries (Continuing Professional Education) Regulations 2010

Notaries (Post-Admission) Rules 2009

NOTARIES (QUALIFICATION) RULES 2017

WE CHARLES RICHARD GEORGE One of Her Majesty's Counsel Commissary or Master of the Faculties of the Most Reverend Father in God Justin Portal by Divine Providence Lord Archbishop of Canterbury Primate of All England and Metropolitan in exercise of the powers conferred by section 4 of the Public Notaries Act 1843 and section 57 of the Courts and Legal Services Act 1990 and of all other powers Us enabling hereby make the following Rules:

PART I: Preliminary

1. **Citation and Commencement**

    1.1   These rules may be cited as the Notaries (Qualification) Rules 2017

    1.2   These rules shall come into force on the 1st day of April 2017.

2. **Interpretation**

    In these rules:

    'the Board' means the Qualifications Board established under rule 6;

    'the Company' means the Incorporated Company of Scriveners of London;

    'Degree' means a qualification awarded following a post secondary course of at least three years' duration (or of an equivalent duration part time) at a university or an establishment of higher education or an establishment of similar level;

    'the Directive' means the Directive 2005/36/EC of the European Parliament and of the Council of 7th September 2005 as amended from time to time;

    'the Faculty Office' means the Registry of the Court of Faculties;

    'the Master' means the Master of the Faculties;

    'the Notarial Practice Course' means a course approved from time to time by the Master comprising the prescribed subjects set out in paragraphs 9, 10 and 11 of schedule 2;

    'the Office Practice Course' means a course approved from time to time by the Master comprising the matters set out in schedule 5; and

    'the Registrar' means the Registrar of the Court of Faculties.

PART II: General provisions as to admission

3. Qualification for Admission as a Notary Public
No person shall be admitted as a notary public to practise in England and Wales unless such person:

3.1 Is at least 21 years of age and has satisfied the requirements of these rules;

3.2 Has taken the oath of allegiance and the oath required by Section 7 of the Public Notaries Act 1843; and

3.3 Is, except where such application is made under rule 4 (ecclesiastical notaries) or rule 8 (European Economic Area notaries) either a solicitor of the Senior Courts of England and Wales, or a barrister at law or holds a Degree.

4. Ecclesiastical Notaries
Any person appointed as registrar of either of the provinces of Canterbury or York, as registrar to the Archbishop of Wales, as legal adviser to the General Synod to the Church of England, as legal secretary to the Governing Body of the Church in Wales, as registrar of any diocese in England or Wales, as an officer of the ecclesiastical court in Jersey or Guernsey, or as the deputy to any such officer, may apply for admission as a notary public for ecclesiastical purposes only, upon satisfying the Master of the fact of such an appointment.

5. General Notaries
Any person who satisfies the requirements of rule 3 and who has obtained the qualifications required under Part III of these rules may apply for admission as a general notary to practise in England and Wales.

PART III: Qualifications

6. Qualifications Board and Fees for Applications
6.1 There shall be established a Qualifications Board constituted in accordance with schedule 1.

6.2 The functions of the Board shall be:
6.2.1 To advise the Master whether a degree or other qualification should be approved by him for the purpose of these rules.
6.2.2 To advise the Master on the standard of the qualifications of any person applying for admission as a general notary under these rules.
6.2.3 To advise the Master on the qualifications and experience of persons applying for recognition that they are eligible for admission as a general notary under rule 8.
6.2.4 To advise any other body concerned with the administration or regulation of the notarial profession in England and

Wales or any part of it on matters relating to qualifications and experience.

6.3   The Master may by Order delegate to the Board any of his functions under these rules relating to the approval or recognition of degrees, qualifications and experience.

6.4   The Master may from time to time by Order prescribe fees or the maximum fees which may be charged in respect of any application to the Master under these rules and such fees may be applied by the Faculty Office towards meeting the expenses of the Board but subject thereto the expenses of the Board and of its members shall be paid from and such fees shall form part of the general notarial income of the Faculty Office.

7.   Practical Qualifications

7.1   Any person wishing to be admitted as a general notary under rule 5 shall have undertaken and attained a satisfactory standard in a course or courses of studies covering all of the subjects listed in schedule 2.

7.2   Whether a particular course of studies satisfies the requirements of these rules and whether a person has obtained a satisfactory standard in that course shall be determined by the Master after seeking the advice of the Board.

7.3   The Master after seeking the advice of the Board may by Order direct that the award of a particular qualification meets the requirements of these rules as to some or all of the subjects listed in schedule 2.

7.4   The Master may as a condition of making a direction under rule 7.3 require the body by which the qualification is awarded to issue those pursuing a course of studies leading to that qualification with such information about the notarial profession, these rules and other rules made by the Master and the Company as the Master may specify.

7.5   The Master may by Order add any subjects to the list in schedule 2 or remove any subjects from that list or alter any of the provisions of that schedule but before doing so he shall consult the Board.

8.   Notaries from jurisdictions outside England and Wales

8.1   This rule applies to a person who:

(a)   holds the office of notary public in a jurisdiction other than England and Wales, or

(b)   holds all the qualifications and has completed all the practical training necessary for appointment or admission to that office in such a jurisdiction but has not yet been so appointed or admitted.

8.2   Any person to whom this rule applies may apply to the Master for recognition that he is qualified for the purposes of rule 9.1 for admission as a general notary to practise anywhere in England and Wales and such application shall be made to the Faculty Office in such form and accompanied by such information as the Master may from time to time by Order prescribe.

8.3

    8.3.1   Any person applying to the Master for recognition under this rule shall satisfy the Master, in consultation with the Board, that:

        (a)   he can demonstrate a knowledge sufficient for a notary to practise in England and Wales in those subjects contained in schedules 3 and 4 either through examinations set by such institution or body recognised by the Board for the purpose taken within the last 5 years in those subjects, or from the applicant's own practical experience of the areas of law covered by those subjects; and

        (b)   he can demonstrate a competence in Notarial Practice with respect to the practice of a notary in England and Wales, and in particular the matters listed in paragraph 11 of schedule 2.

    8.3.2   Where an applicant is unable to demonstrate the requisite knowledge or experience set out in 8.3.1 above, he may be required:

        (a)   to take an aptitude test by way of an examination or examinations in such form and set by an institution or body recognised by the Board as may be prescribed from time to time by the Master; or

        (b)   undertake a period of supervision under a qualified and admitted notary for such period as may be specified by the Master not exceeding 3 years and such period may include a requirement to undertake further training and assessment.

8.4   Where an application is made to the Master under rule 8.2 he shall determine the application as soon as possible and communicate the outcome to the applicant in a reasoned decision within four months of the production of all the certificates and documents relating to the applicant as the Board shall reasonably require.

8.5   If the Master refuses an application under rule 8.2 or has not determined the application within the time prescribed by rule 8.4 the Master shall be deemed to have refused an application for a faculty and the applicant may pursue the remedy provided for in the Ecclesiastical Licences Act 1533 and mentioned in section 5 of the Public Notaries Act 1843.

PART IV: Procedure for admission

9.   **Application for Admission**

9.1   A person qualified for admission as a notary under these rules shall apply in writing to the Faculty Office on such form as the Master may from time to time specify.

9.2   The application shall be accompanied by:

(a)   A certificate of fitness in such form as the Master may from time to time prescribe to be given by a notary public to the effect that the applicant is known to him and that having made due enquiry to the best of his knowledge and belief the applicant is a fit and proper person to be created a notary public; and

(b)   A certificate of good character in such form as the Master may from time to time prescribe to be given by a person who is qualified under paragraph 9.3 testifying to the good character, honesty, reliability, diligence and trustworthiness of the applicant and stating that the person giving the certificate knows of no reason why the applicant should not be created a notary public;

(c)   Evidence that the applicant has successfully completed the Notarial Practice Course within a period not exceeding two years prior to the date of the application provided that this requirement shall not apply to an applicant under rule 8.2 who has demonstrated to the satisfaction of the Master his knowledge and competence in accordance with rule 8.3, the application to be accompanied by evidence that such demonstration was within the same period.

9.3   A person is qualified to give the certificate of good character required by paragraph 9.2(b) of this rule if he is a person of good standing and character, he has known the applicant for a period of not less than five years, he is not related to the applicant by blood, marriage or adoption, and he is not a professional partner, employer or employee of the applicant.

9.4   In the case of a person qualified under rule 4 the certificate of fitness shall further state that the applicant is conformable to the doctrine and discipline of the Church of England as by law established (or, in the case of a person qualified only by reason of holding an ecclesiastical appointment in Wales, the doctrine, discipline and constitution of the Church in Wales).

9.5   The certificate of fitness and the certificate of good character may be given in the case of a person qualified under rule 8 by suitably qualified persons in the applicant's home jurisdiction.

9.6   The application shall be accompanied by such fee as the Master may from time to time prescribe.

10.   Publicity, Refusal of Applications and Admissions

10.1   The Master may give, or require an applicant to give, such publicity to an application made under rule 9 as in the circumstances appear to the Master to be necessary.

10.2   Any representations made to the Master following such publicity shall be notified to the applicant, and the Master shall consider any response thereto made by the applicant before deciding whether a faculty shall be granted.

10.3   Any decision by the Master to refuse an application under rule 9 shall be notified to the applicant by the Registrar in writing to enable the applicant to pursue (if so advised) the remedy provided for in The Ecclesiastical Licences Act 1533 and mentioned in Section 5 of the Public Notaries Act 1843.

10.4   Upon the Master deciding to grant an application under rule 9, the Registrar shall cause a faculty to pass the seal in accustomed form. The applicant shall appear personally before the Registrar to make the oaths mentioned in rule 3.2 and the Registrar shall then admit him by delivering the faculty to him and causing his name to be entered upon the roll of notaries. The Master may appoint a Commissioner to act in place of the Registrar for this purpose.

10.5   Before admitting the applicant in accordance with rule 10.4 the Registrar shall be satisfied that the applicant has successfully completed the Office Practice Course.

PART V: Repeals and Savings

11.   The following Rules are hereby revoked:

12.1   The Notaries (Qualification) Rules 2013

12.   Subject to any further Order of the Master, the certificates of fitness and of good character prescribed by the Master's Orders of 27th August 1992 and

13th September 1993 respectively shall be the certificates prescribed for the purposes of rule 9.2. (a) and (b) of these rules.

Dated this 9th day of March 2017

Signed   C R GEORGE
....
            MASTER

SCHEDULE 1

QUALIFICATIONS BOARD

The Board shall comprise not more than 10 persons appointed by the Master after consultation with the Company, the Society of Scrivener Notaries and the Notaries Society and such other persons or bodies as the Master may consider appropriate.

1. The Master shall appoint one member of the Board to be Chairman for such period as the Master may determine.

2. Members of the Board, including the Chairman, shall hold office for such period as the Master may determine and may be removed from office by the Master at any time.

3. The Registrar shall act as Clerk to the Board or may appoint or nominate another person to act as Clerk in his place.

4. The Board shall meet as often as may be necessary and, in any event, not less than once each year.

5. The Board may delegate any of its functions under these rules to a subcommittee comprising not fewer than three of its members.

SCHEDULE 2

PRESCRIBED SUBJECTS

1. **Public & Constitutional Law**
    - The nature and sources of constitutional law
    - Conventions
    - The sovereignty of parliament
    - Introduction to the objectives and structure of the European Union
    - Human Rights and Freedom of Expression
    - Administrative Law

2. **The Law of Property**
    - The definition of "land" and the distinction between real and personal property
    - The nature of legal and equitable interests
    - Registered and unregistered land
    - Estates and interests in land: freehold, leases, mortgages, easements, covenants relating to land, licences
    - Principles relating to the transfer of legal estates and interest in land, and contracts enforceable in equity
    - Trusts of land, joint tenancies and tenancies in common

3. **The Law of Contract**
   - Formation of a contract: offer, acceptance, consideration, intention to create legal relations
   - Contents of a contract: express and implied terms
   - Exemption clauses and unfair terms
   - Vitiating factors: duress, undue influence, non-disclosure, misrepresentation, mistake
   - Discharge of contracts: performance, agreement, breach, frustration
   - Remedies: damages, specific performance, injunction

4. **The Law of the European Union**
   - Evolution of the European Union
   - The institutions of the European Union
   - The law making process
   - Sources and hierarchy of law in the European Union
   - The supremacy of European Union law
   - Overview of the substantive law of the European Union

5. **Equity and the Law of Trusts**
   - Equity and equitable principles
   - Formation of trusts: the three certainties; the beneficiary principle
   - Formal requirements to create a trust
   - Legality of a trust: perpetuities and accumulations
   - Completely and incompletely constituted trusts
   - Implied, resulting and constructive trusts
   - Trusts of land
   - Charitable trusts
   - Appointment, retirement and removal of trustees
   - Trustees' powers and duties
   - Rights of beneficiaries under a trust
   - Variation of trusts
   - Remedies for breach of trust

6. **Conveyancing**
   - Land registration and third-party rights
   - Conflicts of interest, undertakings and professional negligence
   - Contract: formation and enforceability
   - Deducing and investigating title
   - Pre-contract searches and enquiries
   - Mortgages
   - Planning considerations
   - Exchange of contracts
   - Pre-completion searches steps, completion and post-completion
   - Investigation of Title - registered and unregistered
   - Delayed completion and remedies
   - Leasehold properties

- Commonhold

7.   The Law and Practice of Companies and Partnerships
- Company formation
- Articles of association
- Shares and debentures
- The members of a company, including rights of minority shareholders
- Company directors and other officers
- Administration
- Winding up
- Formation of partnerships
- Relationship between partners, including partners as agents
- Dissolution
- Limited Liability Partnerships

8.   Wills Probate and Administration
- The nature and validity of wills
- Intestacy
- Planning and drafting a will
- Construction of wills
- Taxation and accounts for taxation purposes
- Applying for the grant
- Family provision claims
- Duties and powers of personal representatives
- Completion of the administration
- Beneficiaries' rights and remedies

9.   Roman Law as an Introduction to Civil-Law Systems
- The different areas of law: property, obligations, family, agency, succession
- The use of written instruments in Roman practice - the tabellio and the notarius
- The reception of Roman law in medieval Europe and its continuing relevance to modern civil-law jurisdictions
- The civil-law courts in England
- The role of Roman law in the development of the English common law
- The development of the modern European notariat

10.   Private International Law
- The structure and elements of private international law
- EU and common law rules on jurisdiction
- Recognition and enforcement of judgments under EU law and the common law
- Authentic instruments
- Arbitration and alternative dispute resolution

- Choice of law rules: contractual and non-contractual obligations, moveable and immoveable property, insolvency, marriages and civil partnerships, and succession
- The meaning and use of nationality, domicile and habitual residence as connecting factors
- Characterisation and the distinction between rules of substance and rules of procedure
- The role of public policy and mandatory rules
- The pleading and proof of foreign law

11.   Notarial Practice
- The legislation and rules governing notarial practice
- Personal identity and capacity
- Corporate identity and capacity
- The law of agency and powers of attorney
- Execution of documents and deeds by individuals and bodies corporate
- Forms of notarial act
- Affidavits and statutory declarations
- The noting and protest of bills of exchange
- Document security and record-keeping
- Apostilles and consular legalisation
- The regulation of notarial services
- Appointment, supervision, and continuing professional education
- Professional standards and the Conduct and Discipline Rules

SCHEDULE 3

PRESCRIBED SUBJECTS (Rule 8.3)
(details of subjects as in Schedule 2 above)

1.   Public/Constitutional Law

2.   The Law of Property

3.   The Law of Contract

4.   The Law of the European Union

5.   Equity and the Law of Trusts

6.   Conveyancing

7.   The Law and Practice of Companies and Partnerships

8.   Wills, Probate & Administration

SCHEDULE 4

PRESCRIBED SUBJECTS (Rule 8.3)
(details of subjects as in Schedule 2 above)

PART 1

A. Roman Law as introduction to Civil Law systems
B. Private International Law

PART 2

Notarial Practice (including Bills of Exchange)

In Part 1 of this Schedule, the applicant may be required either to have passed an examination in these subjects, or to have undertaken supervised practice in these subjects under a qualified and admitted notary or otherwise satisfied the Master of his proficiency by practice as a notary in another member state.

In Part 2, the applicant shall have satisfied the Master either by examination or by supervised practice under a qualified and admitted notary in these areas.

SCHEDULE 5

OFFICE PRACTICE COURSE

*   The practical aspects of preparing notarial acts, including the function of a newly qualified notary's supervisor and the use of other resources

*   The application in practice of the Notaries Practice Rules

*   Consular legalisation and apostilles

*   Record-keeping, with particular reference to notarial acts in the public form, and accounts

*   Client care and handling complaints

*   The Conduct and Discipline Rules

NOTARIES PRACTICE RULES 2014 (As Amended)

WE CHARLES RICHARD GEORGE One of Her Majesty's Counsel Commissary or Master of the Faculties of the Most Reverend Father in God JUSTIN PORTAL by Divine Providence Lord Archbishop of Canterbury Primate of All England and Metropolitan in exercise of the powers conferred by section 4 of the Public Notaries Act 1843 and section 57 of the Courts and Legal Services Act 1990 and of all other powers Us enabling hereby make the following Rules:

PART I: PRELIMINARY

1.   Citation and Commencement

   1.1   These rules may be cited as the Notaries Practice Rules 2014.

   1.2   These rules shall come into force on 1st May 2014 save for rule 20 which shall come into force on a date to be appointed by the Master by Order made under these rules.

   1.3   Rules 18 and 19 were amended in March 2017 and will come into force on 1st April 2017.

   1.4   Rule 21.5 was added on 13th July 2017 and came into force on 13 August 2017.

2.   Interpretation

   2.1   In these rules:-

   "approved regulator" has the meaning given to it in section 20 of the Legal Services Act 2007;

   "arrangement" means any express or tacit agreement between a notary and another person whether contractually binding or not;

   "client" includes any person who has instructed a notary to carry out a reserved legal activity within the meaning of section 12 of the Legal Services Act 2007;

   "firm" includes a sole practitioner and professional partnership (which expression shall include a limited liability partnership and any other body corporate) the members of which are authorised to conduct legal practice as such;

   "holding company" and **"subsidiary company"** have the meanings assigned to them by the Companies Act 2006, and two companies are "associated" where they are subsidiary companies of the same holding company;

   "the Master" means the Master of the Faculties;

"notarial act" means any act that has validity by virtue only of its preparation performance authentication attestation or verification by a notary and includes any such act carried out by electronic means;

"notary" includes a firm of notaries;

"performance" includes execution completion and carrying out;

"person" includes a body corporate or unincorporated association or group of persons;

"principles" means the general principles set out in rule 4;

"qualified legal practitioner" means
(i)   a person qualified to provide legal services to the public in England and Wales; or
(ii)   a person qualified to provide legal services to the public under the laws of any other jurisdiction who practises as such in England and Wales;

"the Registrar" means the Registrar of the Court of Faculties;

2.2   for the purposes of these rules:

2.2.1   a notary's practice includes the preparation and performance of notarial acts and any other service undertaken as a notary whether or not such service may only be undertaken by a notary;

2.2.2   for the avoidance of doubt the Interpretation Act 1978 applies to these rules as it applies to an Act of Parliament;

2.2.3   reference to any other rules or regulations which govern the practice of a notary in England and Wales and made by the Master shall include any rules and regulations made in substitution therefor;

2.2.4   words importing the masculine gender shall include the feminine gender and words importing the singular shall where the context so admits include the plural and vice versa

PART II: PRACTICE AS A NOTARY

3.   Oath of Office and Recognition of Notarial Acts
3.1   A notary shall exercise the office of public notary in accordance with the Oath or Declaration made by him at the time of the grant of his Notarial Faculty as set out in section 7 of the Public Notaries

Act 1843 and shall offer appropriate notarial services to any person lawfully and reasonably requiring the same.

3.2 A notary in possession of a valid practising certificate issued pursuant to the Notaries (Practising Certificate) Rules 2012 may issue notarial acts in the public or private forms intended for use in England and Wales and in any other jurisdiction.

4. General Principles

4.1 Without prejudice to rule 3.1 above a notary shall exercise his office at all times in accordance with the principles set out below and these rules shall be read in accordance with such principles.

4.2 A notary shall:

4.2.1 uphold the rule of law and the proper administration of justice;

4.2.2 act with integrity;

4.2.3 maintain his independence and impartiality;

4.2.4 provide a prompt and proper standard of service for all clients;

4.2.5 act in a way that maintains the trust in the office of notary which the public may reasonably expect;

4.2.6 comply with all legal and regulatory obligations and cooperate with the Master and any persons or body appointed by him in exercise of the Master's regulatory functions;

4.2.7 operate his notarial practice in accordance with proper governance and sound financial and risk management principles; and

4.2.8 operate his notarial practice in such a way as to provide equality of opportunity and respect for diversity.

5. Code of Practice

5.1 A notary shall at all times have regard to any code or codes of practice approved by the Master from time to time.

5.2 Failure to comply with this rule may amount to "Notarial Misconduct" as defined by rule 2 of the Notaries (Conduct and Discipline) Rules 2011.

6. Bankruptcy

A notary who is bankrupt may not practice as a notary on his own behalf or as the sole member of a professional partnership until he is discharged from bankruptcy, provided that this rule shall not prevent him from practicing as the employee of another notary.

7. Obtaining Instructions

A notary shall not directly or indirectly obtain or attempt to obtain instructions for professional work or permit another person to do so on his behalf, or do anything in the course of practising as a notary, in any manner which compromises or impairs or is likely to compromise or impair any of the following:

7.1   the principles;

7.2   a person's freedom to instruct a notary of their choice;

7.3   the notary's ability to act in the best interests of the client;

7.4   the good repute of the notary or of the notarial profession;

7.5   the notary's proper standard of work;

7.6   the notary's duty of care to persons in all jurisdictions who may place legitimate reliance on his notarial acts.

8.   Duty to inform instructing person of right to complain

8.1   When a notary accepts instructions for professional work or changes the terms on which he is acting he must provide the client with a copy of a form of words prescribed by the Master from time to time (the "prescribed form of words") which explains that the client has a right to make a complaint under Part II of the Notaries (Conduct and Discipline) Rules 2015 and how to make such a complaint.

8.2   The prescribed form of words may be provided to the client electronically.

9.   Conflicts of Interest

9.1   Conflicts of Interest (General)

9.1.1   In the conduct of his practice a notary shall not favour the interests of one client over those of another and shall not favour his own interests or those of any other person over those of his clients.

9.2   Conflicts of Interest (Conveyancing Transactions)

9.2.1   A notary conducting a conveyancing transaction in the capacity of a solicitor, or a licensed conveyancer, or member of another professional body with an approved regulator, is subject to the rules and any guidance relating to (a) conflicts of interest and (b) relations with third parties laid down by the approved regulator of that professional body and should comply with such rules and have regard to any such guidance accordingly.

9.2.2   A notary conducting a conveyancing transaction in the capacity of a notary must not act for both seller and buyer in a transaction relating to property situated in England and Wales unless:

(a)   the notary is satisfied that no conflict of interest exists or is likely to arise during the course of the transaction, whether or not the transaction is between parties at arm's length; and

(b)   both parties are established clients in that they have instructed the notary on previous occasions; or

(c)   the consideration does not exceed £10,000 in an individual transaction; and

(d)   both clients are informed of the advantages of separate representation before they give their written consent to the notary acting for both of them; and

(e)   both parties consent in writing.

9.2.3 For the avoidance of doubt this rule shall apply to a notary acting for one party in his capacity under rule 9.2.1 and another party in his capacity under rule 9.2.2.

9.3   Relations with third parties

9.3.1 A notary shall not communicate directly by any means whatsoever with any other party to a conveyancing transaction where that party is represented by a lawyer except:

(a)   to obtain information about the name and address (including e-mail address) of that lawyer; or

(b)   with the consent of that lawyer; or

(c)   after notifying the lawyer of the intention to contact the party direct because the other party's lawyer has refused or without good reason failed to pass on messages or to reply to communications; or

(d)   in exceptional circumstances where it is impracticable to contact that party's lawyer; provided that any communication under (a) to (d) of this rule shall be in writing.

9.3.2 A notary who is dealing with any unrepresented party to a conveyancing transaction must not take unfair advantage of that party, and where it is necessary for practical reasons to communicate orally with an unrepresented party the notary should immediately thereafter make a written note of the communication and should as soon as possible confirm the substance of it in writing to the unrepresented party.

9.4   Conflicts of Interest (notarial activities other than conveyancing transactions)

9.4.1 In respect of notarial activities other than conveyancing transactions, a notary may act for both parties to a transaction but only if:

(a)   each party has consented in writing to the notary so acting; and

(b)   the notary is satisfied that there is no conflict of interest between the parties.

9.4.2 For the avoidance of doubt a notary does not act for both parties to a transaction merely by preparing or authenticating a notarial act in his capacity as a public certifying officer even though that act may concern two or more parties.

10. Duty to Act Impartially in respect of Notarial Acts

A notary must act impartially and in particular must not perform any notarial act which involves or may affect:

10.1   his own affairs, including matters in which he is personally interested jointly with another person;

10.2   the affairs of his spouse or partner or a person to whom the notary is engaged to be married (for the purpose of this sub-rule, "partner" means a person with whom the notary cohabits or with whom he has a sexual relationship and includes a partner of the same sex);

10.3   the affairs of a person to whom he is directly and closely related;

10.4   the affairs of a person with whom he is in a professional partnership or by whom he is employed or from whom he receives a benefit by being provided with office accommodation or other facilities for his notarial practice;

10.5   the affairs of a person who has appointed the notary to be his attorney which concern a matter within the scope of the power of attorney granted;

10.6   the affairs of a trust of which he is a trustee or of an estate where he is a personal representative of the deceased;

10.7   the affairs of a body corporate of whose board of directors or governing body he is a member;

10.8   the affairs of an employee of the notary;

10.9   the affairs of a partnership of which he is a member or of a company in which the notary holds shares either exceeding five percent of the issued share capital or having a market value exceeding such figure as the Master may from time to time specify.

11. Employed Notaries

11.1   Save as permitted by rule 11.2 a notary who is the employee of a non-notary shall not perform any notarial act as part of his employment or do or perform any notarial act for his employer or his employer's holding, associated or subsidiary company.

11.2   A notary may act for a person who is also the client of the qualified legal practitioner or firm of qualified legal practitioners by which he is employed but he shall take all proper and reasonable steps in the exercise of his notarial practice to maintain his independence of his employer and in particular he shall:

11.2.1   ensure that his independence and integrity as a notary is fully recognised in writing in any contract of employment entered into by him; and

11.2.2 annually send to his employer a written statement of professional independence in a form approved by the Master from time to time and shall declare in his application for a notarial practising certificate that he has complied with this rule.

12. Language

12.1 Notarial acts shall normally be drawn up in the English language.

12.2 A notary may upon request or in appropriate circumstances prepare a notarial act in a language other than English if he has sufficient knowledge of the language concerned.

12.3 A notary may not authenticate by means of a notarial act a document drawn up in a language other than English unless he has satisfied himself as to its meaning but this does not prevent a notary from authenticating the execution or signature of a document in any language.

12.4 A notary may not certify the accuracy of a translation that has been made by someone other than himself unless he has knowledge of the language sufficient to satisfy himself as to the accuracy of the translation but this does not prevent a notary from attesting a translator's affidavit or authenticating a verification.

13. Undertakings

13.1 Any notary giving an undertaking, whether oral or in writing, shall be personally liable for that undertaking, and the implementation of any such undertaking is required as a matter of conduct. Save in exceptional cases a failure by a notary to honour an undertaking will constitute Notarial Misconduct as defined in rule 2 of the Notaries (Conduct and Discipline) Rules 2011.

13.2 An undertaking given by a notary in writing or confirmed in writing shall be signed by the notary giving it.

14. Publicity

A notary may advertise his practice and seek to obtain directly or indirectly clients and business in any manner and through any medium whether informative or promotional with the exception of unsolicited telephone calls or unsolicited visits to persons or organisations provided that:

14.1 the principles are upheld;

14.2 the client's freedom to instruct a qualified person of the client's choice is not thereby unduly restricted;

14.3 the notary's good reputation for integrity and professional standards of work is not thereby damaged;

14.4 he complies with any relevant non-statutory code of advertising standards and practice currently in force;

but nothing in this rule shall be construed as authorising the use of the word "notary" or any word designating or indicating notarial services in any publicity for activities which are not of a notarial nature.

15. Scrivener Notaries

No notary shall describe himself professionally as a Scrivener or a Scrivener notary unless he holds the qualifications to practise as a Scrivener notary from time to time prescribed by the Incorporated Company of Scriveners.

16. Introductions and Referrals

When a notary enters into an arrangement with another person for the introduction of clients to the notary or by the notary to the other person he must ensure:

16.1   that the client is informed in writing of the arrangement and of any commission or other benefit the notary may be receiving or pay;

16.2   that he either obtains the client's written agreement as to the destination of the commission or accounts to the client for the commission;

16.3   that he remains able to advise the client independently in accordance with these rules and continues to do so regardless of his own interests.

17. Offering Services other than as a Notary

17.1   Where a notary by himself or with any other person operates, actively participates in or controls any business, other than a notary's practice, the notary shall ensure:

17.1.1   that the name of that business has no substantial element in common with the name of any practice of the notary;

17.1.2   that the words "notary", "notaries," "attorney(s)" or "lawyer(s)" or any words designating or indicating a notarial or legal practice are not used in connection with the notary's involvement with that business;

17.1.3   that any client referred by any practice of the notary to the business is informed in writing that, as a customer of that business, he does not enjoy any protection attaching to the client of a notary, and that where that business shares premises or reception staff with any practice of the notary, every customer of the business is informed in writing that, as a customer of that business, he does not enjoy the protection attaching to the client of a notary.

17.2   Rule 17.1 does not apply to the practice of a qualified legal practitioner.

18. Fees

18.1 A notary may charge a professional fee for all notarial work undertaken by him, and the basis upon which that fee will be calculated or the fee to be charged for the work done, shall be made known in advance to any new client.

18.2 Subject to rule 18.3 below a notary shall not share or agree to share his professional fees with any person not entitled to act as a notary; provided that this rule shall not prohibit the payment of any allowance or allowances, sum or sums of money, that are or shall be agreed to be made or paid to the widows or children of any deceased notary or notaries, by any surviving partner or partners of such deceased notary or notaries.

18.3 A notary who also practises as a qualified legal practitioner either in a professional partnership or as an employee may share professional fees provided that:

18.3.1 his professional partners or employer are also qualified legal practitioners;

18.3.2 the notary shall keep accounts which enable the income and expenditure arising from his practice as a notary to be distinguished from the income and expenditure arising from his practice or employment as a qualified legal practitioner; and

18.3.3 shall furnish the Faculty Office with such additional information as to his professional partnership and accounting arrangements or his employment as may be prescribed in rules or orders of the Master.

18.4 A notary who practises as such within or on behalf of a limited company or limited liability partnership may share his professional fees, or collect them through, that company or partnership provided that the equity of that company or partnership is wholly owned by the notary or notaries who are the directors or partners of the company or partnership.

19. Name of a Firm of Notaries

19.1 A notary shall notify the Registrar of the name under which he practises, or the firm of notaries within which he practises:

19.1.1 at the time of his admission;

19.1.2 at any time the name is to change; and

19.1.3 annually when he applies for a practising certificate pursuant to Rule 4 of the Notaries (Practising Certificates) Rule 2012

19.2 A notary shall not practise under a name which is likely to mislead (whether intentionally or unintentionally) or bring the notarial profession into disrepute.

20. Investment Business
[This rule came into force by Order of the Master made on 20 August 2014]

20.1 In this rule "appointed representative", "investment" and "regulated activity" have the meanings assigned to them by the Financial Services and Markets Act 2000 and the Financial Services and Markets Act 2000 (Regulated Activities) Order 2001 as extended by the Financial Services Act 2012.

20.2 A notary shall not in connection with any regulated activity:

    20.2.1 have an exclusive arrangement with a provider of financial services nor with a provider of financial services advice (whether of independent advice or restricted advice or both) under which the notary could be constrained to recommend, introduce or refer clients or effect for them (or refrain from so doing) transactions or contracts:

        a. in some investments or markets but not others;
        b. with some persons or companies but not others;
        c. through the agency of some persons or companies but not others.

    20.2.2 be an appointed representative.

20.3 Notwithstanding any provision in rule 17 a notary shall not by himself or with any other person set up, operate, actively participate in or control any separate business which is an appointed representative.

20.4 For the avoidance of doubt a notary shall comply with this rule in connection with regulated activity carried on within England and Wales and in any other jurisdiction

21. Supervision of a Notary's Office

21.1 A notary shall take reasonable steps to ensure that every office where he practises is and can be seen to be:

    21.1.1 open, save exceptionally and for a good reason, during normal office hours for the provision of appropriate notarial services to members of the public; and

    21.1.2 properly supervised. In particular a notary shall ensure that he or another notary holding a Practising Certificate shall spend sufficient time at such office to ensure adequate control of the staff employed there and afford requisite facilities for consultation with clients. Such notary may be a principal, employee or consultant of the firm or a locum tenens.

21.2 In determining whether or not there has been compliance with the requirement as to supervision in rule 21.1, account shall be taken of, inter alia, the arrangements for the principals to see or be apprised of incoming communications.

21.3 Where the operation or supervision of a notary's office in accordance with this rule is prevented by illness, accident or other sufficient or unforeseen cause for a prolonged period, suitable alternative arrangements shall be made without delay to ensure compliance.

21.4 In cases where a notary is not in attendance on days when his office is normally open to the public, he shall make adequate arrangements to ensure the provision of notarial services to persons requiring the same.

21.5 A notary shall not employ within his professional practice a person who is, or has been, a member of a Specified Profession within the meaning of rule 24 and the Schedule to the Notaries (Conduct and Discipline) Rules 2015 without the express written permission of the Registrar where that person has had a finding of professional misconduct made against him by the Relevant Body of the Specified Profession.

22. Continuing Professional Education
22.1 After commencing practice and having satisfactorily completed the required period of supervision, a notary shall, within every such successive period as shall be determined by the Master, participate in such programmes, courses or seminars approved by the Master as may be necessary to acquire the number of credit points determined by the Master.

22.2 Upon determination by the Master of the periods and number of credit points, they shall be included in regulations made by the Master under this rule from time to time.

PART III: RECORDS AND INSPECTIONS

23. Duty to Keep Records
23.1 A notary shall keep proper records of his notarial acts in accordance with this rule.

23.2 The records so kept must clearly identify:
23.2.1 the date of the act;
23.2.2 the person at whose request the act was performed;
23.2.3 the person or persons, if any, intervening in the act and, in the case of a person who intervened in a representative capacity, the name of his principal;

126

23.2.4 the method of identification of the party or parties intervening in the notarial act, and in the case of a party intervening in a representative capacity, any evidence produced to the notary of that party's entitlement so to intervene;

23.2.5 the nature of the act;

23.2.6 the fee charged.

23.3 In the case of a notarial act in the public form, the notary shall place an original of the act or a complete photographic copy of the same in a protocol which shall be preserved permanently by the notary and for the avoidance of doubt such preservation may be by means of a suitable digital or other electronic system providing for the storage of documents in an indelible and unalterable format.

23.4 Records of acts not in public form kept in accordance with rule 23.2 shall be preserved for a minimum period of twelve years and for the avoidance of doubt such preservation may be by means of a suitable digital or other electronic system providing for the storage of documents in an indelible and unalterable format.

23.5 A notary who preserves records by means of a digital or other electronic system in accordance with rules 23.3 and 23.4 shall notify the Registrar of any username and password required for access to such digital or electronic system and the Registrar shall keep such information confidential.

23.6 A copy of a notarial act or of the record of a notarial act preserved in accordance with rules 23.3 and 23.4 shall, upon payment of a reasonable fee, be issued upon the application of any person or authority having a proper interest in the act unless prevented by order of a competent court.

23.7 Any question as to whether a person has a proper interest in an act for the purposes of rule 23.6 shall be determined by the Master.

24. Inspections of Records and Practice

24.1 A notary's premises, records and practice may be inspected from time to time on behalf of the Master and as directed by him

24.2 The records which may be inspected in accordance with rule 24.1 shall include all documents in the notary's possession relating in any way to his practice as a notary, whether or not they also relate to non-notarial matters and shall include documents stored by means of a digital or other electronic system.

24.3 Copies of documents inspected in accordance with rule 24.1 may be taken for onward transmission to the Master where requested by the person carrying out the inspection.

24.4 Inspections shall be carried out in accordance with regulations to be made by the Master from time to time under this rule.

25. Notaries Ceasing to Practise

25.1 When a notary ceases to practise as such then he, or failing him his continuing notarial partners or the person having possession or custody of the records maintained by him pursuant to rule 23, shall arrange for such records to be transferred:

    25.1.1 to another notary in practice appointed by him or by his continuing notarial partners;

    25.1.2 to another notary in practice appointed, with the approval of the Master, by the persons having possession or custody of the records; or

    25.1.3 to any archive designated for the purpose under regulations made by the Master from time to time;

and the persons making such transfer shall give written particulars to the Registrar of the date of transfer and the person or archive to which the records were transferred.

25.2 The provisions of rules 23 and 24 shall apply to a notary or archive to which the records of any notary are transferred pursuant to this rule as they apply to the notary himself.

26. Application to Ecclesiastical Notaries

The provisions of this Part shall apply to notaries appointed for ecclesiastical purposes only subject to the following modifications:

26.1 The requirement of rule 23 to keep a record of notarial acts shall apply only to such ecclesiastical acts as law or custom requires to be performed in the presence of a public notary and recorded in writing.

26.2 Any act or transaction properly recorded in the Act Book of any Archbishop or Bishop, or in the Minute Book of any Cathedral Chapter, shall be deemed to have been properly recorded in accordance with rule 23.

26.3 Rule 25 shall not apply to ecclesiastical notaries, but upon a person ceasing for any reason to hold the office in respect of which he was appointed an ecclesiastical notary, any records kept by him pursuant to this Part shall be transferred to the succeeding holder of that office (being an ecclesiastical notary) upon his appointment.

PART IV: MISCELLANEOUS

27. Waivers

The Master shall have power to waive any of the provisions of these rules in any particular case or classes of case for the purpose expressed in such waiver, and to revoke such waiver.

28.   Repeals and Savings

28.1   Subject to rule 28.2 the Notaries Practice Rules 2009, with the exception of Rule 17 thereof, are hereby revoked. [NPR2009 Rule 17 was revoked by an Order of the Master dated 20 August 2014]

28.2   Rule 28.1 does not absolve any notary from the duty to comply with the Notaries Practice Rules 2009 prior to the coming into force of these rules and records maintained by a notary in accordance with Rules 20-23 of the Notaries Practice Rules 2009 prior to the coming into force of these rules shall continue to be so maintained by him and rules 23.5, 23.6, 24, 25 and 26 of these rules shall apply to such records.

Rule 28.1 does not absolve any notary from the duty to comply with the Notaries Practice Rules 2009 prior to the coming into force of these rules and records maintained by a notary in accordance with Rules 20-23 of the Notaries Practice Rules 2009 prior to the coming into force of these rules shall continue to be so maintained by him and rules 23.5, 23.6, 24, 25 and 26 of these rules shall apply to such records.

C R George

The Right Worshipful Charles R George, Q.C.
Master   **March 2017**

NOTARIES (CONDUCT AND DISCIPLINE) RULES 2015 (As Amended)

WE CHARLES RICHARD GEORGE One of Her Majesty's Counsel Commissary or Master of the Faculties of the Most Reverend Father in God Justin Portal by Divine Providence Lord Archbishop of Canterbury Primate of All England and Metropolitan in exercise of the powers conferred by section 4 of the Public Notaries Act 1843 and section 57 of the Courts and Legal Services Act 1990 and of all other powers Us enabling hereby make the following Rules:

ARRANGEMENT OF RULES

Part I: Preliminary

Part II: The Court and its Officers

Part III: Complaints Generally

Part IV: Disciplinary Procedure

PART I: PRELIMINARY

1.   Citation and Commencement

1.1   These rules may be cited as the Notaries (Conduct and Discipline) Rules 2015

1.2   The rules come into force on the 1st day of November 2015

2.   Interpretation

2.1   In these rules:

- **'1993 Rules'** means the Public Notaries (Conduct and Discipline) Rules 1993.

- **'2000 Rules'** means the Notarial Appeals and Hearings Rules 2000.

- **'2009 Rules'** means the Notaries (Conduct and Discipline) Rules 2009.

- **'2011 Rules'** means the Notaries (Conduct and Discipline) Rules 2011.

- **'2012 Rules'** means the Notaries (Practising Certificate) Rules 2012.

- **'Approved Procedure'** means a complaints resolution procedure approved under Rule 7 of these rules, Rule 3 of the 1993 Rules, Rule 3 of the 2009 Rules or Rule 3 of the 2011 Rules.

- **'Client'** includes any person who has instructed a notary to carry out a reserved legal activity within the meaning of section 12 of the Legal Services Act 2007 and any person who has placed legitimate reliance on a Notarial Act.

- **'Commissary'** and **'Deputy Commissary'** mean respectively the Commissary and Deputy Commissary appointed by the Archbishop of Canterbury under section 3 of the Ecclesiastical Licences Act 1533 to be the Commissary and Deputy Commissary for the purposes of these rules.

- **'Competent Complainant'** means:-
  (1) A Nominated Notary, or
  (2) A Client where the complaint relates to Notarial Misconduct arising from notarial acts or other professional services performed by the notary in question.

- **'The Contingency Fund'** means the fund referred to in the Notarial Contingency Fund Rules 1981.

- **'The Court'** means the Court of Faculties.

- **'Designated Society'** means the Notaries Society and the Incorporated Company of Scriveners and such other bodies as the Master may from time to time designate for the purposes of these rules.

- **'Document'** means anything in which information of any description is recorded.

- **'Lay Assessor'** means an Assessor who is not a notary.

- **'The Master'** means the Master of the Faculties.

- **'Nominated Notary'** means a notary appointed by the Registrar under Rule 6 of these rules.

- **'Notarial Act'** means any act that has validity by virtue only of its preparation performance authentication attestation or verification by a notary and includes any such act carried out by electronic means.

- **'Notary Assessor'** means an Assessor who is a notary.

- **'Notarial Misconduct'** means

  (1) Fraudulent conduct,
  (2) Practising as a notary without a valid Notarial Practising Certificate or in breach of a condition or limitation imposed on a Notarial Practising Certificate, or
  (3) Serious misconduct which may inter alia include failure to observe the requirements of these rules or of the Notaries Practice Rules 2014 or falling seriously below the standard

of service reasonably to be expected of a notary or persistent failure to provide the standard of service reasonably to be expected by a notary.

- **'The Registrar'** means the Registrar of the Court of Faculties or an officer of the Court acting with the Registrar's authority.

- **'Specified Profession'** and **'Relevant Body'** have the meanings specified in Rule 24.

- **'Statement'** means a written statement (including a witness statement) containing a statement of truth.

- **'The Schedule'** and **'the Appendix'** mean respectively the Schedule and the Appendix to these rules.

2.2   References in these rules to a "notary" are references to a public notary enrolled on the Roll of Notaries maintained by the Court.

2.3   Reference to any other rules or regulations made by the Master shall include any rules and regulations made in substitution therefore.

2.4   References in these rules to forms are to the forms set out in the Appendix, references in Part IV (Disciplinary Procedure) to the **Complainant** and the **Respondent** are to the person bringing a complaint and the notary against whom a complaint is brought respectively and references in Part V (Reviews) to the Applicant and the **Respondent** are to the notary applying for review and the person or body appointed to act as respondent to the application respectively.

2.5   The Interpretation Act 1978 applies to these rules as it applies to an Act of Parliament.

PART II: THE COURT AND ITS OFFICERS

3.   Permanent officers of the Court

3.1   The Commissary shall be the principal judge of the Court for the purposes of these rules.

3.2   If for any reason the Commissary is unable or unwilling to perform his functions under these rules in relation to any matter, that matter shall be assigned by the Registrar to a Deputy Commissary.

3.3   Where a matter has been assigned under these rules to a Deputy Commissary that Deputy Commissary shall perform all of the functions in relation to that matter which would have been performed by the Commissary.

3.4 The Registrar shall act as the clerk of the Court.

4. **Assessors**

4.1 There shall be established a panel of assessors comprising at least six persons of whom one half shall be notaries who have held a Notarial Practising Certificate for not less than ten consecutive years at the date of their appointment and one half shall be persons of good standing who are not notaries.

4.2 The members of the panel shall be appointed by the Master for a term of five years (which may be renewed for further terms of five years on expiry) but an Assessor who is involved in an appeal or hearing shall continue in office until the conclusion of that appeal or hearing notwithstanding the expiry of his term of office.

4.3 An Assessor's appointment may be terminated by the Master with the consent of the Commissary for gross misconduct.

5. **Composition of the Court**

5.1 In respect of an appeal or hearing to which these rules apply interlocutory issues shall be dealt with by the Commissary but the matter will be heard by the Commissary sitting with two Assessors chosen by him, one being a Notary Assessor and the other being a Lay Assessor.

5.2 Where the Commissary is sitting with Assessors questions of law shall be determined by the Commissary alone but all other issues shall be determined by a majority decision.

5.3 Where the Master is required to hear any application, appeal or other matter whether under rules made by him or under his inherent jurisdiction he may direct that the matter shall be heard by the Commissary.

5.4 Where the Master has made a direction under Rule 5.3 the Commissary shall determine whether to hear the matter alone or with Assessors.

5.5 On assessment of costs the Commissary shall determine whether to make the assessment alone or with Assessors.

6. Nominated Notaries and their functions

6.1 A Nominated Notary appointed by the Registrar under these rules shall be a notary who holds a Notarial Practising Certificate and has held such a Certificate for not less than five years.

6.2 A Nominated Notary may be appointed by the Registrar to carry out the functions conferred on a Nominated Notary by these rules.

6.3 A Nominated Notary appointed under this Rule shall be independent of and not personally acquainted with the notary who is the subject of the allegation of Notarial Misconduct to be investigated.

6.4 If the Registrar is unable to identify a Nominated Notary who fulfils the requirements in Rule 6.3 the Master shall appoint an independent person, who need not be a notary, to act in place of a Nominated Notary for the purposes of Rule 6.1, and that person shall carry out all functions conferred on a Nominated Notary by these rules.

6.5 Subject to Rule 6.6 on order by the Master a Nominated Notary shall have the power in the course of an investigation to inspect Documents in the power possession or control of or believed to be in the power possession and control of the notary who is the subject of the allegation or evidence of Notarial Misconduct.

6.6 A Nominated Notary may not use a Document or Documents or the information contained therein obtained pursuant to the power given by Rule 6.5 for any purpose other than in the investigation of the allegation or evidence and shall not disclose such Document or Documents or information except to the Court without the leave of the Court unless necessary:
6.6.1 for the prevention or detection of crime,
6.6.2 the investigation of a criminal offence or
6.6.3 the conduct of a prosecution either nationally or internationally in which case such Document, Documents or information may be disclosed by the Nominated Notary to the law enforcement and prosecuting authorities.

PART III: COMPLAINTS GENERALLY

7. Complaints Resolution Procedures

7.1 The Master may from time to time approve by written notice a complaints resolution procedure produced by a Designated Society or any amendment or variation thereof and may at any time by written notice withdraw approval of any procedure or amendment or variation.

7.2   An Approved Procedure may include provision:

7.2.1   for the informal resolution of disputes between members of the public and notaries concerning notarial acts done by a notary or the conduct of a notary's practice,

7.2.2   for the informal resolution of disputes between members of the public and notaries concerning the charges made by notaries for notarial services,

7.2.3   for dealing with complaints referred to a Designated Society by the Registrar about the conduct or practice of a notary who is a member of that Designated Society,

and for such other matters as the Master may from time to time specify.

7.3   Where a dispute with or complaint against a notary is dealt with in accordance with an Approved Procedure it shall be a duty of the notary to cooperate with the Designated Society in the operation of the procedure.

7.3.1   At the end of the Approved Procedure a notary shall comply with any reasonable action proposed by the Designated Society in its conclusion unless the notary does not accept on reasonable grounds the action proposed.

7.3.2   A notary shall offer the client an alternative remedy which is reasonable in the circumstances of the complaint if he does not accept on reasonable grounds the conclusion of the Designated Society.

7.3.3   An apology, an offer of treatment or other redress shall not of itself amount to an admission of Notarial Misconduct.

7.4   A notary shall give the Office of Legal Complaints all such assistance requested by that Office in connection with the investigation, consideration or determination of complaints under the ombudsman scheme established under section 115 of the Legal Services Act 2007 as he is reasonably able to give.

7.5   Where a dispute with or complaint against a notary is received by the Registrar and there is no Approved Procedure available to deal with the complaint, the Registrar shall refer the matter to a member of a panel of not less than four notaries each of whom has held a Notarial Practising Certificate for a minimum of ten years appointed for this purpose by the Registrar to carry out the functions set out in Rule 7.2.

7.5.1 the notary carrying out these functions shall be entitled to a fixed fee to be specified by the Master from time to time which shall be payable by the notary complained against,

7.5.2 the notary carrying out these functions may not be appointed a Nominated Notary under Rule 8.2 in relation to the same dispute or complaint.

8. Handling of Allegations

8.1 Where the Registrar receives evidence or an allegation concerning the conduct or practice of a notary which in his opinion does not amount to an allegation of Notarial Misconduct or where the precise nature of the allegation is unclear he shall refer the matter to a Designated Society or to a notary appointed under Rule 7.5, to be dealt with in accordance with an Approved Procedure.

8.2 Where the Registrar receives evidence of or an allegation concerning the conduct or practice of a notary which appears to him to amount to an allegation of Notarial Misconduct he shall appoint a Nominated Notary to investigate pursuant to Rule 8.3.

8.3 A Nominated Notary appointed under Rule 8.2 shall diligently and expeditiously investigate evidence of or an allegation of Notarial Misconduct and shall make a complaint under Rule 11.1 and prepare and prosecute disciplinary proceedings against a notary in the Court under Part IV of these rules, if after investigation, the Nominated Notary reasonably believes that there is a prima facie case of Notarial Misconduct to be answered.

8.4 If the Nominated Notary upon investigating the evidence or an allegation of Notarial Misconduct considers that there is a prima facie case of Notarial Misconduct he shall make a written report to the Registrar stating the reasons for his decision.

8.5 The Master on the application of the Registrar may discharge a Nominated Notary from his investigatory and prosecutorial functions with respect to a specific allegation or evidence of Notarial Misconduct if the Registrar considers that the Nominated Notary is not acting uprightly, diligently or expediently in fulfilling his duties in the matter and appoint another Nominated Notary in his place.

9. Interim suspensions by the Registrar

9.1 Where the Registrar receives evidence concerning a notary which amounts to prima facie evidence of Notarial Misconduct, the Registrar, if he is satisfied that it is required for the protection of the public, may make an interim order to suspend the notary from practice or restrict or limit or impose conditions on the notary's practice pending the conclusion of disciplinary proceedings under Part IV of these rules.

9.2 A suspension given under this Rule may be renewed by the Registrar for any number of times but each suspension shall be for no longer than a period of three months.

9.3 The notary may appeal to the Master against the Registrar's decision within seven days of the issue of that interim order and on such appeal the Master shall have the same power as the Registrar has under this Rule 9.1.

9.4 The Registrar's power under this Rule 9 shall not be exercisable after the receipt by the Registrar of the answer in Form 4 or the end of the twenty-one day period specified in Rule 11.5 (time for delivery of reply to complaint), whichever is the earlier.

9.5 If following appointment by the Registrar:
9.5.1 the Nominated Notary decides not to bring a complaint under Rule 11.1 and makes his written report to the Registrar in accordance with Rule 8.5 or
9.5.2 a complaint is withdrawn with the leave of the Court under Rule 15 or
9.5.3 the decision is taken by the Court that disciplinary proceedings are to cease in respect of the complaint,
the suspension and/or any conditions imposed on the notary's practice shall automatically lapse.

9.6 Any interim order made under this Rule 9 may be discharged or varied by the Commissary on application made to him after the end of the twenty-one day period specified in Rule 11.5.

10. Referral of Allegations by Designated Societies

Where an allegation against a notary comes to the attention of a Designated Society (whether or not in the course of the operation of an Approved Procedure) and it appears that such allegation amounts to an allegation of Notarial Misconduct the Designated Society shall refer the allegation to the Registrar for consideration in accordance with Rule 8.2.

PART IV: DISCIPLINARY PROCEDURE

11. Making of complaints of Notarial Misconduct

11.1 A complaint of Notarial Misconduct may be made to the Court by any Competent Complainant.

11.2 Where:

11.2.1 Evidence of or an allegation of misconduct concerning the practice of a notary has been received by or brought to the attention of the Registrar and he has not appointed a Nominated Notary to investigate that evidence or allegation under Rule 8.2 of these rules within 28 days of receiving the evidence or allegation, or

11.2.2 The Registrar has appointed a Nominated Notary to investigate that evidence or allegation and the Nominated Notary has determined not to make a complaint of Notarial Misconduct to the Court in respect of the allegation or has not so made a complaint within 112 days of his appointment or the referral of the allegation (as the case may be);

then a complaint of Notarial Misconduct in respect of that allegation or evidence may be made to the Court by any notary who holds a Notarial Practising Certificate and such notary shall be deemed to be a Competent Complainant for the purposes of these rules.

11.3 A complaint of Notarial Misconduct howsoever arising shall be made to the Registrar by a written complaint in form 1 delivered to the Registrar and shall be supported by a Statement setting out the allegations and the facts and matters supporting the complaint and each allegation in form 2.

11.4 On receiving a written complaint and Statement in support the Registrar shall issue the complaint and serve a copy of each document together with notice of proceedings in form 3 on the Respondent.

11.5 Within twenty-one days of service of the notice of proceedings on him the Respondent shall deliver to the Registrar an answer to the complaint in form 4 stating whether or not the Respondent intends to contest the proceedings in whole or in part and if only part which part and on receipt of an answer the Registrar shall serve a copy on the complainant.

12. Respondent's reply to complaint

Within forty-two days of service of the notice of proceedings on him and provided the Respondent has delivered to the Registrar an answer the Respondent shall, if he intends to continue to contest the proceedings, deliver to the Registrar a Statement in reply to the complaint stating which facts in the complaint are agreed and which are not and on receipt of such Statement the Registrar shall send a copy to the complainant.

13. Further Statements or allegations

13.1 With the leave of the Court the Complainant may file supplementary Statements with the Registrar containing additional facts or matters on which the complainant seeks to rely in support of the complaint or containing further allegations and facts or matters in support of the further allegations. Any supplementary Statement containing further allegations against the Respondent shall be treated as though it were a complaint for the purposes of Rule 12.

13.2 On receiving a supplementary Statement the Registrar shall serve a copy on the Respondent.

14. Agreed statements

14.1 The Respondent and Complainant may engage in "without prejudice" communications between themselves with a view to determining whether the parties can come to an agreed settlement as to facts and issues of the complaint.

14.2 If under this Rule the Respondent and the Complainant agree on certain facts and issues of the complaint they may set these down in writing and by mutual agreement present the agreed statement to the Court.

14.3 The agreed statement under this Rule may contain an admission by the Respondent of Notarial Misconduct and propose a sanction to be imposed upon the Respondent and/or an offer of redress to be made by him.

14.4 Except in circumstances where the agreed statement under this Rule is clearly wrong, the Court shall accept the veracity of the statement and shall have regard to it as evidence when making its findings but the Court shall retain full discretion to find whether or not the Respondent is guilty of misconduct and, if so, what order should be made by penalty or otherwise in consequence of the finding.

15. Withdrawal of complaints

The complainant may withdraw the complaint with the leave of the Court.

16. Hearing and case management directions

16.1 If the Respondent fails to deliver an answer within the time prescribed by Rule 12 the Registrar shall appoint a date for the hearing of the complaint, where possible with the agreement of the parties or, failing that, by direction of the Court and give notice to both parties in form 5.

16.2   If the Respondent delivers an answer and the reply pursuant to Rule 12 within the time prescribed the Registrar shall refer the papers to the Commissary who shall make such directions for the future conduct of the complaint as he thinks fit including directions:-

    16.2.1   for the filing and service of further evidence including the Statement evidence of witnesses,

    16.2.2   for the preparation and disclosure of lists of documents and for the inspection of such documents,

    16.2.3   for the filing of skeleton arguments,

    16.2.4   for a preliminary hearing to consider any point of law or procedure which may be raised by the proceedings or to consider the making of further directions,

    16.2.5   for the hearing of the complaint and the attendance of witnesses at the hearing,

and the Registrar shall serve a copy of the Commissary's directions and notice of any hearing (which shall be in form 5) on each party.

17.   Witnesses and witness evidence

17.1   If a party to the complaint requires the witness to any Statement filed to attend at the hearing of the complaint he shall give notice to the Registrar and to the other party not less than fourteen days before the date appointed for the hearing.

17.2   If a witness who has been so required to attend the hearing does not attend the onus shall be on the party seeking to rely on the evidence of that witness contained in the Statement to show why the Statement should be accepted in evidence.

18.   Procedure

18.1   Whether on application or of its own motion the procedure adopted at the hearing shall take such form as the Court thinks fit in all the circumstances of the case but shall ensure that both parties are given an opportunity to state their case to the Court and to cross-examine any witnesses giving evidence in person at the hearing.

18.2   The Court may dispense with any requirements of these Rules in respect of notices, Statements, witnesses, service or time in any case where it appears to the Court to be just so to do.

18.3   The Court may issue practice directions under the authority of the Commissary concerning the practices or procedures of the Court as are consistent with these Rules and as shall seem appropriate.

18.4 The complaint shall be decided on the basis of the Statements filed and the evidence of any witnesses.

18.5 At any time prior to the conclusion of a hearing the Court may, if it thinks it expedient to do so, adjourn the hearing and give such further directions as it thinks fit.

18.6 After hearing the complaint the Court may give its decision at the hearing or reserve judgment and the Registrar shall give notice to the parties of the Court's Order in form 6. In either case the Court's decision will be delivered or handed down in such a way that its contents are made public (this may include making the decision available to access on the website of the Court).

18.7 The forms set out in the Appendix with such variations or additions thereto as the Master may from time to time approve shall be used in all proceedings before the Court to which these rules relate.

18.8 Forms 3, 5, 6, 8 and 10 set out in the Appendix shall be issued by the Registrar under the seal of the Court but any omission to affix the seal of the Court shall not invalidate a form or any proceedings to which it relates.

18.9 The hearing of a complaint or application under these rules shall take place at such venue as the Commissary may direct and each party shall be entitled to be present and to be represented by a notary, a solicitor or counsel or (but only with the permission of the Court) any other person.

18.10 Every hearing shall take place in public unless:

18.10.1 The Court considers that a hearing in public will cause exceptional hardship or exceptional prejudice to a party, a witness or any person affected by the application, or

18.10.2 in the Court's view a hearing in public would be prejudicial to justice

in which case the hearing or part of it may be held in private and the Court shall make such order as shall appear to it to be just and proper.

18.11 It shall be within the discretion of the Registrar to grant to a party to proceedings before the Court such extension to any of the time limits contained in Parts IV and V of these Rules as appears to him to be reasonable.

19. Standard of proof

The Court shall make findings of facts on the balance of probabilities.

20. Service of documents

20.1 Any notice or document required by these rules to be delivered to the Registrar shall be delivered to him at the Court of Faculties, 1 The Sanctuary, Westminster, London SW1P 3JT and shall be deemed to be delivered on the day on which it is actually received by the Registrar.

20.2 Any notice or document required by these Rules to be served by the Registrar may be served:

20.2.1 personally or
20.2.2 by sending it by ordinary first class post or
20.2.2 document exchange or
20.2.3 the Royal Mail's Special Delivery service

to such address as may have been specified by the party concerned as his address for service or, if no such address has been specified for a notary, to the address appearing for him on the Roll of Notaries, and any notice or document so sent shall be deemed to have been served on the second working day after dispatch by post or document exchange and in the case of personal service, the next working day.

21. Interim suspension by the Court

21.1 If the Complainant wishes to apply to the Court for an order suspending the Respondent from practice or restricting or limiting or imposing conditions on the Respondent's practice pending the determination of the complaint he shall make the application in form 7 and shall lodge a Statement in support of the application.

21.2 Subject to Rule 21.8, on receiving an application in form 7 and Statement in support the Registrar shall serve a copy of each document on the Respondent and appoint a date for the hearing of the application (which shall be not less than fourteen days after the date on which the documents are served on the Respondent) and shall give notice to the parties in form 8.

21.3 If the Respondent wishes to oppose the application he shall, within seven days of its service upon him, deliver to the Registrar a Statement in response and the Registrar shall serve a copy of the response on the Complainant.

21.4 When the application has been determined by the Court the Registrar shall give notice to the parties of the Court's order in form 6.

21.5 Unless the Court orders otherwise the costs of the parties to the application shall be reserved to the hearing of the substantive complaint.

21.6 An application under this Rule shall be heard by the Commissary or a Deputy Commissary alone and when the application has been heard by the Commissary or a Deputy Commissary the Commissary or (as the case may be) the Deputy Commissary in question shall not sit on the hearing of the substantive complaint.

21.7 At the hearing of an application under this Rule the Court may, if it considers it appropriate to do so, give directions under Rule 15.2 for the hearing of the substantive complaint.

21.8 Where it appears to him to be necessary for the protection of the public the Commissary or Deputy Commissary to whom an application under this Rule is referred may direct such modifications to the procedure as he thinks fit including the making of an interim order to suspend the Respondent from practice or restrict or limit or impose conditions on the Respondent's practice pending the hearing of the application pursuant to Rule 21.2.

21.9 Where a complaint against a notary has been made to the Court under Rule 11.1 and the notary has been struck off or suspended from legal practice by a Relevant Body, as defined in Rule 24, following a finding of misconduct, the Court may of its own initiative, or on the application of the Complainant, suspend the notary from practice or make an order restricting or limiting or imposing conditions on the notary's practice pending the determination of the complaint, provided that the Court first considers any representations which the notary wishes to make about any such suspension or order.

22. Disciplinary Sanctions

22.1 Where the Court after hearing a complaint of Notarial Misconduct against a notary finds that it has been proved it may:

22.1.1 Order that the notary be struck off the Roll of Notaries,

22.1.2 Order that the notary be suspended from practice as a notary for a specified period or until certain conditions have been met or indefinitely,

22.1.3 Impose conditions as to the future scope or conduct of the notarial practice of the notary or conditions relating to the

144

monitoring or supervision of his practice and direct that his Practising Certificate be endorsed,

22.1.4 Impose conditions as to the training that the notary must complete or further examination or examinations that he must pass before he may continue or resume practice as a notary, or

22.1.5 Order that the notary be admonished.

22.2 In addition to imposing any of the penalties listed in Rule 22.1 above the Court may order that the notary:-

22.2.1 Indemnifies any Client of the notary whom the Court finds to have suffered actual loss as a result of the Notarial Misconduct in question and;

22.2.2 Pays a monetary sum not exceeding £10,000 (or such higher sum as the Master may from time to time specify for the purpose of these rules) such sum to be paid to whomsoever the Court may direct.

22.3 The Respondent shall be entitled to make any submissions by way of mitigation in respect of any sanction (including any order for costs) which the Court may impose.

22.4 The Registrar may decide to advertise any sanction against a notary under this Rule in a newspaper circulating in the area of the notary's practice or former practice or in the London Gazette, a publication of a Designated Society, or in any other relevant publication as the Registrar sees fit.

23. Costs

23.1 Subject to Rule 23.3 it shall be within the discretion of the Court to order:

23.1.1 that the costs of either party arising from or incidental to the complaint be paid by the other party,

23.1.2 that the costs of the Court be paid by either party or by both parties (whether in equal or unequal shares),

23.1.3 that costs incurred unnecessarily be disallowed,

23.1.4 that the costs of either party or of the Court shall be paid from the Contingency Fund,

23.1.5 that a party against whom an order for Costs is made shall, instead of paying those costs to the other party or the Court, pay them into the Contingency Fund, and

23.1.6 that either party pay a sum to the Contingency Fund for monies paid out to a Nominated Notary acting in the exercise of his functions under these rules, in relation to costs incurred at any time after the earlier of the appointment of the Nominated Notary or the making of a complaint under Rule 11.1.

23.2 The Court may make an order as to costs under this Rule where any application is withdrawn including the complaint itself.

23.3 The Court shall not make any order for costs against a Nominated Notary who shall in all cases be entitled to an order for costs in his favour such costs to be paid from the Contingency Fund.

23.4 The Master shall by Order, after consultation with the Commissary, approve a table of costs which will be applied by the Court, save in exceptional cases, in relation to orders for costs made under this Rule, and may, after consultation with the Commissary, issue directions or guidance about the manner in which such a table is to be applied by the Court.

23.5 Where a Nominated Notary investigates an allegation of Notarial Misconduct referred to him by the Registrar but such investigation does not lead to the issue of disciplinary proceedings in the Court the Nominated Notary shall be entitled to be paid such fixed fee as may have been previously authorised by the Registrar or such fee as the Registrar may determine should be paid for work properly done after considering a bill and other representations submitted by the Nominated Notary and such fee shall be paid by the Registrar out of the Contingency Fund.

24. Specified Professions and Relevant Bodies

24.1 For the purposes of these rules a 'Specified Profession' means a profession specified in the Schedule and in respect of a Specified Profession 'Relevant Body' means the disciplinary body named for that profession in the Schedule.

24.2 The Master may by order add to or amend the Schedule.

24.3 It shall be the duty of any notary who is also a member of a Specified Profession and against whom a complaint has been made to the Relevant Body, and where such complaint has been found by that body to be substantiated (whether in part or in whole), to report such finding forthwith to the Registrar (whether or not a penalty is imposed by the Relevant Body and without regard to the nature of such penalty).

24.4 Where it comes to the attention of the Registrar that a Relevant Body has found a complaint against a notary to be substantiated, the Registrar shall appoint a Nominated Notary to investigate the matter and if he thinks fit to prepare and prosecute disciplinary proceedings as if he were acting under Rule 8.

24.5   In proceedings under these rules the written decision of a Relevant Body shall be evidence of the facts stated in that decision.

PART V: REVIEWS

25.   Application for Review

25.1   Where as a result of an Order made under these rules or the 1993 Rules, or the 2009 Rules or the 2011 Rules a notary:

25.1.1   has been struck off the Roll of Notaries other than pursuant to proceedings under Rule 10 of the 1993 Rules, under Rule 10 of the 2009 Rules, or under Rule 10 of the 2011 Rules or under Rule 24 of these rules, and a period of not less than twelve months has elapsed since the date of striking off, or

25.1.2   has been suspended from practice for a period exceeding twelve months or for an indefinite period and a period of not less than twelve months has elapsed since the date of the suspension,

25.1.3   has had conditions imposed as to the future scope or conduct of his notarial practice, or conditions relating to the monitoring or supervision of his practice, or

25.1.4   has been struck off the Roll of Notaries pursuant to proceedings under Rule 10 of the 1993 Rules, or under Rule 10 of the 2009 Rules, or under Rule 10 of the 2011 Rules, or under Rule 24 of these rules, and has since been restored to the Roll of Solicitors, or, where relevant, the equivalent record of practitioners maintained by a Specified Profession,

the notary may apply to the Court to review the Order.

25.2   In the case of an application under Rule 25.1.1, Rule 25.1.2 or Rule 25.1.4 above it shall be for the notary to prove to the satisfaction of the Court that circumstances have changed since the Order was made and that it is not contrary to the public interest or the interest of the notarial profession that the order be reviewed and, in the case of a petition under Rule 25.1.3, it shall be for the notary to prove to the satisfaction of the Court that as a result of a change in circumstances the conditions imposed are no longer necessary or desirable in the public interest.

25.3   An application under this Rule shall be made in form 9 and shall be accompanied by a Statement or Statements setting out in full the grounds of the application and the evidence in support.

25.4   On receiving an application brought under this Rule the Registrar shall appoint a Nominated Notary to act as Respondent to the application.

25.5   Upon receiving an application and Statements in support the Registrar shall issue the application and serve a copy of each document on the Nominated Notary appointed as Respondent under Rule 25.4 and the Registrar shall also serve on both parties notice of hearing of the application in form 10.

25.6   Where the Order which the applicant is seeking to review was made as a result of a complaint brought by a person who was a Competent Complainant as a person who had been a Client of the notary the Registrar shall also send copies of the above documents and notice and any Statement delivered under Rule 25.3 to the Complainant who shall be entitled to attend the hearing and (if the Court so permits) to address the Court.

25.7   The Registrar may decide to advertise the notary's application under this Rule in a newspaper circulating in the area of the applicant's practice or former practice or in the London Gazette, a publication of a Designated Society or in any other relevant publication as the Registrar sees fit.

25.8   Any person may, no later than 10 days before the hearing date of an application to which this Rule applies, serve on the Court and the parties to the application notice of his intention to oppose the grant of the application and the Court may allow that person to appear before the Court at the hearing of the application, call evidence and make representations upon which the Court may allow him to be cross-examined.

25.9   The function of the Respondent shall be to ensure that the applicant is put to proof of his case and to bring to the attention of the Court all such facts and matters as the Respondent thinks should be before the Court and if the Respondent wishes to present to the Court a Statement or Statements in reply to the application he shall deliver the same to the Registrar not less than twentyeight days before the date of the hearing and the Registrar shall forthwith serve copies on the applicant.

25.10   At the hearing the Court shall consider all documents and evidence which were before the Court before making the order which the applicant is seeking to review and shall consider the Statement filed in support of and any Statements filed in answer to the application and the applicant may give evidence in person. The Court shall also consider representations made to it by the parties.

25.11 If the Court is satisfied that notice of the hearing was served on the applicant in accordance with these Rules, the Court shall have the power to hear and determine an application notwithstanding that the applicant fails to attend in person or is not represented at the hearing.

25.12 After hearing the petition the Court may give its decision at the hearing or reserve judgment and the Registrar shall give notice to the parties of the Court's Order in form 6.

25.13 Except in exceptional circumstances the costs of the Respondent to an application brought under this Rule and of the Court shall be paid by the applicant regardless of the outcome; in all other respects the provisions of Rule 23 shall apply mutatis mutandis.

25.14 Upon hearing an application brought under this Rule the Court may:

25.14.1 In the case of an application under Rule 25.1.1 or 25.1.4 order that the notary be restored to the Roll of Notaries either immediately or on some specified future date;

25.14.2 In the case of an application under Rule 25.1.2 order that the suspension be lifted either immediately or on some specified future date;

25.14.3 In the case of an application under Rule 25.1.3 order that the conditions imposed be lifted or that different conditions be imposed;

25.14.4 Impose such conditions upon any order or require such undertakings to be given by the petitioner as it thinks fit, or

25.14.5 Dismiss the application.

26. Revocation, Savings and Consequential Amendments

26.1 Subject to Rule 26.2 the 2011 Rules and the 2000 Rules are hereby revoked.

26.2 Where any proceedings before the Court had been commenced under the 2011 Rules or the 2000 Rules prior to the coming into force of these rules the 2011 Rules and the 2000 Rules (as the case may be) shall continue to have effect in respect of those proceedings.

26.3 In Rule 3.3 of the Notaries (Prevention of Money Laundering) Rules 2007 "Public Notaries (Conduct and Discipline) Rules 2011" is omitted and "Notaries (Conduct and Discipline) Rules 201[-]" substituted therefor.

26.4 References to the 1993 Rules, the 1997 Rules and the 2011 Rules and in other rules and regulations made by the Master shall be construed by reference to the corresponding Rule in these Rules.

THE SCHEDULE

Specified Profession	Relevant Body
Solicitor of the Senior Courts of England and Wales	The Solicitors Disciplinary Tribunal
Barrister in England and Wales	A Panel or Disciplinary Tribunal operated by the Bar Standards Board
Chartered Legal Executive	The Investigating Committee or the Disciplinary Tribunal of the Chartered Institute of Legal Executives
Licensed Conveyancer	The Investigating Committee established under section 24 of the Administration of Justice Act 1985 or the Discipline and Appeals Committee established under section 25(1) of that Act
Avocat or other legal practitioner in a country outside England and Wales	The body responsible for exercising disciplinary regulation over the avocat or other legal practitioner in the country in question
Any other Authorised Person as defined by Section 18 of the Legal Services Act 2007 authorised to carry out reserved legal services	The body responsible for exercising disciplinary regulation over the Authorised Person in question with respect to that reserved legal service

APPENDIX

Form 1: Written Complaint

IN THE COURT OF FACULTIES
In the Matter of [AB] a notary and
In the matter of the Notaries (Conduct and Discipline) Rules 201[-]
To the Registrar
I, the undersigned [CD] of [address] do hereby make complaint that the said [AB] of [address] has been guilty of Notarial Misconduct within the meaning of the said rules in that he/she has …(insert summary of allegation(s) of misconduct).
……………………………………………………………………………………

Details of my complaint are contained in the statement of truth which companies this written complaint.
DATED this ………… day of ………….. 20...
Signed
Address for service

Form 2: Statement of truth in support of Written Complaint

IN THE COURT OF FACULTIES
In the matter of [AB] a notary and
In the matter of the Notaries (Conduct and Discipline) Rules 201[-]
I [CD] of [address] make the following statement as follows:-

1.   I am a Competent Complainant within the meaning of the said rules as [specify how the deponent is a Competent Complainant].
2   I make this statement in support of my written complaint against the above named [AB] a notary of [address]
3.   [Here state the facts concisely in numbered paragraphs and show the complainant's means of knowledge.]
4.   I believe that the facts stated in this [witness] statement are true.

Form 3: Notice of Proceedings I

N THE COURT OF FACULTIES
In the matter of [AB] a notary and
In the matter of the Notaries (Conduct and Discipline) Rules 201[-]
TO: [AB] a notary of [address]
TAKE NOTICE that a written complaint has been received by the Court alleging that you have been guilty of Notarial Misconduct. A copy of the complaint and the statement of truth supporting it are attached to this notice.
You are required:-
1.   Within twenty-one days of service of this notice upon you to deliver to me an answer to the complaint in the form prescribed by the above rules, and

2.   If you intend to contest these proceedings, to deliver to me within forty-two days of service of this notice upon you a statement of truth in reply to the complaint.

If you fail to comply with these requirements I will proceed to appoint a date for the hearing of the complaint.

All communications should be addressed to "The Registrar, The Court of Faculties, 1 The Sanctuary, Westminster, London SW1P 3JT".

DATED this ……… day of ……………… 20...

Form 4: Answer to Complaint

IN THE COURT OF FACULTIES
In the matter of [AB] a notary and
In the matter of the Notaries (Conduct and Discipline) Rules 201[-]
To the Registrar
I, [AB] in answer to the complaint of [CD], say that:-
1.   I intend to contest the complaint OR I intend to contest the following parts of the complaint:- [specify] OR I do not intend to contest the complaint [and I consent to being struck off the Roll of Notaries] [delete as applicable]
2.   My address for service is
DATED this ……… day of ……………… 20...

Form 5: Notice of Hearing

IN THE COURT OF FACULTIES
In the matter of [AB] a notary and
In the matter of the Notaries (Conduct and Discipline) Rules 201[-]
To the above named respondent [AB] of [address] and to the complainant [CD] of [address]
TAKE NOTICE that this complaint will be heard by the Court on ……………..…..
day the ………………… day of ……………….. at [time of day] at
…………………………………. when you are required to attend.
If you do not attend the hearing may proceed in your absence.
DATED this ……… day of ……………… 20...
Signed
Registrar

Form 6: Order

IN THE COURT OF FACULTIES
In the matter of [AB] a notary and
In the matter of the Notaries (Conduct and Discipline) Rules 201[-]
To the above named [respondent/petitioner] [AB] of [address] and to the [complainant/respondent] [CD] of [address]
The Court having heard this [complaint] [application] on the ……. day of
………………… 200..
THE COURT ORDERS as follows:-
DATED this ……… day of ……………… 20...

Signed
Registrar

Form 7: Application for Suspension etc pending determination of Complaint

IN THE COURT OF FACULTIES

In the Matter of [AB] a notary and
In the matter of the Notaries (Conduct and Discipline) Rules 201[-]
To the Registrar
I, the undersigned complainant [CD] of [address] apply to the Court for an order that pending the determination of this complaint [the said respondent [AB] of [address] be suspended from practice as a notary] OR [the practice of the said respondent [AB] of [address] be restricted or limited as follows: [specify restrictions or limitations] OR [the following conditions be imposed on the practice of the said respondent [AB] of [address]: [specify conditions]]
The grounds of this application are contained in the accompanying statement of truth.
DATED this .... day of .... 20...
Signed
Address for service

Form 8: Notice of Hearing of Application

IN THE COURT OF FACULTIES
In the matter of [AB] a notary and
In the matter of the Notaries (Conduct and Discipline) Rules 201[-]
To the above named respondent [AB] of [address] and to the complainant [CD] of [address]
TAKE NOTICE that the complainant's application that the respondent be suspended from practice as a notary or that the practice of the respondent be restricted or limited or that conditions be imposed on the practice of the respondent will be heard by the Court on .... day the .... day of .... at [time of day] at .... when you are required to attend.
The Court may also give directions for the hearing of the substantive complaint.
If you do not attend the hearing may proceed in your absence.
DATED this .... day of .... 20...
Signed
Registrar

Form 9 Application under Rule [-]

IN THE COURT OF FACULTIES
In the matter of [AB] a notary and
In the matter of the Notaries (Conduct and Discipline) Rules 201[-]
To the Registrar I [AB] of [address for service] apply to the Court as follows:-
1.   By an Order of the Court made on [date] it was ordered that [set out the terms of the Order other than terms as to costs]

2.   I now apply that the said Order be reviewed pursuant to Rule [-] of the said rules.
3.   The grounds of this application and the evidence in support of it are fully set out in the accompanying statement[s] of truth

DATED this .... day of .... 20...
Signed
Petitioner

Form 10 Notice of Hearing of Petition under Rule [-]

IN THE COURT OF FACULTIES
In the matter of [AB] a notary and
In the matter of the Notaries (Conduct and Discipline) Rules 201[-]
To the above named applicant [AB] of [address] and to [CD] of [address] appointed to act as respondent to this application.
TAKE NOTICE that this application will be heard by the Court on .... day the .... day of .... 20... at [time of day] at .... when you are required to attend. If you do not attend the hearing may proceed in your absence.
DATED this .... day of .... 20...
Signed
Registrar

C R GEORGE
....
MASTER

NOTARIES (CONDUCT AND DISCIPLINE) FEES AND COSTS ORDER 2015

WE CHARLES RICHARD GEORGE One of Her Majesty's Counsel Commissary or Master of the Faculties of the Most Reverend Father in God Justin Portal by Divine Providence Lord Archbishop of Canterbury Primate of All England and Metropolitan so far as We lawfully can or may do hereby make the following ORDER pursuant to the provisions of Rule 23 of the Notaries (Conduct and Discipline) Rules 2015:

Part I: Preliminary

Part II: Costs and fees payable - general

Part III: Fees payable to officers of the Court

Part IV: Fees payable to nominated notaries

Part V: Costs recoverable by a party to proceedings

PART I: PRELIMINARY

1. Citation and Commencement

1.1 This Order may be cited as the Notaries (Conduct and Discipline) Fees and Costs Order 2015

1.2 This Order comes into force on the 1st day of November 2015

2. Interpretation

2.1 In these rules:-

- **"Advocate"** means a notary, a barrister, a solicitor, or a chartered legal executive.

- **"Court"** means the Court of Faculties.

- **"Fee Earner"** means a Litigator, or person employed by a Litigator, who undertakes work on a case;

- **"Instructed Advocate"** means—

    (a) where leave of the Court has not been given to a party to instruct multiple Advocates, a single Advocate, being the Advocate who for the time being has primary responsibility for the case or the party himself if unrepresented and being an Advocate; or

    (b) where the Court has given leave for a party to be represented by more than one Advocate, each of those Advocates.

- **"Instructed Litigator"** means –

    (a) where leave of the Court has not been given to a party to instruct multiple Litigators, a single Litigator, being the Litigator who for the time being has primary responsibility for the case or the party himself if unrepresented; or

    (b) where the Court has given leave for a party to be represented by more than one Litigator, each of those Litigators;

- **"Judge"** means the Commissary or a Deputy Commissary of the Court, and if sitting with Assessors, those Assessors as well;

- **"Litigator"** means the person representing a party, being a solicitor, firm of solicitors or a person authorised under the Legal Services Act 2007 to conduct litigation or the party himself if unrepresented;

- **"Nominated Notary"** means a person appointed by the Registrar under rule 6 of the Notaries (Conduct and Discipline) Rules 2015;

- **"Party"** means either a complainant, applicant or a respondent in proceedings before the Court;

- **"Representative"** means an Instructed Advocate or an Instructed Litigator;

- **"Senior Solicitor"** means a solicitor eight years post qualification experience including at least eight years of litigation or other relevant experience and "Senior Notary" shall have a corresponding meaning;

- **"Solicitor, Notary, Legal Executive or Fee Earner of equivalent experience"** means a solicitor, notary, Fellow of the Institute of Legal Executives, or equivalent Fee Earner;

- **"Trainee Solicitor or Trainee Notary or Fee Earner of equivalent experience"** means a Trainee Solicitor or Trainee Notary or other Fee Earner who is not a Fellow of the Institute of Legal Executives;

2.2   The fees and rates set out in this Order are exclusive of value added tax.

PART II: COSTS AND FEES PAYABLE - GENERAL

3.   Fees and disbursements payable to officers of the Court

3.1   Part III sets out the fees which are to be paid to the Judges and Registrar in respect of the carrying out by them of the duties of their offices that are specified.

3.2   Officers of the Court are entitled to recover such disbursements as appear to the Judge to have been reasonably incurred in performance of their functions.

4.   Fees payable to Nominated Notaries

4.1   Part IV sets out the fees which are to be paid to Nominated Notaries in respect of the carrying out by them of the duties of their offices that are specified.

4.2 A Nominated Notary must seek the leave of the Court before instructing a Litigator or Advocate and if leave is given Clause 5 applies as appropriate.

5. Costs recoverable by a party to proceedings

5.1 Part V sets out the costs recoverable by a party to proceedings.

5.2 A party is entitled to seek an order for costs under Part V in relation to work carried out by him and disbursements including court fees incurred by him or on his behalf by his Instructed Litigator and/or Instructed Advocate.

5.3 A party must obtain the prior order of the Judge to instruct on a matter

5.3.1 multiple Litigators and/or multiple Advocates; and/or

5.3.2 an Advocate who is a Queen's Counsel

if an application for costs is to be entertained in relation to the costs and disbursements of more than one Litigator or Advocate and/or for the additional costs set out in this Order of an Advocate who is a Queen's Counsel.

5.4 The Judge will not give leave under 5.3 above unless there is a special reason with regards to the novelty, weight and complexity of a case.

5.5 The Judge shall not issue an order for costs in relation to work done or disbursements incurred by a Litigator or Advocate who is not an Instructed Litigator or an Instructed Advocate.

5.6 With the agreement of the parties to proceedings the Judge may order that an order for costs will be in a fixed sum assessed by the Court as representing or being a contribution towards the reasonable costs of the party concerned and that Part V will not apply.

PART III: FEES PAYABLE TO OFFICERS OF THE COURT

6.   Table of Court fees

The following prescribed fees shall apply to orders made by the Judge with respect to the costs of the Court-

		Commissary / Deputy Commissary £	Assessor £	Registrar £
1	Fees payable on the Judge or Court giving directions (otherwise than at the hearing in respect of which fees are payable under paragraph 2 of this Table), such fees to be fixed by the Judge within the limits shown	100 - 400	50 - 350	50 - 350
2	Fees payable where the issue, whether interlocutory or final, is heard in Court or in Chambers— (a) if the hearing lasts half a day or less	500	400	400
	(b) if the hearing lasts a whole day or more than a half (fees on same scale for subsequent days).	1,000	750	750
3	Fee on the Judge preparing a written judgment or drafting the form of order or both, such fee to be at the hourly rate shown and in respect of the number of hours certified by the Judge as spent on such work.	350	250	-
4	On review, a fee, to be fixed by the Judge and paid to the Registrar, in respect of the cost of preparing for the use of the members of the Court copies of all documents required for the use of the Court.			

5	Fee in respect of all other work carried out by the Registrar in his or her capacity as such, in relation to proceedings to which this Table applies, on or after the date on which the proceedings were instituted in accordance with the Notaries (Conduct and Discipline) Rules 2015 or on which a person was authorised to act as complainant in accordance with those Rules (including preparatory and ancillary work and correspondence)-- such fee to be at the hourly rate shown and in respect of the number of hours certified by the Registrar as spent on such work.	250		
6	Fee in respect of all other work carried out by the Registrar of the Court and in his or her capacity as such, in relation to investigations carried out under the Notaries (Conduct and Discipline) Rules 2015 at any time including the appointment of a Nominated Notary in accordance with those Rules (including preparatory and ancillary work and correspondence)-- such fee to be at the hourly rate shown and in respect of the number of hours certified by the Registrar as spent on such work.	250		
7	Fees payable on an assessment of costs to be paid by the party applying for assessment:-			
	(a) where the amount allowed does not exceed £5,000	200	70	70
	(b) where the amount allowed exceeds £5,000			
	(i) for the first £5,000	200	70	70
	(ii) for every £200 or fraction thereof over £5,000.	10	6	6

PART IV: FEES PAYABLE TO NOMINATED NOTARIES

7. Table of fees to be paid to nominated notaries

The following prescribed fees shall apply to fees payable to Nominated Notaries:-

		£
1	Fee on the investigation of the evidence or allegation of Notarial Misconduct referred to him by the Registrar such fee to be fixed by the Registrar within the limits shown.	2,000- 3,000
2	Fee for the written report to the Registrar following investigation of evidence or allegation of Notarial Conduct such fee to be fixed by the Registrar within the limits shown.	500 - 750
3	Fees in respect of carrying out any and all interim directions prior to the hearing of the case such fee to be fixed by the Registrar within the limits shown.	500 - 1,000
4	Fee for preparation and prosecution of case such fee to be fixed by the Registrar within the limits shown.	1,000 - 3,000
5	Fees payable where the issue, whether interlocutory or final, is heard in Court or in Chambers such fee to be fixed by the Registrar within the limits shown:-	
	(a) if the hearing lasts half a day or less	500 - 1,000
	(b) if the hearing lasts a whole day or more than a half (fees on same scale for subsequent days).	1,000 - 2,000
6	Fees payable in respect of attending on the giving of judgment and matters arising in respect of the judgment including preparation of papers for an assessment of costs and attendance on that assessment such fee to be fixed by the Registrar within the limits shown	500 - 1,000

PART V: COSTS RECOVERABLE BY A PARTY TO PROCEEDINGS

8. General Provisions

    8.1   In determining costs the Court has an absolute discretion and, subject to the provisions of this Part V can—

        8.1.1   take into account all the relevant circumstances of the case including the nature, importance, complexity or difficulty of the work and the time involved; and

8.1.2 allow a reasonable amount in respect of all work necessarily carried out and properly, actually and reasonably done.

8.2 The Court cannot allow costs whether or not at the prescribed rates if those costs exceed the amount payable to the Litigator or Advocate by the applicant.

8.3 Where a party to the proceedings is acting as the Litigator or the Advocate the rate at which fees are to be awarded to him for acting in that capacity may be reduced by such proportion as the Court thinks fit.

9. Claims for Litigators' fees and disbursements

9.1 Subject to Paragraph 19 no claim in relation to the fees and disbursements of a Litigator in respect of work done in proceedings in the Court may be entertained unless the represented party submits it within one month of the final decision of the Court after the hearing of the complaint.

9.2 Subject to Paragraph 9.3, a claim for fees in proceedings in the Court must be submitted to the Court in such form and manner as the Judge may direct and must be accompanied by any receipts or other documents in support of any disbursement claimed.

9.3 A claim must-

9.3.1 summarise the items of work done by a Fee Earner in respect of which fees are claimed according to the classes specified in Paragraph 14;

9.3.2 state, where appropriate, the dates on which the items of work were done, the time taken, the sums claimed and whether the work was done for more than one party;

9.3.3 specify, where appropriate, the level of Fee Earner who undertook each of the items of work claimed;

9.3.4 specify any disbursements claimed, the circumstances in which they were incurred and the amounts claimed in respect of them;

9.3.5 state whether the applicant claims that Paragraph 15 applies in relation to an item of work, and must give full particulars in support of the claim;

9.3.6 specify any special circumstances which the applicant considers should be drawn to the attention of the Court;

9.3.7 supply such further information and documents as the Judge may require;

9.3.8 contain a certificate of accuracy in the prescribed form from a partner, member or director of the Litigator verifying the disbursements made and all sums claimed;

9.3.9 state whether the applicant is unable to recover the VAT or any proportion of it as an input tax and provide a certificate signed by the Litigator in the prescribed form to that effect in cases where a Litigator has been instructed.

10. Determination for Litigators' fees

10.1 The Judge may allow work done in the following classes by Fee Earners-

10.1.1 preparation, including taking instructions, interviewing witnesses, drafting and finalising witness statements, preparing list of documents and providing appropriate bundles for use in connection with any court hearing, ascertaining the case, advising, preparing and perusing documents, dealing with letters and telephone calls which are not routine, preparing for advocacy, instructing an Advocate and expert witnesses, conferences, consultations, views and work done in connection with advice on appeal;

10.1.2 advocacy, including applications to the Court;

10.1.3 attending at Court where an Advocate is assigned, including conferences with the Advocate at Court;

10.1.4 travelling and waiting; and

10.1.5 writing routine letters and dealing with routine telephone calls;

10.1.6 any other steps necessarily and properly taken for the proper conduct of proceedings before the Court.

10.2 The Judge must consider the claim; any further information or documents submitted for the Fee Earner under Paragraph 10.1 and any other relevant information and must allow—

10.2.1 such work as appears to the Judge to have been properly proportionate to the issues in question and done in connection with the matter (including any representation or advice which is deemed to be work done pursuant to the matter) by a 9 Fee Earner, classifying such work according

163

to the classes specified in Paragraph 10.1 as the Judge considers appropriate; and

10.2.2 such time in each class of work allowed by him (other than routine letters written and routine telephone calls) as the Judge considers reasonable.

10.2.3 The fees allowed in accordance with this Part V are those appropriate to such of the following grades of Litigator as the Judge considers reasonable-

(a) Senior Solicitor or Senior Notary;
(b) Solicitor, Notary, Legal Executive or Fee Earner of equivalent experience; or
(c) Trainee or Fee Earner of equivalent experience.

11. Determination for Litigators' disbursements

The Judge must allow such disbursements claimed under Paragraph 10 as appear to the Judge to have been reasonably incurred, provided that—

11.1.1 if they are abnormally large by reason of the distance of the Court or the person's residence or both from the Litigator's place of business, the Judge may limit reimbursement of the disbursements to what otherwise would, having regard to all the circumstances, be a reasonable amount; and

11.1.2 the cost of a transcript, or any part thereof, of the proceedings in the Court obtained otherwise than through the Registrar must not be allowed except where the Judge considers that it is reasonable in all the circumstances for such disbursement to be allowed.

12. Claims for fees of Advocates

12.1 Subject to Paragraph 19 a claim for fees for work done by an Advocate in proceedings in the Court may not be entertained unless the applicant submits it within one month of the final decision of the Court after the hearing of the complaint or it is submitted in accordance with paragraph 9.1 as part of the claim of a Litigator's for fees.

12.2 Where the applicant claims that Paragraph 15 applies in relation to an item of work the Advocate must give full particulars in support of his claim.

12.3 Subject to Paragraph 12.4 a claim for the fees of an Advocate by an applicant in proceedings in the Court must be submitted to the Judge in such form and manner as the Judge may direct.

12.4   A claim must-

12.4.1   summarise the items of work done by an Advocate in respect of which fees are claimed according to the classes specified in Paragraph 16;

12.4.2   state, where appropriate, the dates on which the items of work were done, the time taken, the hourly rate charged and the sums claimed for each item and whether the work was done for more than one assisted person; and

12.4.3   give particulars of any work done in relation to more than one hearing.

12.4.4   The Advocate must specify any special circumstances which the Advocate considers should be drawn to the attention of the Court.

12.4.5   The applicant must supply such further information and documents as the Judge may require.

12.5   The Court may make such orders and directions as it sees fit to deal with the claim.

13.   Determination for Advocates' fees

13.1   The Judge must consider the claim; any further particulars and information submitted for an Advocate under Paragraph 12 and any other relevant information and must allow such work as appears to the Judge to have been reasonably done.

13.2   The Judge may allow any of the following classes of fee to an Advocate in respect of work allowed by him under this Paragraph-

13.2.1   a basic fee for preparation including preparation for a pre-trial review and, where appropriate, the first day's hearing including, where they took place on that day, short conferences, consultations, applications and appearances, views and any other preparation;

13.2.2   a refresher fee for any day or part of a day during which a hearing continued, including, where they took place on that day, short conferences, consultations, applications and appearances;

13.2.3 subsidiary fees for-

(a) written advice on evidence, plea or appeal or other written work; and

(b) attendance at directions hearings, applications and appearances not covered by Paragraph 13.2.1 or 13.2.2.

13.2.4 Where the Court has not given leave for a party to be represented by a QC and a QC agrees to appear as the single Advocate or as a leading junior, the remuneration of the QC must be determined as if the Advocate were not a QC.

14. Litigators' fees for proceedings in the Court

14.1 For proceedings in the Court the Judge must allow fees for work by Litigators at the following prescribed rates—

Class of work	Grade of Fee Earner	Rate	Variations
Preparation	Senior Solicitor or Senior Notary	£240 per hour	Up to £400 per hour for a Litigator whose office is situated within the City of London or a London borough
	Solicitor, Notary, Legal Executive or Fee Earner of equivalent experience	£200 per hour	Up to £300 per hour for a Litigator whose office is situated within the City of London or a London borough
	Trainee or Fee Earner of equivalent experience	£120 per hour	Up to £150 per hour for a Litigator whose office is situated within the City of London or a London borough
Advocacy	Senior Solicitor or Senior Notary	£360 per hour	Up to £410 per hour for a Litigator whose office is situated within the City of London or a London borough
	Solicitor, Notary, Legal Executive or Fee Earner of equivalent	£300 per hour	Up to £350 per hour for a Litigator whose office is situated within the City of London or a London

Attendance at court where more than one Instructed Litigator present	Senior Solicitor or Senior Notary	£300 per hour	
	Solicitor, Notary, Legal Executive or Fee Earner of equivalent experience	£250 per hour	
	Trainee or Fee Earner of equivalent experience	£100 per hour	
Travelling and waiting	Senior Solicitor or Senior Notary	£250 per hour	
	Solicitor, Notary, Legal Executive or Fee Earner of equivalent experience	£200 per hour	
	Trainee or Fee Earner of equivalent experience	£80 per hour	
Routine letters written and routine telephone calls		£10 per item	£12 per item for a Litigator whose office is situated within the City of London or a London borough

14.2   In respect of any item of work, the Court may allow fees at less than the relevant prescribed rate specified in the table following Paragraph 14.1 where it appears to the Judge reasonable to do so having regard to the competence and despatch with which the work was done.

15. Allowance of Litigators' fees at more than the prescribed rate

15.1 The Judge may allow fees at more than the prescribed rate where it appears to the Judge, taking into account all the relevant circumstances of the case, that—

15.1.1 the work was done with exceptional competence, skill or expertise;

15.1.2 the work was done with exceptional despatch; or

15.1.3 the case involved exceptional complexity or other exceptional circumstances.

15.2 Where the Judge considers that any item or class of work should be allowed at more than the prescribed rate, the Judge must apply to that item or class of work a 13 percentage enhancement in accordance with the following provisions of this paragraph.

15.3 In determining the percentage by which fees should be enhanced above the prescribed rate the Court may have regard to-

15.3.1 the degree of responsibility accepted by the Fee Earner;

15.3.2 the care, speed and economy with which the case was prepared; and

15.3.3 the novelty, weight and complexity of the case.

15.4 The percentage above the relevant prescribed rate by which fees for work may be enhanced must not exceed 35%.

16. Advocates' fees for proceedings in the Court

16.1 Subject to sub-Paragraph 16.3, for proceedings in the Court the Judge must allow a reasonable fee for work by Advocates, not to exceed at the following maximum rates—

Advocate other than QC

Types of proceedings	Basic fee	Full day refresher	Subsidiary fees		
			Attendance at consultation, conferences and views	Written work	Attendance at directions hearings, applications and other appearances
All cases	Maximum amount: £1,500 per case	Maximum amount: £1,500 per day	Maximum amount: £350 per hour, maximum	Maximum amount: £400 per hour,	Maximum amount: £1,500 per appearance

			amount per case: £2,000	maximum amount per case £3,000	

QC

Types of proceedings	Basic fee	Full day refresher	Subsidiary fees		
		Attendance at consultation, conferences and views	*Written work*	*Attendance at directions hearings, applications and other appearances*	
All cases	Maximum amount: £3,000 per case	Maximum amount: £3,000 per day	Maximum amount: £500 per hour, maximum amount per case: £3,000	Maximum amount: £550 per hour, per hour, maximum amount per case, £3,500	Maximum amount: £2,500 per appearance

16.2 Where a refresher fee is claimed in respect of less than a full day, the Court must allow such fee as appears to the Court reasonable having regard to the fee which would be allowable for a full day.

16.3 Where it appears to the Judge, taking into account all the relevant circumstances of the case, that owing to the exceptional circumstances of the case the amount payable by way of fees in accordance with the table following Paragraph 16.1 would not provide reasonable remuneration for some or all of the work the Judge has allowed, the Judge may allow such amounts as appear to the Judge to be reasonable remuneration for the relevant work.

17. Authorisation of expenditure

17.1 Where it appears to a Litigator necessary for the proper conduct of proceedings in the Court for costs to be incurred in relation to representation by taking any of the following steps—

17.1.1 obtaining a written report or opinion of one or more experts;

17.1.2 employing a person to provide a written report or opinion (otherwise than as an expert);

17.1.3 obtaining any transcripts or recordings; or

17.1.4 performing an act which is either unusual in its nature or involves unusually large expenditure, the Litigator may apply to the Court for prior authority to do so.

17.2 Where the Judge authorises the taking of any step referred to in Paragraph 17.1, the Judge shall also authorise the maximum to be paid in respect of that step.

17.3 A Representative in any proceedings in the Court may apply to the Judge for prior authority for the incurring of travelling and accommodation expenses in order to attend at a hearing in those proceedings.

17.4 No question as to the propriety of any step or act in relation to which prior authority has been obtained under this Paragraph 17 may be raised on any determination of disbursements unless the Litigator knew or ought reasonably to have known that the purpose for which the authority was given had failed or had become irrelevant or unnecessary before the disbursements were incurred.

17.5 Where disbursements are reasonably incurred in accordance with and subject to the limit imposed by a prior authority given under this Paragraph 17, no question may be raised on any determination of fees as to the amount of the payment to be allowed for the step or act in relation to which the authority was given.

17.6 Where disbursements are incurred in taking any steps or doing any act for which authority may be given under this Paragraph 17, without such authority having been given or in excess of any fee so authorised, payment in respect of those disbursements may nevertheless be allowed on a determination of disbursements payable under Paragraph 11.

18   Expert services

18.1 Subject to Paragraph 18.2, the Judge may provide for the payment of expert services (such rates to be reasonable in respect of the time properly and necessarily taken and the qualifications and expertise of the relevant person instructed to provide those services) normally not to exceed the following rates-

Expert	Non-London - hourly rate unless stated to be a fixed fee	London - hourly rate unless stated to be a fixed fee
Any expert service saves for provision of medical report	£250	£300
GP (medical report)	£100 fixed fee	£150 fixed fee

18.2 The Judge may, in relation to a specific claim, make an additional allowance if he/she considers it reasonable to do so but in particular where the expert's evidence is key to the client's case and either—

    18.2.1 the complexity of the material is such that an expert with a high level of seniority is required; or

    18.2.2 the material is of such a specialised and unusual nature that only very few experts are available to provide the necessary evidence.

18.3 Any additional allowance authorised under Paragraph 18.2 must not exceed 35% of the rate set out in Paragraph 18.1.

19. Time limits

19.1 Subject to Paragraph 19.2, the time limit within which any act is required or authorised to be done under this Order, may for good reason, be extended by the Judge.

19.2 Where a Representative without good reason has failed (or, if an extension were not granted, would fail) to comply with a time limit, the Judge, may, in exceptional circumstances, extend the time limit where the application to extend the time has been made prior to its expiration and must consider whether it is reasonable in the circumstances to reduce the fees payable to the Representative under this Order, and make an Order for the costs incurred by and incidental to the application in favour of the other parties provided that the fees must not be reduced unless the Representative has been allowed a reasonable opportunity to show cause orally or in writing why the fees should not be reduced.

C R GEORGE

....

MASTER

NOTARIES (INSPECTIONS) REGULATIONS 2014

These Regulations are made pursuant to Rule 24 of the Notaries Practice Rules 2014 and Rule 12 of the Notaries Accounts Rules 1989 (as amended) & Rule 11 of the Notaries Trust Accounts Rules 1989.

The Regulations to be known as The Notaries (Inspections) Regulations 2014.

1. The Registrar will select annually the notaries whose records and practices shall be inspected pursuant to these Regulations. The number of such inspections shall be determined annually by the Master.

2. The inspections shall be carried out by an inspector selected by the Registrar from a panel of inspectors appointed for the purpose by the Master. Inspectors shall be notaries who have been in practice as notaries and have held a practicing certificate continuously for not less than 10 years.

3. The Registrar shall ensure, so far as practicable, that the inspector and the notary whose practice is to be inspected are in different geographical locations, are not known to each other personally, and that there is no likelihood of a professional or commercial conflict of interest arising between them.

4. A notary whose records and practice is to be inspected shall be given notice of such inspection by the Registrar of not less than seven days.

5. The inspector shall be entitled to a fixed fee for each inspection carried out, such fee to be set by Order of the Master from time to time, together with reasonable expenses of travel and accommodation to be assessed by the Registrar.

6. The inspection shall be carried out using a pro-forma questionnaire to be approved by the Master from time to time. The inspector shall also prepare a written summary of his findings in a report for the Registrar.

7. The notary whose records and practice is to be inspected shall co-operate with the inspector in providing access to such records files accounts ledgers and other papers ("the inspected documents") as shall be requested to enable the inspector to complete the questionnaire and report. The inspector shall at all times respect the confidentiality of the inspected documents and shall not disclose information concerning the inspected documents or the clients of the notary save to the Master or Registrar as may be necessary. Any breach of this Regulation shall be deemed to be Notarial Misconduct for the purposes of the Notaries (Conduct and Discipline) Rules 2011.

8.   Following the inspection, the inspector shall within 14 days file a copy of his report and the completed questionnaire with the Registrar and send a copy of both documents to the notary.

9.   The notary shall have 14 days from the receipt of the copy report and questionnaire to file any comments he or she may have on the report and questionnaire with the Registrar and with the inspector.

10.   The Registrar may then seek any clarification which he considers necessary from the inspector and/or the notary before sending the completed questionnaire, the report and the notary's comments (if any) to the Master.

11.   The Master may give such directions as he thinks fit which may include (but without limitation) ordering a further inspection or inspections of the notary's practice, a requirement to undertake further training or the supervision by a notary appointed by the Master of the notary's practice, or aspects of it, for such period as may be directed by the Master.

12.   Where the inspector's report discloses matters which may amount to an allegation of Notarial Misconduct, as defined by Rule 2.1 of the Notaries (Conduct and Discipline) Rules 2011, then the Registrar shall proceed to appoint a Nominated Notary to investigate the allegation pursuant to Rule 5 of those Rules. In that case the report shall be referred to the Master in accordance with Regulation 10 and the Master shall give such directions under Regulation 11 as he thinks fit but excluding those matters which are the subject of the allegation of Notarial Misconduct. The inspector may not be appointed as Nominated Notary in such a case.

13.   Where following an inspection under these Regulations a further inspection of a notary's accounts is ordered pursuant to Rule 12 of the Notaries Accounts Rules 1989 (as amended) the provisions of that Rule shall apply together with such directions as may be given by the Master or Registrar in the particular case.

14.   Where following an inspection under these Regulations a further inspection of a notary's trust accounts is ordered pursuant to Rule 11 of the Notaries Trust Accounts Rules 1989 the provisions of that Rule shall apply together with such directions as may be given by the Master or Registrar in the particular case.

C R George

The Right Worshipful Charles R George, Q.C.
Master
         10 April 2014

NOTARIES (PRACTISING CERTIFICATES) RULES 2012

WE CHARLES RICHARD GEORGE One of Her Majesty's Counsel Commissary or Master of the Faculties of the Most Reverend Father in God Rowan Douglas by Divine Providence Lord Archbishop of Canterbury Primate of All England and Metropolitan in exercise of the powers conferred by section 4 of the Public Notaries Act 1843 and section 57 of the Courts and Legal Services Act 1990 and of all other powers Us enabling hereby make the following Rules:

1. **Citation and Commencement**
    1.1 These Rules may be cited as the Notaries (Practising Certificates) Rules 2012.

    1.2 These Rules shall come into force on 1st October 2013.

2. **Interpretation**
    In these Rules

    "the Master" means the Master of the Faculties

    "the Registrar" means the Registrar of the Court of Faculties

    "the Court" means the Court of Faculties

    "the Faculty Office" means the Registry or Office of the Court of Faculties

    "the Commissary" has the meaning assigned by the Notarial Appeals and Hearings Rules 2000

    the Contingency Fund" means the fund established under the Notarial Contingency Fund Rules 1981 (as amended)

    "a Notary" means a Public Notary whose name appears on the Roll of Notaries of England and Wales maintained by the Faculty Office

    "Notarial Act" means any act that has validity by virtue only of its preparation, performance, authentication, attestation or verification by a Notary, and includes any such act carried out by electronic means

    "Practising Certificate Year" means the 1st day of November in a calendar year until the 31st day of October in the following calendar year

    "Reserved Legal Activity" has the meaning set out in the Legal Services Act 2007

    "Specified Profession" and "Relevant Body" have the meanings set out in Rule 10 and the Second Schedule of the 2011 Rules

"a Finding" means a decision or decisions of the Relevant Body of a Specified Profession

"the 1998 Rules" means the Notaries (Qualifications) Rules 1998 or any subsequent amendment or replacement thereof

"the 2011 Rules" means the Notaries (Conduct & Discipline) Rules 2011 or any subsequent amendment or replacement thereof.

3.   **Duty to hold a practising certificate**
3.1   A Notary practising as such within England and Wales must at all times hold a practising certificate issued out of the Faculty Office save for those Notaries appointed for Ecclesiastical purposes only pursuant to Rule 4 of the 1998 Rules.

3.2   No Notary empowered to practise within England and Wales may do or perform any Notarial Act or any other Reserved Legal Activity which a Notary is authorised to perform unless in possession of a valid practising certificate save for those Notaries appointed for Ecclesiastical purposes only pursuant to Rule 4 of the 1998 Rules.

3.3   Practising as a Notary without a valid practising certificate is an offence unders Section 14 of the Legal Services Act 2007 and Notarial Misconduct for the purposes of Rule 2.1 of the 2011 Rules.

3.4   A practising certificate as a Notary shall be valid and have effect for a single Practising Certificate Year subject to the exceptions set out in Rules 3.5 and 3.6 and the provisions of Rule 4.4 below.

3.5   Where a Notary has been admitted during a Practising Certificate Year his or her first practising certificate shall be dated on the day he or she was duly admitted and received their notarial faculty and run until the 31st day of October following.

3.6   In all other cases the date shall be determined by the Registrar in the circumstances of the case and having regard to the information provided by the Notary as to his or her insurance and practice arrangements.

3.7   Notwithstanding the provisions of Rule 4.1 below, if a Notary fails to apply to renew or has not received his or her renewed practising certificate by the 31st day of December in a Practising Certificate Year they shall no longer be authorised to practise as a Notary and shall have their details removed from the list of practising Notaries published on the website of the Faculty Office.

4. Application

4.1 The application for a practising certificate as a Notary shall be in such form as the Master may direct by Order from time to time and, save for any Notary to whom Rule 3.5 or 3.6 above applies, shall be lodged with the Faculty Office no later than the commencement of the relevant Practising Certificate Year.

4.2 The application shall be accompanied by:

4.2.1 the payment of such fee for the issue of a practising certificate as the Master may direct by Order from time to time;

4.2.2 the payment of such sum as a contribution to the Contingency Fund as the Master may direct by Order from time to time;

4.2.3 evidence of the insurance cover held by the Notary in compliance with the provisions of either Rule 6 or Rule 7 of these Rules;

4.2.4 a copy of the CPE Training Record maintained by the Notary for the preceding Practising Certificate Year pursuant to the Notaries (Continuing Professional Education) Regulations 2012;

4.2.5 if required pursuant to Rule 11A of the Notaries Accounts Rules 1998 (as amended), an Accountant's Report as therein defined; and

4.2.6 if required pursuant to Rule 8.2 of the Notaries Practice Rule 2009, confirmation that the Notary has sent to his or her employer a written statement of professional independence together with such other documentation as the Master may direct by Order or request from time to time.

4.3 Where a Notary is also a member of a Specified Profession he or she shall lodge with the Faculty Office a copy of their annual practising certificate or other evidence of their entitlement to practise as such within 21 days of receipt of the same from the relevant issuing authority.

4.4 Where a Notary has lodged an application for the renewal of his or her practising certificate in accordance with Rule 4.1 above but has not received the renewed practising certificate then the practising certificate issued for the immediately preceding Practising Certificate Year shall remain valid for the purpose of Rule 3.2 until 31st December in the new Practising Certificate Year or for the period until he or she receives the renewed practising certificate whichever shall be the shorter.

5. Form of practising certificate

A practising certificate as a Notary shall be issued in such form as the Master may direct by Order from time to time.

6.   **Insurance**

6.1   All Notaries in practice as such within England and Wales (save for those Notaries appointed for Ecclesiastical purposes only pursuant to Rule 4 of the 1998 Rules) shall at all times hold insurance covering their notarial practice for the following:

6.1.1   insurance against civil liability for professional negligence incurred by the Notary in connection with his or her practice as a Notary; and

6.1.2   insurance against financial loss suffered by a third party in consequence of any dishonest or fraudulent act or any omission by the Notary in connection with his or her practice as a Notary.

6.2   The minimum level of insurance cover in respect of 6.1.1 and 6.1.2 above shall be fixed from time to time by Order of the Master and shall come into force on the 1st day of November immediately following.

7.   Where a Notary practises also as a member of a Specified Profession and as a member of such profession holds insurance cover in respect of Rule 6.1.1 and 6.1.2 and provided that the Registrar is satisfied that such insurance cover will extend to the holder's practice as a Notary then the requirements of Rule 6 shall have been satisfied.

8.   If the insurance cover held by a Notary in accordance with Rules 6 or 7 above ceases at any time after 1st November in any Practising Certificate Year he or she shall forthwith provide the Registrar with details of the replacement policy or policies of insurance and if the Registrar is not satisfied that the replacement insurance cover is sufficient to comply with the said Rules 6 or 7 the practising certificate as a Notary shall cease to have effect immediately.

9.   **Restriction of practising certificate**

9.1   The Registrar may on the issue of any practising certificate under these Rules, having regard to the provisions of these Rules and of any general direction given by the Master, restrict or endorse the certificate as to the matters in which the holder is entitled to practise as a Notary and the wording of the certificate or endorsement shall be as the Registrar shall direct.

9.2   Any Notary whose practising certificate has been restricted or endorsed as above may appeal to the Master against the imposition of such a restriction or endorsement by giving notice to the Faculty Office of such appeal within 14 days of the Registrar's decision.

9.3   Any appeal made by a Notary under Rule 9.2 may be heard by the Master in person or may be disposed of on the basis of written representations if the Notary so agrees.

9.4 Upon hearing such an appeal under Rule 9.3 the Master may either

    9.4.1 direct the Registrar to issue a practising certificate to the Notary without condition or endorsement;

    9.4.2 direct the Registrar to issue a practising certificate to the Notary containing conditions or endorsements imposed by the Master as he sees fit; or

    9.4.3 dismiss the appeal.

9.5 Where a practising certificate held by a Notary has been suspended or restricted pursuant to Rule 6.5 of the 2011 Rules any appeal to the Master or application to the Commissary in respect of such restriction or endorsement shall be referred to the Court.

9.6 Where a practising certificate held by a Notary has been suspended or restricted pursuant to Rule 9.1 of the 2011 Rules any application to review the Order (as therein defined) under Rule 11 of the 2011 Rules shall be referred to the Court.

9.7 In the event that a Notary fails to provide the information required pursuant to Rule 4.2 above a practising certificate will not be issued. A Notary may appeal against the decision of the Registrar not to issue a practising certificate and the time limit in Rule 9.2 above shall apply. The appeal shall be conducted in accordance with Rules 9.3 and 9.4 above.

10. Where a Notary is a member of a Specified Profession and the Relevant Body of which has made a Finding against that Notary and such Finding discloses evidence of gross misconduct the Registrar may make an order ("an Interim Order") to suspend the Notary's practising certificate or restrict or limit the Notary's practice pending the conclusion of the procedures set out in Rule 10.4 or 10.5 of the 2011 Rules.

11. Where the Registrar has made an Interim Order the Notary may appeal to the Master and the procedure set out in Rule 6.5 of the 2011 Rules shall apply *mutatis mutandis* save that if disciplinary proceedings have been commenced in the Court of Faculties against the Notary any application shall be made to the Commissary.

12. Revocations

12.1 The following Order of the Master and Rules are hereby revoked:

- Order of the Master dated 16th June 1982
- The Public Notaries (Practising Certificates) Rules 1982
- The Public Notaries (Practising Certificates) Rules 1991
- The Public Notaries (Practising Certificates)(Amendment) Rules 1993
- The Public Notaries (Practising Certificates)(Amendment) Rules 1995

- The Public Notaries (Practising Certificates)(Amendment) Rules 1999

12.2 Any practising certificate issued pursuant to the rules which are hereby revoked for the Practising Certificate Year ending 31st October 2013 shall remain valid until that date or as provided in Rule 4.4. above.

Dated this 21st day of December 2012

Signed   C R GEORGE
             MASTER

NOTARIES (CONTINUING PROFESSIONAL EDUCATION) REGULATIONS 2010

WE CHARLES RICHARD GEORGE One of Her Majesty's Counsel Commissary or Master of the Faculties of the Most Reverend Father in God Rowan Douglas by Divine Providence Lord Archbishop of Canterbury Primate of All England and Metropolitan do make the following Regulations pursuant to Rule 19 of Our Notaries Practice Rules 2009:

PART I: PRELIMINARY

1.   Citation and Commencement

    1.1.   These regulations are made under Rule 19 of the Notaries Practice Rules 2009.

    1.2.   These regulations may be cited as the Notaries (Continuing Professional Education) Regulations 2010.

    1.3.   These regulations shall come into force on 1st May 2010.

2.   Interpretation

In these regulations:-

the "continuing professional education period" is a recurring period which commences on 1st November in each year and ends on 31st October a year later except as otherwise provided by these regulations.

"continuing professional education" is participation in such programmes, courses or seminars accredited by the Master as may be necessary to acquire the number of credit points determined by the Master, and "continuing professional education activity" shall be construed accordingly.

"the Master" means the Master of the Faculties, or where the Master has delegated his functions under these regulations, the delegated person or persons.

"the Registrar" means the Registrar of the Court of Faculties.

"notary" means a public notary admitted by the Master of the Faculties to practice in England and Wales or any other person authorised to act as a notary in accordance with Directive 98/5/EC but does not include a notary serving a period of supervision under rule 3 of the Notaries (Post-Admission) Rules 2009 nor an ecclesiastical notary appointed under rule 4 of the Notaries (Qualification) Rules 1998.

"notarial activities" means those activities customarily carried on by virtue of enrolment as a notary in accordance with section 1 of the Public

Notaries Act 1801 (c. 79), but not including probate activities or conveyancing.

"probate activities" means preparing any probate papers for the purposes of the law of England and Wales or in relation to any proceedings in England and Wales, on which to found or oppose-

(a)   a grant of probate, or

(b)   a grant of letters of administration.

"conveyancing" means:-

(a)   preparing any instrument of transfer or charge for the purposes of the Land Registration Act 2002 (c. 9);

(b)   making an application or lodging a document for registration under that Act;

(c)   preparing any other instrument to real property for the purposes of the law of England and Wales including a contract for the sale or other disposition of land (except a contract to grant a short lease), but does not include an agreement not intended to be executed as a deed, other than a contract that is included by virtue of the preceding provisions of this sub-paragraph,

In this paragraph a "short lease" means a lease such as is referred to in section 54(2) of the Law of Property Act 1925 (c. 20) (short leases).

For the avoidance of doubt the Interpretation Act 1978 applies to these regulations as it applies to an Act of Parliament.

PART II: THE REQUIREMENT

3.   Basic Requirement in Notarial Practice

3.1   A notary who practises during the continuing professional education period is required to obtain six credit points of continuing professional education in Notarial Practice during the same continuing professional education period.

3.2   At least 3 credits of this requirement must be obtained by participation in an accredited activity.

4.   Special Requirement in Conveyancing

4.1   A notary who carries out Conveyancing in his capacity as a notary during the continuing professional education period is required to obtain six credit points of continuing professional education in Conveyancing during the same continuing professional education period.

4.2   At least 3 credits of this requirement must be obtained by participation in an accredited activity.

5.   Special Requirement in Probate Activities

5.1   A notary carries out Probate Activities in his capacity as a notary during the continuing professional education period is required to obtain six credit points of continuing professional education in Probate Activities during the same continuing professional education period.

5.2   At least 3 credits of this requirement must be obtained by participation in an accredited activity.

6.   **Requirement to keep Records**
A notary is required to keep a record of the continuing professional education that he has completed during the continuing professional education period in the form set out in Schedule 2 of these regulations a copy of which he must submit to the Registrar on applying for a notarial practising certificate and on request.

7.   **Investigation by Registrar**
The Registrar may call upon the notary to produce such evidence as may reasonably be required in order to ascertain that the information in the continuing professional education record is faithful and accurate.

PART III: CREDIT POINTS AND ACCREDITED COURSES

8.   **Credit Points**
8.1   One credit point represents one hour of continuing professional education.

8.2   Credit points may not be carried over from one continuing professional education period to another except as provided by these regulations.

9.   **Credit Points Claimed Otherwise Than by Accredited Activities**
9.1   A notary may claim credit points for activities which have not been accredited under these regulations by completing activities listed in Schedule 1 of these regulations.

9.2   Such activities that are listed in Schedule 1 must be completed at an appropriate level and contribute to a notary's professional skill and knowledge in the basic and special continuing professional education requirements, and not merely advance a particular fee-earning matter.

10.   **Credit Points Claimed by Completing Accredited Activities**
A notary may claim the number of credit points which are awardable by completing an accredited activity.

11.   **Application for Accreditation to Award Credit Points**
11.1   A person who provides a continuing professional education activity may apply to the Master in order that the activity provided be accredited for the purpose of awarding credit points in one or more

of the basic or special continuing professional education requirements.

11.2   A person may apply to the Master in order that a continuing professional education activity provided by another person be accredited for the purpose of awarding credit points in one or more of the basic or special continuing professional education requirements.

11.3   On receiving an application for accreditation the Master will inform the applicant whether or not the application has been successful and specify a number of credit points which will be awarded to any notary who completes that activity.

11.4   The Master may in specific cases award credit points to notaries who participated on an accredited course before it became accredited provided that the application for accreditation is made no later than six months after the event.

12.   Content of Accredited Courses

12.1   An accredited course must be relevant to the subject matter of the basic or special continuing professional education requirement.

12.2   An accredited course must have written learning objectives relevant to the basic or special continuing professional education requirement and a form of written assessment to evaluate the notary's achievement of those objectives.

12.3   A written assessment may take the form of a structured self-evaluation such as the completion of a questionnaire.

12.4   An accredited course should take one or more of the following forms:-
(a)   physical attendance at a lecture or seminar;
(b)   a course provided wholly or partly at a distance that involves assessment by dissertation or written assessment.

13.   Completion of Accredited Activities

13.1   A notary completes an accredited activity and is awarded the number of credit points which belong to that activity if he completes the activity.

13.2   Completion of the accredited activity occurs if the following are satisfied:-
(a)   the notary participates in an accredited activity which includes delivering or attending the activity; and
(b)   attendance is attendance at the complete course. Partial attendance does not constitute completion.

13.3 The person providing an accredited activity shall give a certificate to any notary who completes the activity and such a certificate shall contain the following particulars:
(a) the name of the person who provided the accredited activity;
(b) the name of the notary who completed the activity;
(c) the date on which the activity was completed;
(d) a brief description of the activity;
(e) that the activity is accredited by the Master for the purpose of these regulations;
(f) the basic or special requirement in which the activity is accredited;
(g) the number of credit points which have been awarded.

14. Removal of Accreditation

The Master may at any time remove the accreditation of an activity by notice to the provider in writing, which will specify whether the revocation will have immediate effect or will take place at a specified future date.

PART IV: MISCELLANEOUS PROVISIONS

15. Master's Waiver

The Master may in writing waive the requirements of these regulations in whole or in part or revoke such a waiver and any such waiver may be general or specific to one or more individual notaries.

16. Master's Delegation

The Master may in writing delegate his functions under these regulations in whole or in part to another person or persons and revoke in writing such a delegation at any time.

17. Transitional Provisions

17.1 The first continuing professional education period commences on 1st November after the commencement of these regulations and ends on 31st October two years later.

17.2 In the first continuing educational period the notary must complete 12 credit points in each of the basic and special requirements which apply to him.

17.3 After the date of the commencement of these regulations a notary may obtain credit points which shall then be carried into the first continuing professional education period and providers of activities may apply to the Master to become accredited.

SCHEDULE 1: CREDIT POINTS AWARDED OTHERWISE THAN BY ACCREDITED COURSES

Activity	Explanation/comments
Lectures and seminars	• Preparing and delivering or attending a lecture or seminar relevant to the subject matter of the basic or special CPE requirement • Actual time may be claimed
Coaching and mentoring sessions	• Structured coaching sessions and structured mentoring sessions relevant to the subject matter of the basic or special CPE requirement, delivered face to face, of a duration of thirty minutes or more • Includes acting as a supervisor for the purpose of the Notaries (Post-Admission Rules) 2009 • Actual time may be claimed up to one hour per basic or CPE requirement
Coaching and mentoring sessions delivered at a distance	• Structured coaching sessions and structured mentoring sessions relevant to the subject matter of the basic or special CPE requirement, delivered at a distance (eg by telephone, email or fax), of a duration of thirty minutes or more • Actual time may be claimed up to one hour per basic or CPE requirement
Writing on law or practice	• Legal writing on a subject matter relevant to the basic or special CPE requirement intended for publication either in hard copy form or on the Internet • Actual time may be claimed

Research on law or practice	• Legal research on a subject matter relevant to the basic or special CPE requirement which results in a form or written document including precedents, memorandums, questionnaires/surveys • Actual time may be claimed
Watching, reading or listening to material which is produced by a legal education provider.	• Watching, reading or listening to material which is produced by a legal education provider on a subject matter relevant to the basic or special CPE requirement • Actual time may be claimed
Work shadowing	• Participation in structured work shadowing schemes with clear aims and objectives on a subject matter relevant to the basic or special CPE requirement and requiring feedback or reflection on the shadowing activity • Actual time may be claimed
Participation in the development of specialist areas of law and practice	• Participation in the development of specialist areas of law and practice on a subject matter relevant to the basic or special CPE requirement by attending specialist committees and/or working parties of relevant professional or other competent bodies charged with such work • Actual time may be claimed
Study towards professional qualifications	• Study towards professional qualifications relevant to the basic or special CPE requirement • Actual time spent in study may be claimed
Setting, marking or moderation of examinations in professional qualifications	• Setting, marking or moderation in professional qualifications relevant to the basic or special CPE requirement • Actual time may be claimed

Schedule 2

Notaries (Continuing Professional Education) Regulations 2010
CPE Training Record

A copy of this form is to be submitted with your application for a practicing certificate

The original is to be retained for a period of at least six years

Name:...

CPE year: ....

Declaration (to be completed when submitting a copy of this form to the Registrar)

I practise in the following areas *as a notary*: probate activity / conveyancing (delete as inapplicable)

The information in this CPE record is faithful and accurate to the best of my knowledge and belief

Signature of notary: Date:

Date attended	Name of CPE activity and provider	Please indicate whether activity was accredited or non-accredited	Number of credit points awarded	Comments
Notarial Practice				

	Date attended	Name of CPE activity and provider	Please indicate whether activity was accredited or non-accredited	Number of credit points awarded	Comments
Probate Activity					
Conveyancing					

NB. You may continue on separate sheets in necessary, affixing the loose papers to this form

CHARLES GEORGE

MASTER
21st April 2010

NOTARIES (POST-ADMISSION) RULES 2009
(As amended by Order of the Master dated the second day of February 2012

We, CHARLES RICHARD GEORGE One of Her Majesty's Counsel, Commissary or Master of the Faculties of the Most Reverend Father in God Rowan Douglas by Divine Providence Lord Archbishop of Canterbury Primate of All England and Metropolitan in exercise of the powers conferred by section 57 of the Courts and Legal Services Act 1990 and of all other powers Us enabling hereby make the following rules:

Citation and Commencement
1.   These rules may be cited as the Notaries (Post-Admission) Rules 2009 and shall come into force on the 20th day of March 2009.

1A.   Paragraphs 3A, 3B, 3C, 3D and 3E of Rule 3 paragraphs 1A, 1B, 1C 1D and 1E of Rule 4 and paragraphs 2(c) and 3(c) of Rule 5 shall come into force on the second day of February 2012.

Interpretation
2.   In these Rules
        '1991 Rules' means the Notaries (Post-Admission) Rules 1991 as amended by the Notaries (Qualification) Rules 1998;

        'The Faculty Office' means the Registry of the Court of Faculties;

        'The Master' means the Master of the Faculties;

        'The Registrar' means the Registrar of the Court of Faculties.

Period of practice under supervision
3.   (1)   This Rule shall apply to all notaries admitted to practise in England and Wales (other than notaries for ecclesiastical purposes only) on or after 13th day of June 1990

        (2)   A notary to whom this Rule applies shall be required to complete a period of practice under supervision in accordance with these Rules which shall commence
                (a)   in the case of a notary admitted after the date on which this Rule comes into effect, or of a notary admitted before that date but not in practice on that date, on the date on which he commences or resumes practice as a notary; or
                (b)   in any other case, as soon as arrangements for supervision can practicably be made, but not in any event later than two months after this Rule comes into effect.

        (3)   Subject to paragraph (4) of this Rule, the duration of the period of practice under supervision shall be two years, less either of the following:

189

(a) any period of apprenticeship served pursuant to section 2 of the Public Notaries Act 1801 or pursuant to requirements of the Incorporated Company of Scriveners of London imposed under Section 57(11)(b) of the Courts and Legal Services Act 1990;

(b) any period spent in actual practice as a notary, prior to the coming into effect of these Rules, by a district notary appointed pursuant to the Public Notaries Act 1833.

(3A) A notary admitted to practise after 2 February 2012 who carries out conveyancing in his capacity as a notary shall be required to complete a period of practice under supervision of three years commencing no later than the first date that instructions for conveyancing are accepted by the notary in his capacity as a notary.

(3B) A notary admitted to practise after 2 February 2012 who carries out probate in his capacity as a notary shall be required to complete a period of practice under supervision of three years commencing no later than the first date that instructions for probate are accepted by the notary in his capacity as a notary.

(3C) Paragraph 3A of this Rule shall not apply to a notary who is a member of a professional partnership as defined in Rule 2 of the Notaries Practice Rules 2009 or who is an employee of that partnership where at least one other member of that professional practice also carries out conveyancing whether as a notary or by otherwise being entitled.

(3D) Paragraph 3B of this Rule shall not apply to a notary who is a member of a professional partnership as defined in Rule 2 of the Notaries Practice Rules 2009 or who is an employee of that partnership where at least one other member of that professional practice also carries out probate whether as a notary or by otherwise being entitled.

(3E) If a notary has already completed a period of supervision under this Rule but that supervision did not comply with Rules 3A-3D (additional supervision for notaries carrying out conveyancing and probate) and wishes to accept instructions to carry out conveyancing or probate in his capacity as a notary he shall apply to the Master to set a period of supervision of three years or less relating solely to conveyancing or probate or both.

(4) The Master may direct that the period of practice under supervision be extended in any particular case, either

(a) as a condition of approving a change of supervisor under paragraph (5) of Rule 4, or

(b) following his consideration of a report submitted pursuant to paragraph (3) of Rule 7, or

(c) following disciplinary proceedings.

Selection of supervisor

4. (1) During the period of practice under supervision the notary to whom this Rule applies ("the supervised notary") shall practise as a notary only under the supervision (as defined in Rule 5) of another notary ("the supervisor") who holds a current practising certificate entered in or issued from the Court of Faculties, and who has been engaged in actual practice as a notary for a minimum period of five years from the date of admission as a notary.

(1A) A notary acting as a supervisor for a notary to which paragraph 3A of Rule 3 applies shall have carried out conveyancing as a substantial part of his practice for the previous five years whether as a notary or by otherwise being entitled.

(1B) A notary acting as a supervisor for a notary to which paragraph 3B of Rule 3 applies shall have carried out probate as a substantial part of his practice for the previous five years whether as a notary or by otherwise being entitled.

(1C) For the purposes of paragraphs 1A and 1B of this Rule a notary may have more than one supervisor.

(1D) A notary requiring supervision to whom either or both paragraphs 3A and 3B of Rule 3 applies may obtain supervision from a solicitor or (in the case of paragraph 3A of Rule 3 only) a licensed conveyancer who has been in practice as such for a minimum period of five years.

(1E) If for the purposes of paragraphs 1A and 1B of this Rule a notary has more than one supervisor each of those supervisors shall carry out the full extent of supervision required by these rules save that an additional supervisor may restrict his supervision to supervising the conveyancing or probate practice of the notary (or both) for which reason he has been appointed.

(2) A notary (or solicitor or licensed conveyancer where paragraph 1D of this Rule applies) acting as a supervisor shall be located within a reasonable distance from the office at which the supervised notary proposes to practise so as to enable the supervisor to visit that office from time to time as required by Rule 5(2).

191

(3)   It shall be the duty of a supervised notary to notify the Faculty Office upon request of the name and address of his supervisor; and it shall be the duty of any notary to notify the Faculty Office upon request of the names and addresses of all notaries of whom he is the supervisor.

(4)   A supervised notary shall, upon the death or retirement from practice of his supervisor, forthwith make arrangements for another notary qualified under this Rule to supervise his practice for the remainder of the required period; and any time between the death or retirement of the former supervisor and the coming into effect of such arrangements shall not count towards the period of supervised practice.

(5)   If for any reason other than the death or retirement of the supervisor, either party wishes the appointment of a particular supervisor to be terminated before the expiry of the required period of supervised practice, application shall be made for that purpose to the Master, who may terminate the supervision upon such conditions as he shall think fit.

Extent of supervision

5.   (1)   The following aspects of a notary's practice shall be excluded from the general requirement of supervision (but not from the obligation to produce records and accounts under paragraph (2) of this Rule):

(a)   conveyancing and probate, in the case of a notary who is also a solicitor and who would be entitled to carry out conveyancing and probate as a solicitor without supervision, or who does in fact receive such supervision in relation to his practice as a solicitor as is required by the Solicitors Act 1974 and rules made thereunder;

(b)   conveyancing, in the case of a notary who is also a licensed conveyancer and who would be entitled to carry out conveyancing as such without supervision, or who does in fact receive such supervision in relation to his practice as a licensed conveyancer as is required by the statutes and rules governing that profession.

(2)   The supervisor shall visit the office of the supervised notary

(c)   within one month after the supervised notary has been admitted as a notary and has been issued with a practising certificate from the Court of Faculties, and

(d)   for a second time within twelve months from the date of the visit under subparagraph (a) of this Rule, and

(e)   in respect of a supervised notary to whom rule 3(A) and/or Rule 3(B) applies for a third time within twelve months from the date of the visit under sub paragraph (b) of this Rule and shall on each visit inspect the records and accounts of the supervised notary which the supervised notary shall (subject to paragraph (4) of this Rule) produce to the supervisor on request.

(3) The supervised notary shall visit the office of the supervisor
    (a) no later than six months after the supervisor's visit required by paragraph (2)(a) of this Rule, and
    (b) for a second time no later than six months after the supervisor's visit required by paragraph (2)(b) of this Rule, and
    (c) in respect of a supervised notary to whom rule 3(A) and/or Rule 3(B) applies for a third time no later than six months after the supervisor's visit required by paragraph (2)(c) of this Rule,

and shall (subject to paragraph (4) of this Rule) produce to the supervisor for inspection the records and accounts of the supervised notary relating to the period since the supervisor's last visit to the supervised notary's office.

(4) If it appears to a supervised notary that papers relating to the business of a particular client cannot be shown to his supervisor without causing a breach of the duty of confidentiality owed to that client (whether on account of a relationship between the client and the supervisor, or because the supervisor is known to act for a person in competition with the client, or for any other reason), he shall inform the supervisor of that fact. The supervisor may nominate another notary (qualified to be a supervisor under Rule 4(1) but not subject to the same objections of confidentiality as respects the client concerned) and the notary nominated shall, if willing to act, have the supervisor's rights and duties in relation to those papers.

(5) The supervisor shall make himself available at all reasonable times to offer advice and guidance to the supervised notary on matters covered by the supervision and shall make enquiries of the supervised notary at least once in every three months period by e-mail or other means of communication as to the notary's progress and any matter of concern to the supervised notary, and the supervised notary shall within one week of receipt of the supervisor's communication provide the supervisor by e-mail or other means of communication a short report about the notary's progress and shall include any request for advice and guidance as necessary, and both the supervisor and the supervised notary shall keep a record of these communications.

(6) The supervisor shall take particular care to ensure (so far as he is able) that the supervised notary is aware of, and complies with, all Rules and Orders made by the Master under section 57 of the Courts and Legal Services Act 1990 and conducts himself in a

manner calculated to maintain the reputation of the office and profession of a public notary.

Post-Admission Education

6. Every supervised notary shall, during each year of his period of practice under supervision, attend

    (a) one full day course or seminar approved by the Master covering the topics of Bills of Exchange, Notarial Practice and Professional Conduct;

    (b) if desiring to carry out conveyancing as part of his notarial practice, one full day continuing education course or seminar in conveyancing approved by the Master; and

    (c) if desiring to carry out probate work as part of his notarial practice, one full day continuing education course or seminar in probate approved by the Master;

    and shall make a report to his Supervisor on the course or seminar attended.

Records and reporting

7. (1) A report of every visit and inspection made pursuant to paragraphs (2) and (3) of Rule 5 shall be made by the supervisor and shall be inserted in the Register or other permanent record kept by each notary pursuant to the Notaries (Records) Rules 1991.

    (2) The supervisor shall enter in the Register or other permanent record kept by him pursuant to the Notaries (Records) Rules 1991 a note of any advice or guidance given to a supervised notary pursuant to paragraph (4) of Rule 5.

    (3) Upon the completion of a period of practice under supervision (or upon the retirement from practice of a supervisor during such a period), the supervisor shall report the fact of such completion to the Master in writing and shall indicate the courses or seminars attended by the supervised notary pursuant to Rule 6, and whether in his opinion the supervised notary shall thereafter be permitted to practise without supervision. The supervisor and the supervised notary shall respond in writing to any questions put by the Master in relation to the period of supervision and produce to the Faculty Office such documents as the Master may require.

Fees

8. A notary agreeing to act as a supervisor shall be entitled to charge the supervised notary a fee not exceeding the level prescribed from time to time in Regulations made by the Master (which may include provision for expenses), together with the amount of any Value Added Tax due thereon. If for any reason the appointment of the supervisor ceases before the end of the period of supervision, the fee shall be apportioned pro rata or as the Master may direct.

Dispensations

9. The Master may, upon such application made to him as he deems sufficient, for good cause dispense any notary from the requirement of supervision under these Rules or permit such lesser supervision as he considers practicable in the circumstances of any particular case.

10. The provisions of these Rules shall not apply to any Notary who, immediately prior to his admission, was recognised by the Master as qualified for admission under the provision of Rule 9 of the Notaries (Qualification) Rules 1998.

Revocation and Savings

11. (1) Subject to Rule 11(2) the 1991 Rules are hereby revoked.

    (2) Where a notary has commenced a period of practice under supervision prior to the coming into force of these Rules the 1991 Rules, as amended, shall continue to have effect in respect of that period of practice under supervision.

DATED this second day of February 2012.

CHARLES GEORGE

MASTER

LEGISLATION RELEVANT TO NOTARIES

Public Notaries Act 1801

Public Notaries Act 1843

Powers of Attorney Act 1971

Bills of Exchange Act 1882

Mental Capacity Act 2005

Oaths Act 1978

Commissioner for Oaths Act 1889

Limited Liability Partnerships (Application of Companies Act 2006) Regulations 2009

Companies Act 2006

Consular Relations Act 1968

Access to Justice Act 1999

Courts and Legal Services Act 1990

Banking and Financial Dealings Act 1971

Statutory Declaration Act 1835

Courts and Legal Services Act 1990

Legal Services Act 2007

Law of Property (Miscellaneous Provisions) Act 1989

Law of Property Act 1925

Fraud Act 2006

The Perjury Act 1911

Proceeds of Crime Act

Public Notaries Act 1801
(Sections 1 & 4)

No person in England to act as a Public Notary unless duly admitted

1.　　WHEREAS it is expedient, for the better preventing of illiterate and inexperienced persons being created to act as, or admitted to the faculty of Public Notaries, that the said faculty should be regulated in England: Be it therefore enacted &c., that from and after the first day of August, 1801, no person in England shall be created to act as a Public Notary, or use and exercise the office of a Notary, or do any notarial act, unless such person shall have been duly sworn, admitted, and enrolled in the court wherein Notaries have been accustomarily sworn, admitted and enrolled.

Act not to extend to proctors, secretaries to bishops, etc.

14.　　Nothing in this Act contained shall extend, or be construed to extend, to any proctor in any ecclesiastical court in England; not to any secretary or secretaries to any bishop or bishops, merely practising as such secretary or secretaries; or to any other person or persons necessarily created a Notary Public for the purpose of holding or exercising any office or appointment, or occasionally performing any public duty or service under Government, and not as general practitioner or practitioners; anything hereinbefore contained to the contrary notwithstanding.

Public Notaries Act 1843
(Sections 4, 5, 7, 8 &10)

An Act for removing Doubts as to the Service of Clerks or Apprentices to Public Notaries, and for amending the Laws regulating the Admission of Public Notaries.

[Preamble recites the Public Notaries Act 1801.]

Master of the faculties may require testimonials of ability, etc.

4.   The master of the faculties for the time being may make any general rule or rules requiring testimonials, certificates, or proofs as the character, integrity, ability and competency of any person who shall hereafter apply for admission or readmission as a public notary to practise either in England or in any of her Majesty's foreign territories, colonies, settlements, dominions, forts, factories, or possessions, whether such person shall have served a clerkship or not, and from time to time alter and vary such rules as the master of the facilities shall seem meet, and may admit or reject any person applying, at his discretion, any law, custom, usage, or prescription to the contrary so withstanding.

Proceedings in case of refusal of master of faculties to grant a faculty

A1-04   5.   Provided always that if the master of the faculties shall refuse to grant any faculty to practise as a public notary to any person without just and reasonable cause, then the chancellor of England or the lord keeper of the great seal for the time being, upon complaint thereof being made, shall direct the Queen's writ to the said master of the faculties to the effect and shall proceed thereon according to the intent and meaning of the Act of Parliament of the twenty-fifth year of the reign of King Henry the Eighth, intituled "An Act concerning peterpence and dispensations", and in manner and form as is therein provided and set forth in case of the refusal of any licences, dispensations, faculties, instruments, or other writings, as fully and effectually, and with the same powers and authority, as if the same were here inserted and re-enacted.

Oath on admission of notary

A1-05   7.   Every person to be admitted and enrolled a public notary shall, before a faculty is granted to him authorising him to practise as such, make oath before the said master of the faculties, his surrogate or other proper officer, in substance and to the effect following:
"I A.B. do swear, that I will faithfully exercise the office of a public notary: I will faithfully make contracts or instruments for or between any party or parties requiring the same, and I will not add or diminish anything without the knowledge and consent of such party or parties that may alter the substance of the fact; I will not make or attest any act, contract, or instrument in which I shall know there is violence or fraud; and in all things I will act uprightly and justly in the business of a public notary, according to the best of my skill and ability. So help me GOD."

Master of the faculties may issue commissions to take oaths, etc., required before the grant of faculties, marriage licences, etc.

A1-06   8.   The master of the faculties for the time being, or his surrogate, shall and he is hereby authorised and empowered to issue commissions to take any oaths, affidavits, affirmations, or declarations required by law to be taken before the grant of any faculty, marriage licence, or other instrument issuing from the said office of faculties; and all oaths, affidavits, affirmations, or declarations taken before the commissioner so appointed, and the faculty, marriage licence, or other instrument granted in pursuance thereof, shall be valid and effectual as if such oaths, affidavit, affirmation, or declaration was taken before the said master or his surrogate, anything in any Act or law to the contrary thereof notwithstanding.

Persons not duly authorised practising as notaries to be guilty of offence

A1-07   10.- (1)   In any case any person shall, in his own name or in the name of any other person, make, do, act, exercise, or execute or perform, any act, matter, or thing whatsoever of or in any wise appertaining or belonging to the office, function, or practice of a public notary, for or in expectation of any gain, fee, or reward, without being able to prove, if required, that he is duly authorised so to do, he shall be guilty of an offence and liable on summary conviction to a fine not exceeding level 3 on the standard scale.

(2)   Notwithstanding anything in section 127(1) of the Magistrates' Courts Act 1980, proceedings for an offence under this section may be commenced within 12 months from the time when the offence was committed.

Powers of Attorney Act 1971

An Act to make new provision in relation to powers of attorney and the delegation by trustees of their trusts, powers and discretions.   [12th May 1971]

BE IT ENACTED by the Queen's most Excellent Majesty, by and with the advice and consent of the Lords Spiritual and Temporal, and Commons, in this present Parliament assembled, and by the authority of the same, as follows:-

1. -   (1)   An instrument creating a power of attorney shall be signed and sealed by, or by direction and in the presence of, the donor of the power.

(2)   Where such an instrument is signed and sealed by a person by direction and in the presence of the donor of the power, two other persons shall be present as witnesses and shall attest the instrument.

(3)   This section is without prejudice to any requirement in, or having effect under, any other Act as to the witnessing of instruments creating powers of attorney and does not affect the rules relating to the execution of instruments by bodies corporate.

2. -   (1)   As from the commencement of this Act no instrument creating a power of attorney, and no copy of any such instrument, shall be deposited or filed at the central office of the Supreme Court or at the Land Registry under section 25 of the Trustee Act 1925, section 125 of the Law of Property Act 1925 or section 219 of the Supreme Court of Judicature (Consolidation) Act 1925.

(2)   This section does not affect any right to search for, inspect or copy, or to obtain an office copy of, any such document which has been deposited or filed as aforesaid before the commencement of this Act.

3. -   (1)   The contents of an instrument creating a power of attorney may be proved by means of a copy which-

(a)   is a reproduction of the original made with a photographic or other device for reproducing documents in facsimile; and

(b)   contains the following certificate or certificates signed by the donor of the power or by a solicitor or stockbroker, that is to say-

(i)   a certificate at the end to the effect that the copy is a true and complete copy of the original; and

(ii)   if the original consists of two or more pages, a certificate at the end of each page of the copy to the effect that it is a true and complete copy of the corresponding page of the original.

(2)   Where a copy of an instrument creating a power of attorney has been made which complies with subsection (1) of this section, the contents of the instrument may also be proved by means of a copy of that copy if the further copy itself complies with that sub-

section, taking references in it to the original as references to the copy from which the further copy is made.

(3)   In this section "stockbroker" means a member of any stock exchange within the meaning of the Stock Transfer Act 1963 or the Stock Transfer Act (Northern Ireland) 1963.

(4)   This section is without prejudice to section 4 of the Evidence and Powers of Attorney Act 1940 (proof of deposited instruments by office copy) and to any other method of proof authorised by law.

(5)   For the avoidance of doubt, in relation to an instrument made in Scotland the references to a power of attorney in this section and in section 4 of the Evidence and Powers of Attorney Act 1940 include references to a factory and commission.

4. -   (1)   Where a power of attorney is expressed to be irrevocable and is given to secure-

    (a)   a proprietary interest of the donee of the power; or

    (b)   the performance of an obligation owed to the donee, then, so long as the donee has that interest or the obligation remains undischarged, the power shall not be revoked-

        (i)   by the donor without the consent of the donee; or

        (ii)   By the death, incapacity or bankruptcy of the donor or, if the donor is a body corporate, by its winding up or dissolution.

        (iii)   by the death, incapacity or bankruptcy of the donor or,

(2)   A power of attorney given to secure a proprietary interest may be given to the person entitled to the interest and persons deriving title under him to that interest, and those persons shall be duly be duly constituted donees of the power for all purposes of the power but without prejudice to any right to appoint substitutes given by the power.

(3)   This section applies to powers of attorney whenever created.

5. -   (1)   A donee of a power of attorney who acts in pursuance Protection of the power at a time when it has been revoked shall not, by reason of the revocation, incur any liability (either to the donor or to any other person) if at that time he did not know that the of attorney power had been revoked.

(2)   Where a power of attorney has been revoked and a person, without knowledge of the revocation, deals with the donee of the power, the transaction between them shall, in favour of that person, be as valid as if the power had then been in existence.

(3)   Where the power is expressed in the instrument creating it to be irrevocable and to be given by way of security then, unless the person dealing with the donee knows that it was not in fact given by way of security, he shall be entitled to assume that the power is incapable of revocation except by the donor acting with the consent

of the donee and shall accordingly be treated for the purposes of subsection (2) of this section as having knowledge of the revocation only if he knows that it has been revoked in that manner.

(4) Where the interest of a purchaser depends on whether a transaction between the donee of a power of attorney and another person was valid by virtue of subsection (2) of this section, it shall be conclusively presumed in favour of the purchaser that that person did not at the material time know of the revocation of the power if-

(a) the transaction between that person and the donee was completed within twelve months of the date on which the power came into operation; or

(b) that person makes a statutory declaration, before or within three months after the completion of the purchase, that he did not at the material time know of the revocation of the power.

(5) Without prejudice to subsection (3) of this section, for the purposes of this section knowledge of the revocation of a power of attorney includes knowledge of the occurrence of any event (such as the death of the donor) which has the effect of revoking the power.

(6) In this section "purchaser" and "purchase" have the meanings specified in section 205(1) of the Law of Property Act 1925.

(7) This section applies whenever the power of attorney was created but only to acts and transactions after the commencement of this Act.

6. - (1) Without prejudice to section 5 of this Act, where-

(a) the donee of a power of attorney executes, as transferor, an instrument transferring registered securities; and

(b) the instrument is executed for the purposes of a stock exchange transaction, it shall be conclusively presumed in favour of the transferee that the power had not been revoked at the date of the instrument if a statutory declaration to that effect is made by the donee of the power on or within three months after that date.

(2) In this section "registered securities" and "stock exchange transaction" have the same meanings as in the Stock Transfer Act 1963.

7. - (1) The donee of a power of attorney may, if he thinks fit-

(a) execute any instrument with his own signature and, where of attorney sealing is required, with his own seal, and

(b) do any other thing in his own name, by the authority of the donor of the power; and any document executed or thing done in that manner shall be as effective as if executed or done by the donee with the signature and seal, or, as the case may be, in the name, of the donor of the power.

(2) For the avoidance of doubt, it is hereby declared that an instrument to which subsection (3) or (4) of section 74 of the Law of Property

Act 1925, applies may be executed either as provided in those subsections or as provided in this section.

(3)   This section is without prejudice to any statutory direction requiring an instrument to be executed in the name of an estate owner within the meaning of the said Act of 1925.

(4)   This section applies whenever the power of attorney was created.

8. -   Section 129 of the Law of Property Act 1925 (which contains provisions, now unnecessary, in respect of powers of attorney granted by married women) shall cease to have effect.

9. -   (1)   Section 25 of the Trustee Act 1925 (power to delegate trusts etc., during absence abroad) shall be amended as follows.

(2)   For subsections (1) to (8) of that section there shall be substituted the following subsections-

"(1) Notwithstanding any rule of law or equity to the contrary, a trustee may, by power of attorney, delegate for Powers of Attorney Act 1971 c. 27 a period not exceeding twelve months the execution or exercise of all or any of the trusts, powers and discretions vested in him as trustee either alone or jointly with any other person or persons.

(2) The persons who may be donees of a power of attorney under this section include a trust corporation but not (unless a trust corporation) the only other co-trustee of the donor of the power.

(3) An instrument creating a power of attorney under this section shall be attested by at least one witness.

(4) Before or within seven days after giving a power of attorney under this section the donor shall give written notice thereof (specifying the date on which the power comes into operation and its duration, the donee of the power, the reason why the power is given and, where some only are delegated, the trusts, powers and discretions delegated) to-

(a)   each person (other than himself), if any, who under any instrument creating the trust has power (whether alone or jointly) to appoint a new trustee; and

(b)   each of the other trustees, if any;

but failure to comply with this subsection shall not, in favour of a person dealing with the donee of the power, invalidate any act done or instrument executed by the donee.

(5) The donor of a power of attorney given under this section shall be liable for the acts or defaults of the donee in the same manner as if they were the acts or defaults of the donor."

(3)   Subsections (9) and (10) of the said section 25 shall stand as subsections (6) and (7) and for subsection (11) of that section there shall be substituted the following subsection-

"(8) This section applies to a personal representative, tenant for life and statutory owner as it applies to a trustee except that subsection (4) shall apply as if it required the notice there mentioned to be given-

(a)   in the case of a personal representative, to each of the other personal representatives, if any, except any executor who has renounced probate;

(b)   in the case of a tenant for life, to the trustees of the settlement and to each person, if any, who together with the person giving the notice constitutes the tenant for life;

(c)   in the case of a statutory owner, to each of the persons, if any, who together with the person giving the notice constitute the statutory owner and, in the case of a statutory owner by virtue of section 23(1)(a) of the Settled Land Act 1925, to the trustees of the settlement."

(4)   This section applies whenever the trusts, powers or discretions in question arose but does not invalidate anything done by virtue of the said section 25 as in force at the commencement of this Act.

10. - (1)   Subject to subsection (2) of this section, a general power of attorney in the form set out in Schedule 1 to this Act, of attorney in or in a form to the like effect but expressed to be made under specified form this Act, shall operate to confer-

(a)   on the donee of the power; or

(b)   if there is more than one donee, on the donees acting jointly or acting jointly or severally, as the case may be,

authority to do on behalf of the donor anything which he can lawfully do by an attorney.

(2)   This section does not apply to functions which the donor has as a trustee or personal representative or as a tenant for life or statutory owner within the meaning of the Settled Land Act 1925.

11. - (1)   This Act may be cited as the Powers of Attorney Act 1971.

(2)   The enactments specified in Schedule 2 to this Act are hereby repealed to the extent specified in the third column of that Schedule.

(3)   In section 125(2) of the Law of Property Act 1925 for the words "as aforesaid" there shall be substituted the words "under the Land Registration Act 1925"; and in section 219(2) of the Supreme Court of Judicature (Consolidation) Act 1925 for the words "so deposited" there shall be substituted the words "deposited under this section before the commencement of the Powers of Attorney Act 1971."

(4)   This Act shall come into force on 1st October 1971.

(5)   Section 3 of this Act extends to Scotland and Northern Ireland but, save as aforesaid, this Act extends to England and Wales only.

SCHEDULES

Schedule 1 – Section 10

Form of General Power of Attorney for Purposes of Section 10

THIS GENERAL POWER OF ATTORNEY is made this   day of   19
by AB of   .
I appoint CD of   .
[or CD of   and
EF of   jointly
or

     jointly and severally] to be my attorney[s] in accordance with section 10 of
the Powers of Attorney Act 1971.

In Witness etc,

Schedule 2 – Section 11(2)

REPEALS

Chapter	Short Title	Extent of Repeal
15 & 16 Geo. 5. c. 19.	The Trustee Act 1925.	Section 29.
15 & 16 Geo. 5. c. 20.	The Law of Property Act 1925.	Sections 123 and 124. Section 125(1) Sections 126 to 129.
15 & 16 Geo. 5. c. 49.	The Supreme Court of Judicature (Consolidation) Act 1925.	Section 219(1).
4 & 5 Eliz. 2. c. 46.	The Administration of Justice Act 1956.	Section 18.

Bills of Exchange Act 1882
ARRANGEMENT OF SECTIONS

PART I.

PRELIMINARY

PART II.

BILLS OF EXCHANGE

PART III.
CHEQUES ON A BANKER.

PART IV.
PROMISSORY NOTES.

PART V.
SUPPLEMENTARY.

An Act to codify the law relating to Bills of Exchange, Cheques, and Promissory Notes.

[18th August 1882.]

BE it enacted by the Queen's most Excellent Majesty, by and with the advice and consent of the Lords Spiritual and Temporal, and Commons, in this present Parliament assembled, and by the authority of the same, as follows:

PART I.
PRELIMINARY.

1. This Act may be cited as the Bills of Exchange Act, 1882.

2. In this Act, unless the context otherwise requires,-

" Acceptance " means an acceptance completed by delivery or notification.

" Action " includes counter claim and set off.

" Banker " includes a body of persons whether incorporated or not who carry on the business of banking.

" Bankrupt " includes any person whose estate is vested in a trustee or assignee under the law for the time being in force relating to bankruptcy.

" Bearer " means the person in possession of a bill or note which is payable to bearer.

" Bill " means bill of exchange, and "note " means promissory note.

" Delivery " means transfer of possession, actual or constructive from one person to another.

" Holder " means the payee or indorsee of a bill or note who is in

209

possession of it, or the bearer thereof.

" Indorsement " means an indorsement completed by delivery.

" Issue " means the first delivery of a bill or note, complete in form to a person who takes it as a holder.

" Person " includes a body of persons whether incorporated or not.

" Value " means valuable consideration.

" Written " includes printed, and " writing " includes print.

PART II.
BILLS OF EXCHANGE.

Form and Interpretation.

3.   (1.)   A bill of exchange is an unconditional order in writing, addressed by one person to another, signed by the person giving it, requiring the person to whom it is addressed to pay on demand or at a fixed or determinable future time a sum certain in money to or to the order of a specified person, or to bearer.

(2.)   An instrument which does not comply with these conditions, or which orders any act to be done in addition to the payment of money, is not a bill of exchange.

(3.)   An order to pay out of a particular fund is not unconditional within the meaning of this section; but an unqualified order to pay, coupled with (a) an indication of a particular fund out of which the drawee is to re-imburse himself or a particular account to be debited with the amount, or (b) a statement of the transaction which gives rise to the bill, is unconditional.

(4)   A bill is not invalid by reason-
    (a.)   That it is not dated;
    (b.)   That it does not specify the value given, or that any value has been given therefor;
    (c.)   That it does not specify the place where it is drawn or the place where it is payable.

4.   (1.)   An inland bill is a bill which is or on the face of it purports to be (a) both drawn and payable within the British Islands, or (b) drawn within the British Islands upon some person resident therein. Any other bill is a foreign bill.

For the purposes of this Act " British Islands " mean any part of the United Kingdom of Great Britain and Ireland, the islands of Man, Guernsey, Jersey, Alderney, and Sark, and the islands adjacent to any of them being part of the dominions of Her Majesty.

	(2.)	Unless the contrary appear on the face of the bill the holder may treat it as an inland bill.
5.	(1.)	A bill may be drawn payable to, or to the order of, the drawer; or it may be drawn payable to, or to the order of, the drawee.
	(2.)	Where in a bill drawer and drawee are the same person, or where the drawee is a fictitious person or a person not having capacity to contract, the holder may treat the instrument, at his option, either as a bill of exchange or as a promissory note.
6.	(1.)	The drawee must be named or otherwise indicated in a bill with reasonable certainty.
	(2.)	A bill may be addressed to two or more drawees whether they are partners or not, but an order addressed to two drawees in the alternative or to two or more drawees in succession is not a bill of exchange.
7.	(1.)	Where a bill is not payable to bearer, the payee must be named or otherwise indicated therein with reasonable certainty.
	(2.)	A bill may be made payable to two or more payees jointly, or it may be made payable in the alternative to one of two, or one or some of several payees. A bill may also be made payable to the holder of an office for the time being.
	(3.)	Where the payee is a fictitious or non-existing person the bill may be treated as payable to bearer.
8.	(1.)	When a bill contains words prohibiting transfer or indicating an intention that it should not be transferable, it is valid as between the parties thereto, but is not negotiable.
	(2.)	A negotiable bill may be payable either to order or to bearer.
	(3.)	A bill is payable to bearer which is expressed to be so payable, or on which the only or last indorsement is an indorsement in blank.
	(4.)	A bill is payable to order which is expressed to be so payable, or which is expressed to be payable to a particular person and does not contain words prohibiting transfer or indicating an intention that it should not be transferable.
	(5.)	Where a bill, either originally or by indorsement, is expressed to be payable to the order of a specified person, and not to him or his order, it is nevertheless payable to him or his order at his option.

211

9. (1.) The sum payable by a bill is a sum certain within the meaning of this Act, although it is required to be paid-
   (a.) With interest.
   (b.) By stated instalments.
   (c.) By stated instalments, with a provision that upon default in payment of any instalment the whole shall become due.
   (d.) According to an indicated rate of exchange or according to a rate of exchange to be ascertained as directed by the bill.

   (2.) Where the sum payable is expressed in words and also in figures, and there is a discrepancy between the two, the sum denoted by the words is the amount payable.

   (3.) Where a bill is expressed to be payable with interest, unless the instrument otherwise provides, interest runs from the date of the bill, and if the bill is undated from the issue thereof.

10. (1.) A bill is payable on demand-
    (a.) Which is expressed to be payable on demand, or at sight, or on presentation; or
    (b.) In which no time for payment is expressed.

    (2.) Where a bill is accepted or indorsed when it is overdue, it shall, as regards the acceptor who so accepts, or any indorser who so indorses it, be deemed a bill payable on demand.

11. A bill is payable at a determinable future time within the meaning of this Act which is expressed to be payable-

    (1.) At a fixed period after date or sight.
    (2.) On or at a fixed period after the occurrence of a specified event which is certain to happen, though the time of happening may be uncertain.

    An instrument expressed to be payable on a contingency is not a bill, and the happening of the event does not cure the defect.

12. Where, a bill expressed to be payable at a fixed period after date is issued undated, or where the acceptance of a bill payable at a fixed period after sight is undated, any holder may insert therein the true date of issue or acceptance, and the bill shall be payable accordingly.

    Provided that (1) where the holder in good faith and by mistake inserts a wrong date, and (2) in every case where a wrong date is inserted, if the bill subsequently comes into the hands of a holder in due course the bill shall not be avoided thereby but shall operate and be payable as if the date so inserted had been the true date.

13.   (1.)   Where a bill or an acceptance or any indorsement on a bill is dated, the date shall, unless the contrary be proved, be deemed to be the true date of the drawing, acceptance, or indorsement, as the case may be.

        (2.)   A bill is not invalid by reason only that it is ante-dated or post-dated, or that it bears date on a Sunday.

14.   Where a bill is not payable on demand the day on which it falls due is determined as follows:

        (1.)   Three days, called days of grace, are, in every case where the bill itself does not otherwise provide, added to the time of payment as fixed by the bill, and the bill is due and payable on the last day of grace: Provided that-

            (a.)   When the last day of grace falls on Sunday, Christmas Day, Good Friday, or a day appointed by Royal proclamation as a public fast or Thanksgiving Day, the bill is, except in the case herein-after provided for, due and payable on the preceding business day;

            (b.)   When the last day of grace is a bank holiday (other than Christmas Day or Good Friday) under the Bank Holidays Act, 1871, and Acts amending or extending it, or when the last day of grace is a Sunday and the second day of grace is a Bank Holiday, the bill is due and payable on the succeeding business day.

        (2.)   Where a bill is payable at a fixed period after date, after sight, or after the happening of a specified event, the time of payment is determined by excluding the day from which the time is to begin to run and by including the day of payment.

        (3.)   Where a bill is payable at a fixed period after sight, the time begins to run from the date of the acceptance if the bill be accepted, and from the date of noting or protest if the bill be noted or protested for non-acceptance, or for non-delivery.

        (4.)   The term " month " in a bill means calendar month.

15.   The drawer of a bill and any indorser may insert therein the name of a person to whom the holder may resort in case of need, that is to say, in case the bill is dishonoured by non-acceptance or non-payment. Such person is called the referee in case of need. It is in the option of the holder to resort to the referee in case of need or not as he may think fit.

16.   The drawer of a bill, and any indorser, may insert therein an express stipulation-

        (1.)   Negativing or limiting his own liability to the holder:

(2.)   Waiving as regards himself some or all of the holder's duties.

17.   (1.)   The acceptance of a bill is the signification by the drawee of his assent to the order of the drawer.

    (2.)   An acceptance is invalid unless it complies with the following conditions, namely: -

        (a.)   It must be written on the bill and be signed by the drawee. The mere signature of the drawee without additional words is sufficient.

        (b.)   It must not express that the drawee will perform his promise by any other means than the payment of money.

18.   A bill may be accepted-

    (1.)   before it has been signed by the drawer, or while otherwise incomplete:

    (2.)   When it is overdue, or after it has been dishonoured by a previous refusal to accept, or by non-payment:

    (3.)   When a bill payable after sight is dishonoured by non-acceptance, and the drawee subsequently accepts it, the holder, in the absence of any different agreement, is entitled to have the bill accepted as of the date of first presentment to the drawee for acceptance.

19.   (1.)   An acceptance is either (a) general or (b) qualified.

    (2.)   A general acceptance assents without qualification to the order of the drawer. A qualified acceptance in express terms varies the effect of the bill as drawn.

In particular an acceptance is qualified which is-

        (a.)   conditional, that is to say, which makes payment by the acceptor dependent on the fulfilment of a condition therein stated:

        (b.)   partial, that is to say, an acceptance to pay part only of the amount for which the bill is drawn:

        (c.)   local, that is to say, an acceptance to pay only at a particular specified place:

An acceptance to pay at a particular place is a general acceptance, unless it expressly states that the bill is to be paid there only and not elsewhere:

        (d.)   qualified as to time:

        (e.)   the acceptance of some one or more of the drawees, but not of all.

20. (1.) Where a simple signature on a blank stamped paper is delivered by the signer in order that it may be converted into a bill, it operates as a prima facie authority to fill it up as a complete bill for any amount the stamp will cover, using the signature for that of the drawer, or the acceptor, or an indorser; and, in like manner, when a bill is wanting in any material particular, the person in possession of it has a prima facie authority to fill up the omission in any way he thinks fit.

(2.) In order that any such instrument when completed may be enforceable against any person who became a party thereto prior to its completion, it must be filled up within a reasonable time, and strictly in accordance with the authority given. Reasonable time for this purpose is a question of fact.

Provided that if any such instrument, after completion is negotiated, to a holder in due course it shall be valid and effectual for all purposes in his hands, and he may enforce it as if it had been filled up within a reasonable time and strictly in accordance with the authority given.

21. (1.) Every contract on a bill, whether it be the drawer's, the acceptor's, or an indorser's, is incomplete and revocable, until delivery of the instrument in order to give effect thereto.

Provided that where acceptance is written on a bill, and the drawee gives notice to or according to the directions of the person entitled to the bill that he has accepted it, the acceptance then becomes complete and irrevocable.

(2.) As between immediate parties, and as regards a remote party other than a holder in due course, the delivery-
(a.) in order to be effectual must be made either by or under the authority of the party drawing, accepting, or indorsing, as the case may be:
(b.) may be shown to have been conditional or for a special purpose only, and not for the purpose of transferring the property in the bill.

But if the bill be in the hands of a holder in due course a valid delivery of the bill by all parties prior to him so as to make them liable to him is conclusively presumed.

(3.) Where a bill is no longer in the possession of a party who has signed it as drawer, acceptor, or indorser, a valid and unconditional delivery by him is presumed until the contrary is proved.

Capacity and Authority of Parties.

22.   (1.)   Capacity to incur liability as a party to a bill is co-extensive with capacity to contract.

Provided that nothing in this section shall enable a corporation to make itself liable as drawer, acceptor, or indorser of a bill unless it is competent to it so to do under the law for the time being in force relating to corporations.

(2.)   Where a bill is drawn or indorsed by an infant, minor, or corporation having no capacity or power to incur liability on a bill, the drawing or indorsement entitles the holder to receive payment of the bill, and to enforce it against any other party thereto.

23.   No person is liable as drawer, indorser, or acceptor of a bill who has not signed it as such: Provided that

(1.)   Where a person signs a bill in a trade or assumed name, he is liable thereon as if he had signed it in his own name:

(2.)   The signature of the name of a firm is equivalent to the signature by the person so signing of the names of all persons liable as partners in that firm.

24.   Subject to the provisions of this Act, where a signature on a bill is forged or placed thereon without the authority of the person whose signature it purports to be, the forged or unauthorised signature is wholly inoperative, and no right to retain the bill or to give a discharge therefor or to enforce payment thereof against any party thereto can be acquired through or under that signature, unless the party against whom it is sought to retain or enforce payment of the bill is precluded from setting up the forgery or want of authority.

Provided that nothing in this section shall affect the ratification of an unauthorised signature not amounting to a forgery.

25.   A signature by procuration operates as notice that the agent has but a limited authority to sign, and the principal is only bound by such signature if the agent in so signing was acting within the actual limits of his authority.

26.   (1.)   Where a person signs a bill as drawer, indorser, or acceptor, and adds words to his signature, indicating that he signs or in representative for or on behalf of a principal, or in a representative character, he is not personally liable thereon; but the mere addition to his signature of words describing him as an agent, or as filling a representative character, does not exempt him from personal liability.

216

(2.) In determining whether a signature on a bill is that of the principal or that of the agent by whose hand it is written, the construction most favourable to the validity of the instrument shall be adopted.

The Consideration for a Bill.

27. (1.) Valuable consideration for a bill may be constituted by,-

    (a.) Any consideration sufficient to support a simple contract;

    (b.) An antecedent debt or liability. Such a debt or liability is deemed valuable consideration whether the bill is payable on demand or at a future time.

(2.) Where value has at any time been given for a bill the holder is deemed to be a holder for value as regards the acceptor and all parties to the bill who became parties prior to such time.

(3.) Where the holder of a bill has a lien on it, arising either from contract or by implication of law, he is deemed to be a holder for value to the extent of the sum for which he has a lien.

28. (1.) An accommodation party to a bill is a person who has signed a bill as drawer, acceptor, or indorser, without receiving value therefor, and for the purpose of lending his name to some other person.

(2.) An accommodation party is liable on the bill to a holder for value; and it is immaterial whether, when such holder took the bill, he knew such party to be an accommodation party or not.

29. (1.) A holder in due course is a holder who has taken a bill, complete and regular on the face of it, under the following conditions; namely,

    (a.) That he became the holder of it before it was overdue, and without notice that it had been previously dishonoured, if such was the fact:

    (b.) That he took the bill in good faith and for value, and that at the time the bill was negotiated to him he had no notice of any defect in the title of the person, who negotiated it.

(2.) In particular the title of a person who negotiates a bill is defective within the meaning of this Act when he obtained the bill, or the acceptance thereof, by fraud, duress, or force and fear, or other unlawful means, or for an illegal consideration, or when he negotiates it in breach of faith, or under such circumstances as amount to a fraud.

(3.) A holder (whether for value or not), who derives his title to a bill through a holder in due course, and who is not himself a party to any fraud or illegality affecting it, has all the rights of that holder in due course as regards the acceptor and all parties to the bill prior to that holder.

217

30. (1.) Every party whose signature appears on a bill is prima facie deemed to have become a party thereto for value.

(2.) Every holder of a bill is prima facie deemed to be a holder in due course; but if in an action on a bill it is admitted or proved that the acceptance, issue, or subsequent negotiation of the bill is affected with fraud, duress, or force and fear, or illegality, the burden of proof is shifted, unless and until the holder proves that, subsequent to the alleged fraud or illegality, value has in good faith been given for the bill.

Negotiation of Bills.

31. (1.) A bill is negotiated when it is transferred from one person to another in such a manner as to constitute the transferee the holder of the bill.

(2.) A bill payable to bearer is negotiated by delivery.

(3.) A bill payable to order is negotiated by the indorsement of the holder completed by delivery.

(4.) Where the holder of a bill payable to his order transfers it for value without indorsing it, the transfer gives the transferee such title as the transferor had in the bill, and the transferee in addition acquires the right to have the indorsement of the transferor.

(5.) Where any person is under obligation to indorse a bill in a representative capacity, he may indorse the bill in such terms as to negative personal liability.

32. An indorsement in order to operate as a negotiation must comply with the following conditions, namely:-

(1.) It must be written on the bill itself and be signed by the indorser. The simple signature of the indorser on the bill, without additional words, is sufficient.

An indorsement written on an allonge, or on a " copy " of a bill issued or negotiated in a country where " copies " are recognised, is deemed to be written on the bill itself.

(2.) It must be an indorsement of the entire bill. A partial endorsement, that is to say, an indorsement which purports to transfer to the indorsee a part only of the amount payable, or which purports to transfer the bill to two or more indorsees severally, does not operate as a negotiation of the bill.

(3.) Where a bill is payable to the order of two or more payees or indorsees who are not partners all must indorse, unless the one indorsing has authority to indorse for the others.

(4.) Where, in a bill payable to order, the payee or indorsee is wrongly designated, or his name is mis-spelt, he may indorse the bill as therein described, adding, if he think fit, his proper signature.

(5.) Where there are two or more indorsements on a bill, each indorsement is deemed to have been made in the order in which it appears on the bill, until the contrary is proved.

(6.) An indorsement may be made in blank or special. It may also contain terms making it restrictive.

33. Where a bill purports to be indorsed conditionally the condition may be disregarded by the payer, and payment to the indorsee is valid whether the condition has been fulfilled or not.

34. (1.) An indorsement in blank specifies no indorsee, and a bill so indorsed becomes payable to bearer.

(2.) A special indorsement specifies the person to whom, or to whose order, the bill is to be payable.

(3.) The provisions of this Act relating to a payee apply with the necessary modifications to an indorsee under a special indorsement.

(4.) When a bill has been indorsed in blank, any holder may convert the blank indorsement into a special indorsement by writing above the indorser's signature a direction to pay the bill to or to the order of himself or some other person.

35. (1.) An indorsement is restrictive which prohibits the further negotiation of the bill or which expresses that it is a mere authority to deal with the bill as thereby directed and not a transfer of the ownership thereof, as, for example, if a bill be indorsed " Pay D. only," or " Pay D. for the account of X.," or " Pay D. or order for collection."

(2.) A restrictive indorsement gives the indorsee the right to receive payment of the bill and to sue any party thereto that his indorser could have sued but gives him no power to transfer his rights as indorsee unless it expressly authorise him to do so.

(3.) Where a restrictive indorsement authorises further transfer, all subsequent indorsees take the bill with the same rights and subject to the same liabilities as the first indorsee under the restrictive indorsement.

36. (1.) Where a bill is negotiable in its origin it continues to be negotiable until it has been (a) restrictively indorsed or (b) discharged by payment or otherwise.

(2.) Where an overdue bill is negotiated, it can only be negotiated subject to any defect of title affecting it at its maturity, and thenceforward no person who takes it can acquire or give a better title than that which the person from whom he took it had.

(3.) A bill payable on demand is deemed to be overdue within the meaning and for the purposes of this section when it appears on the face of it to have been in circulation for an unreasonable length of time. What is an unreasonable length of time for this purpose is a question of fact.

(4.) Except where an endorsement bears date after the maturity of the bill, every negotiation is prima facie deemed to have been effected before the bill was overdue.

(5.) Where a bill which is not overdue has been dishonoured any person, who takes it with notice of the dishonour takes it subject to any defect of title attaching thereto at the time of dishonour, but nothing in this sub-section shall affect the rights of a holder in due course.

37. Where a bill is negotiated back to the drawer, or to a prior indorser or to the acceptor, such party may, subject to the provisions of this Act, re-issue and further negotiate the bill, but he is not entitled to enforce payment of the bill against any intervening party to whom he was previously liable.

38. The rights and powers of the holder of a bill are as follows:

(1.) He may sue on the bill in his own name:

(2.) Where he is a holder in due course, he holds the bill free from any defect of title of prior parties, as well as from mere personal defences available to prior parties among themselves, and may enforce payment against all parties liable on the bill:

(3.) Where his title is defective (a) if he negotiates the bill to a holder in due course, that holder obtains a good and complete title to the bill, and (b) if he obtains payment of the bill the person who pays him in due course gets a valid discharge for the bill.

General duties of the Holder.

39. (1.) Where a bill is payable after sight, presentment for acceptance is necessary in order to fix the maturity of the instrument.

(2.)   Where a bill expressly stipulates that it shall be presented for acceptance, or where a bill is drawn payable elsewhere than at the residence or place of business of the drawee it must be presented for acceptance before it can be presented for payment.

(3.)   In no other case is presentment for acceptance necessary in order to render liable any party to the bill.

(4.)   Where the holder of a bill, drawn payable elsewhere than at the place of business or residence of the drawee, has not time, with the exercise of reasonable diligence, to present the bill for acceptance before presenting it for payment on the day that it falls due, the delay caused by presenting the bill for acceptance before presenting it for payment is excused, and does not discharge the drawer and indorsers.

40.   (1.)   Subject to the provisions of this Act, when a bill payable after sight is negotiated, the holder must either present it for acceptance or negotiate it within a reasonable time.

        (2.)   If he do not do so, the drawer and all indorsers prior to that holder are discharged.

        (3.)   In determining what is a reasonable time within the meaning of this section, regard shall be had to the nature of the bill, the usage of trade with respect to similar bills, and the facts of the particular case.

41.   (1.)   A bill is duly presented for acceptance which is presented in accordance with the following rules:

        (a.)   The presentment must be made by or on behalf of the holder to the drawee or to some person authorised to accept or refuse acceptance on his behalf at a reasonable hour on a business day and before the bill is overdue:

        (b.)   Where a bill is addressed to two or more drawees, who are not partners, presentment must be made to them all, unless one has authority to accept for all, then presentment may be made to him only:

        (c.)   Where the drawee is dead, presentment may be made to his personal representative:

        (d.)   Where the drawee is bankrupt, presentment may be made to him or to his trustee:

        (e.)   Where authorised by agreement or usage, a presentment through the post office is sufficient.

        (2.)   Presentment in accordance with these rules is excused, and a bill may be treated as dishonoured by non-acceptance-

        (a.)   Where the drawee is dead or bankrupt, or is a fictitious person or a person not having capacity to contract by bill:

(b.) Where, after the exercise of reasonable diligence, such presentment cannot be effected:

(c.) Where although the presentment has been irregular, acceptance has been refused on some other ground.

(3.) The fact that the holder has reason to believe that the bill, on presentment, will be dishonoured does not excuse presentment.

2. (1.) When a bill is duly presented for acceptance and is not accepted within the customary time, the person presenting it must treat it as dishonoured by non-acceptance. If he do not, the holder shall lose his right of recourse against the drawer and indorsers.

43. (1.) A bill is dishonoured by non-acceptance-

(a.) when it is duly presented for acceptance, and such an acceptance as is prescribed by this Act is refused or cannot be obtained; or

(b.) when presentment for acceptance is excused and the bill is not accepted.

(2.) Subject to the provisions of this Act when a bill is dishonoured by non-acceptance, an immediate right of recourse against the drawer and indorsers accrues to the holder, and no presentment for payment is necessary.

44. (1.) The holder of a bill may refuse to take a qualified acceptance, and if he does not obtain an unqualified acceptance may treat the bill as dishonoured by non-acceptance.

(2.) Where a qualified acceptance is taken, and the drawer or an indorser has not expressly or impliedly authorised the holder to take a qualified acceptance, or does not subsequently assent thereto, such drawer or indorser is discharged from his liability on the bill.

The provisions of this sub-section do not apply to a partial acceptance, whereof due notice has been given. Where a foreign bill has been accepted as to part, it must be protested as to the balance.

(3.) When the drawer or indorser of a bill receives notice of a qualified acceptance and does not within a reasonable time express his dissent to the holder he shall be deemed to have assented thereto.

45. Subject to the provisions of this Act a bill must be duly presented for payment. If it be not so presented the drawer and indorsers shall be discharged.

A bill is duly presented for payment which is presented in accordance with the following rules:-

(1.) Where the bill is not payable on demand, presentment must be made on the day it falls due.

(2.) Where the bill is payable on demand, then, subject to the provisions of this Act, presentment must be made within a reasonable time after its issue in order to render the drawer liable, and within a reasonable time after its indorsement, in order to render the indorser liable.

In determining what is a reasonable time, regard shall be had to the nature of the bill, the usage of trade with regard to similar bills, and the facts of the particular case.

(3.) Presentment must be made by the holder or by some person authorised to receive payment on his behalf at a reasonable hour on a business day, at the proper place as herein-after defined, either to the person designated by the bill as payer, or to some person authorised to pay or refuse payment on his behalf if with the exercise of reasonable diligence such person can there be found.

(4.) A bill is presented at the proper place:-
(a.) Where a place of payment is specified in the bill and the bill is there presented.
(b.) Where no place of payment is specified, but the address of the drawee or acceptor is given in the bill, and the bill is there presented.
(c.) Where no place of payment is specified and no address given, and the bill is presented at the drawee's or acceptor's place of business if known, and if not, at his ordinary residence if known.
(d.) In any other case if presented to the drawee or acceptor wherever he can be found, or if presented at his last known place of business or residence.

(5.) Where a bill is presented at the proper place, and after the exercise of reasonable diligence no person authorised to pay or refuse payment can be found there, no further presentment to the drawee or acceptor is required.

(6.) Where a bill is drawn upon, or accepted by two or more persons who are not partners, and no place of payment is specified, presentment must be made to them all.

(7.) Where the drawee or acceptor of a bill is dead, and no place of payment is specified, presentment must be made to a personal representative, if such there be, and with the exercise of reasonable diligence he can be found.

(8.)   Where authorised by agreement or usage a presentment through the post office is sufficient.

46.   (1.)   Delay in making presentment for payment is excused when the delay is caused by circumstances beyond the control of the holder, and not imputable to his default, misconduct, or negligence. When the cause of delay ceases to operate presentment must be made with reasonable diligence.

    (2.)   Presentment for payment is dispensed with, -
        (a.)   Where, after the exercise of reasonable diligence presentment, as required by this Act, cannot be effected.
                The fact that the holder has reason to believe that the bill will, on presentment, be dishonoured, does not dispense with the necessity for presentment.
        (b.)   Where the drawee is a fictitious person.
        (c.)   As regards the drawer where the drawee or acceptor is not bound, as between himself and the drawer, to accept or pay the bill, and the drawer has no reason to believe that the bill would be paid if presented.
        (d.)   As regards an indorser, where the bill was accepted or made for the accommodation of that indorser, and he has no reason to expect that the bill would be paid if presented.
        (e.)   By waiver of presentment, express or implied.

47.   (1.)   A bill is dishonoured by non-payment (a) when it is duly presented for payment and payment is refused or cannot be obtained, or (b) when presentment is excused and the bill is overdue and unpaid.

    (2.)   Subject to the provisions of this Act, when a bill is dishonoured by non-payment, an immediate right of recourse against the drawer and indorsers accrues to the holder.

48.   Subject to the provisions of this Act, when a bill has been dishonoured by non-acceptance or by non-payment, notice of dishonour must be given to the drawer and each indorser, and any drawer or indorser to whom such notice is not given is discharged;

Provided that-
(1.)   Where a bill is dishonoured by non-acceptance, and notice of dishonour is not given, the rights of a holder in due course subsequent to the omission, shall not be prejudiced by the omission.

(2.)   Where a bill is dishonoured by non-acceptance and due notice of dishonour is given, it shall not be necessary to give notice of a

224

subsequent dishonour by non-payment unless the bill shall in the meantime have been accepted.

49.   Notice of dishonour in order to be valid and effectual must be given in accordance with the following rules:-

(1.)   The notice must be given by or on behalf of the holder, or by or on behalf of an indorser who, at the time of giving it, is himself liable on the bill.

(2.)   Notice of dishonour may be given by an agent either in his own name, or in the name of any party entitled to give notice whether that party be his principal or not.

(3.)   Where the notice is given by or on behalf of the holder, it enures for the benefit of all subsequent holders and all prior indorsers who have a right of recourse against the party to whom it is given.

(4.)   Where notice is given by or on behalf of an indorser entitled to give notice as herein-before provided, it enures for the benefit of the holder and all indorsers subsequent to the party to whom notice is given.

(5.)   The notice may be given in writing or by personal communication and may be given in any terms which sufficiently identify the bill, and intimate that the bill has been dishonoured by non-acceptance or non-payment.

(6.)   The return of a dishonoured bill to the drawer or an indorser is, in point of form, deemed a sufficient notice of dishonour.

(7.)   A written notice need not be signed, and an insufficient written notice may be supplemented and validated by verbal communication. A mis-description of the bill shall not vitiate the notice unless the party to whom the notice is given is in fact misled thereby.

(8.)   Where notice of dishonour is required to be given to any person, it may be given either to the party himself, or to his agent in that behalf.

(9.)   Where the drawer or indorser is dead, and the party giving notice knows it, the notice must be given to a personal representative if such there be, and with the exercise of reasonable diligence he can be found.

(10.)   Where the drawer or indorser is bankrupt, notice may be given either to the party himself or to the trustee.

(11.) Where there are two or more drawers or indorsers who are not partners, notice must be given to each of them, unless one of them has authority to receive such notice for the others.

(12.) The notice may be given as soon as the bill is dishonoured and must be given within a reasonable time thereafter.

In the absence of special circumstances notice is not deemed to have been given within a reasonable time, unless-
(a.) where the person giving and the person to receive notice reside in the same place, the notice is given or sent off in time to reach the latter on the day after the dishonour of the bill.
(b.) where the person giving and the person to receive notice reside in different places, the notice is sent off on the day after the dishonour of the bill, if there be a post at a convenient hour on that day, and if there be no such post on that day then by the next post thereafter.

(13.) Where a bill when dishonoured is in the hands of an agent, he may either himself give notice to the parties liable on the bill, or he may give notice to his principal. If he gives notice to his principal, he must do so within the same time as if he were the holder, and the principal upon receipt of such notice has himself the same time for giving notice as if the agent had been an independent holder.

(14.) Where a party to a bill receives due notice of dishonour, he has after the receipt of such notice the same period of time for giving notice to antecedent parties that the holder has after the dishonour.

(15.) Where a notice of dishonour is duly addressed and posted, the sender is deemed to have given due notice of dishonour, notwithstanding any miscarriage by the post office.

50. (1.) Delay in giving notice of dishonour is excused where the delay is caused by circumstances beyond the control of the party giving notice, and not imputable to his default, misconduct, or negligence. When the cause of delay ceases to operate the notice must be given with reasonable diligence.

(2.) Notice of dishonour is dispensed with-
(a.) When, after the exercise of reasonable diligence, notice as required by this Act cannot be given to or does not reach the drawer or indorser sought to be charged:
(b.) By waiver express or implied. Notice of dishonour may be waived before the time of giving notice has arrived, or after the omission to give due notice:
(c.) As regards the drawer in the following cases, namely, (1) where drawer and drawee are the same person, (2) where the

drawee is a fictitious person or a person not having capacity to contract, (3) where the drawer is the person to whom the bill is presented for payment, (4) where the drawee or acceptor is as between himself and the drawer under no obligation to accept or pay the bill, (5) where the drawer has countermanded payment:

(d.) As regards the indorser in the following cases, namely, (1) where the drawee is a fictitious person or a person not having capacity to contract and the indorser was aware of the fact at the time he indorsed the bill, (2) where the indorser is the person to whom the bill is presented for payment, (3) where the bill was accepted or made for his accommodation.

51. (1.) Where an inland bill has been dishonoured it may, if the holder think fit, be noted for non-acceptance or non-payment, as the case may be; but it shall not be necessary to note or protest any such bill in order to preserve the recourse against the drawer or indorser.

(2.) Where a foreign bill, appearing on the face of it to be such, has been dishonoured by non-acceptance it must be duly protested for non-acceptance, and where such a bill, which has not been previously dishonoured by non-acceptance, is dishonoured by non-payment it must be duly protested for non-payment. If it be not so protested the drawer and indorsers are discharged. Where a bill does not appear on the face of it to be a foreign bill, protest thereof in case of dishonour is unnecessary.

(3.) A bill which has been protested for non-acceptance may be subsequently protested for non-payment.

(4.) Subject to the provisions of this Act, when a bill is noted or protested, it must be noted on the day of its dishonour. When a bill has been duly noted, the protest may be subsequently extended as of the date of the noting.

(5.) Where the acceptor of a bill becomes bankrupt or insolvent or suspends payment before it matures, the holder may cause the bill to be protested for better security against the drawer and indorsers.

(6.) A bill must be protested at the place where it is dishonoured:

Provided that-
(a.) When a bill is presented through the post office, and returned by post dishonoured, it may be protested at the place to which it is returned and on the day of its return if received during business hours, and if not received during business hours, then not later than the next business day:

227

(b.)   When a bill drawn payable at the place of business or residence of some person other than the drawee, has been dishonoured by non-acceptance, it must be protested for n-payment at the place where it is expressed to be payable, and no further presentment for payment to, or demand on, the drawee is necessary.

(7.)   A protest must contain a copy of the bill, and must be signed by the notary making it, and must specify-
(a.)   The person at whose request the bill is protested:
(b.)   The place and date of protest, the cause or reason for protesting the bill, the demand made, and the answer given, if any, or the fact that the drawee or acceptor could not be found.

(8.)   Where a bill is lost or destroyed, or is wrongly detained from the person entitled to hold it, protest may be made on a copy or written particulars thereof.

(9.)   Protest is dispensed with by any circumstance which would dispense with notice of dishonour. Delay in noting or protesting is excused when the delay is caused by circumstances beyond the control of the holder, and not imputable to his default, misconduct, or negligence. When the cause of delay ceases to operate the bill must be noted or protested with reasonable diligence.

52.   (1.)   When a bill is accepted generally presentment for payment is not necessary in order to render the acceptor liable.

(2.)   When by the terms of a qualified acceptance presentment for payment is required, the acceptor, in the absence of an express stipulation to that effect, is not discharged by the omission to present the bill for payment on the day that it matures.

(3.)   In order to render the acceptor of a bill liable it is not necessary to protest it, or that notice of dishonour should be given to him.

(4.)   Where the holder of a bill presents it for payment, he shall exhibit the bill to the person from whom he demands payment, and when a bill is paid the holder shall forthwith deliver it up to the party paying it.

Liabilities of Parties.

53.   (1.)   A bill, of itself, does not operate as an assignment of funds in the hands of the drawee available for the payment thereof, and the drawee of a bill who does not accept as required by this Act is not liable on the instrument. This sub-section shall not extend to Scotland.

(2.)   In Scotland, where the drawee of a bill has in his hands funds available for the payment thereof, the bill operates as an assignment of the sum for which it is drawn in favour of the holder, from the time when the bill is presented to the drawee.

54.   The acceptor of a bill, by accepting it—

(1.)   Engages that he will pay it according to the tenor of his acceptance:

(2.)   Is precluded from denying to a holder in due course:

    (a.)   The existence of the drawer, the genuineness of his signature, and his capacity and authority to draw the bill;

    (b.)   In the case of a bill payable to drawer's order, the then capacity of the drawer to indorse, but not the genuineness or validity of his indorsement;

    (c.)   In the case of a bill payable to the order of a third person, the existence of the payee and his then capacity to indorse, but not the genuineness or validity of his endorsement.

55.   (1.)   The drawer of a bill by drawing it—

    (a.)   Engages that on due presentment it shall be accepted and paid according to its tenor, and that if it be dishonoured he will compensate the holder or any indorser who is compelled to pay it, provided that the requisite proceedings on dishonour be duly taken;

    (b.)   Is precluded from denying to a holder in due course the existence of the payee and his then capacity to indorse.

(2.)   The indorser of a bill by indorsing it-

    (a.)   Engages that on due presentment it shall be accepted and paid according to its tenor, and that if it be dishonoured he will compensate the holder or a subsequent endorser who is compelled to pay it, provided that the requisite proceedings on dishonour be duly taken;

    (b.)   Is precluded from denying to a holder in due course the genuineness and regularity in all respects of the drawer's signature and all previous indorsements;

    (c.)   Is precluded from denying to his immediate or a subsequent indorsee that the bill was at the time of his indorsement a valid and subsisting bill, and that he had then a good title thereto.

56.   Where a person signs a bill otherwise than as drawer or acceptor, he thereby incurs the liabilities of an indorser to a holder as in due course.

57.   Where a bill is dishonoured, the measure of damages, which shall be deemed to be liquidated damages, shall be as, follows:

(1.)   The holder may recover from any party liable on the bill, and the drawer who has been compelled to pay the bill may recover from

the acceptor, and an indorser who has been compelled to pay the bill may recover from the acceptor or from the drawer or from a prior indorser-

(a.)   The amount of the bill:

(b.)   Interest thereon from the time of presentment for payment if the bill is payable on demand, and from the maturity of the bill in any other case:

(c.)   The expenses of noting, or, when protest is necessary, and the protest has been extended, the expenses of protest.

(2.)   In the case of a bill which has been dishonoured abroad, in lieu of the above damages, the holder may recover from the drawer or an indorser, and the drawer or an indorser who has been compelled to pay the bill may recover from any party liable to him, the amount of the re-exchange with interest thereon until the time of payment.

(3.)   Where by this Act interest may be recovered as damages, such interest may, if justice require it, be withheld wholly or in part, and where a bill is expressed to be payable with interest at a given rate, interest as damages may or may not be given at the same rate as interest proper.

58.   (1.)   Where the holder of a bill payable to bearer negotiates it by delivery without indorsing it, he is called a "transferor by delivery".

(2.)   A transferor by delivery is not liable on the instrument.

(3.)   A transferor by delivery who negotiates a bill thereby warrants to his immediate transferee being a holder for value that the bill is what it purports to be, that he has a right to transfer it, and that at the time of transfer he is not aware of any fact which renders it valueless.

59.   (1.)   A bill is discharged by payment in due course by or on behalf of the drawee or acceptor.

"Payment in due course" means payment made at or after the maturity of the bill to the holder thereof in good faith and without notice that his title to the bill is defective.

(2.)   Subject to the provisions herein-after contained, when a bill is paid by the drawer or an indorser it is not discharged; but

(a.)   Where a bill payable to, or to the order of, a third party is paid by the drawer, the drawer may enforce payment thereof against the acceptor, but may not re-issue the bill.

(b.)   Where a bill is paid by an indorser, or where a bill payable to drawer's order is paid by the drawer, the party paying it is remitted to his former rights as regards the acceptor or antecedent parties, and he may, if he thinks fit, strike out his own and subsequent indorsements, and again negotiate the bill.

(3.) Where an accommodation bill is paid in due course by the party accommodated the bill is discharged.

60. When a bill payable to order on demand is drawn on a banker, and the banker on whom it is drawn pays the bill in good faith and in the ordinary course of business, it is not incumbent on the banker to show that the indorsement of the payee or any subsequent indorsement was made by or under the authority of the person whose indorsement it purports to be, and the banker is deemed to have paid the bill in due course, although such indorsement has been forged or made without authority.

61. When the acceptor of a bill is or becomes the holder of it at or after its maturity, in his own right, the bill is discharged.

62. (1.) When the holder of a bill at or after its maturity absolutely and unconditionally renounces his rights against the acceptor the bill is discharged.

The renunciation must be in writing unless the bill is delivered up to the acceptor.

(2.) The liabilities of any party to a bill may in like manner be renounced by the holder before, at, or after its maturity; but nothing in this section shall affect the rights of a holder in due course without notice of the renunciation.

63. (1.) Where a bill is intentionally cancelled by the holder or his agent, and the cancellation is apparent thereon, the bill is discharged.

(2.) In like manner any party liable on a bill may be discharged by the intentional cancellation of his signature by the holder or his agent. In such case any indorser who would have had a right of recourse against the party whose signature is cancelled, is also discharged.

(3.) A cancellation made unintentionally, or under a mistake, or without the authority of the holder is inoperative; but where a bill or any signature thereon appears to have been cancelled the burden of proof lies on the party who alleges that the cancellation was made unintentionally, or under a mistake, or without authority.

64. (1.) Where a bill or acceptance is materially altered without the assent of all parties liable on the bill, the bill is avoided except as against a party who has himself made, authorised, or assented to the alteration, and subsequent indorsers.

Provided that,

Where a bill has been materially altered, but the alteration is not apparent, and the bill is in the hands of a holder in due course, such holder may avail himself of the bill as if it had not been altered and may enforce payment of it according to its original tenour.

(2.) In particular the following alterations are material, namely, any alteration of the date, the sum payable, the time of payment, the place of payment, and, where a bill has been accepted generally, the addition of a place of payment without the acceptor's assent.

Acceptance and Payment for Honour.

65. (1.) Where a bill of exchange has been protested for dishonour by non-acceptance, or protested for better security, and is, not overdue, any person, not being a party already liable thereon, may, with the consent of the holder, intervene and accept the bill supra protest, for the honour of any party liable thereon, or for the honour of the person for whose account the bill is drawn.

(2.) A bill may be accepted for honour for part only of the sum for which it is drawn.

(3.) An acceptance for honour supra protest in order to be valid must-
(a.) be written on the bill, and indicate that it is an acceptance for honour:
(b.) be signed by the acceptor for honour:

(4.) Where an acceptance for honour does not expressly state for whose honour it is made, it is deemed to be an acceptance for the honour of the drawer.

(5.) Where a bill payable after sight is accepted for honour, its maturity is calculated from the date of the noting for non-acceptance, and not from the date of the acceptance for honour.

66. (1.) The acceptor for honour of a bill by accepting it engages that he will, on due presentment, pay the bill according to the tenor of his acceptance, if it is not paid by the drawee, provided it has been duly presented for payment, and protested for non-payment, and that he receives notice of these facts.

(2.) The acceptor for honour is liable to the holder and to all parties to the bill subsequent to the party for whose honour he has accepted.

67. (1.) Where a dishonoured bill has been accepted for honour supra protest, or contains a reference in case of need, it must be protested for non-payment before it is presented for payment to the acceptor for honour, or referee in case of need.

(2.)   Where the address of the acceptor for honour is in the same place where the bill is protested for non-payment, the bill must be presented to him not later than the day following its maturity; and where the address of the acceptor for honour is in some place other than the place where it was protested for non-payment, the bill must be forwarded not later than the day following its maturity for presentment to him.

(3.)   Delay in presentment or non-presentment is excused by any circumstance, which would excuse delay in presentment for payment or non-presentment for payment.

(4.)   When a bill of exchange is dishonoured by the acceptor for honour it must be protested for non-payment by him.

68.   (1.)   Where a bill has been protested for non-payment, any person may intervene and pay it supra protest for the honour of any party liable thereon, or for the honour of the person for whose account the bill is drawn.

(2.)   Where two or more persons offer to pay a bill for the honour of different parties, the person whose payment will discharge most parties to the bill shall have the preference.

(3.)   Payment for honour supra protest, in order to operate as such and not as a mere voluntary payment, must be attested by a notarial act of honour which may be appended to the protest or form an extension of it.

(4.)   The notarial act of honour must be founded on a declaration made by the payer for honour, or his agent in that behalf, declaring his intention to pay the bill for honour, and for whose honour he pays.

(5.)   Where a bill has been paid for honour, all parties subsequent to the party for whose honour it is paid are discharged, but the payer for honour is subrogated for, and succeeds to both the rights and duties of, the holder as regards the party for whose honour he pays, and all parties liable to that party.

(6.)   The payer for honour on paying to the holder the amount of the bill and the notarial expenses incidental to its dishonour is entitled to receive both the bill itself and the protest. If the holder do not on demand deliver them up he shall be liable to the payer for honour in damages.

(7.)   Where the holder of a bill refuses to receive payment supra protest he shall lose his right of recourse against any party who would have been discharged by such payment.

Lost Instruments.

69.   Where a bill has been lost before it is overdue, the person who was the holder of it may apply to the drawer to give him another bill of the same tenor, giving security to the drawer if required to indemnify him against all persons whatever in case the bill alleged to have been lost shall be found again.

If the drawer on request as aforesaid refuses to give such duplicate bill, he may be compelled to do so.

70.   In any action or proceeding upon a bill, the court or a judge may order that the loss of the instrument shall not be set up, provided an indemnity be given to the satisfaction of the court or judge against the claims of any other person upon the instrument in question.

Bill in a Set.

71.   (1.)   Where a bill is drawn in a set, each part of the set being numbered, and containing a reference to the other parts, the whole of the parts constitute one bill.

     (2.)   Where, the holder of a set indorses two or more parts to different persons, he is liable on every such part, and every indorser subsequent to him is liable on the part he has himself indorsed as if the said parts were separate bills.

     (3.)   Where two or more parts of a set are negotiated to different holders in due course, the holder whose title first accrues is as between such holders deemed the true owner of the bill; but nothing in this sub-section shall affect the rights of a person who in due course accepts or pays the part first presented to him.

     (4.)   The acceptance may be written on any part, and it must be written on one part only.

If the drawee accepts more than one part, and such accepted parts get into the hands of different holders in due course, he is liable on every such part as if it were a separate bill.

     (5.)   When the acceptor of a bill drawn in a set pays it without requiring the part bearing his acceptance to be delivered up to him, and that part at maturity is outstanding in the hands of a holder in due course, he is liable to the holder thereof.

     (6.)   Subject to the preceding rules, where any one part of a bill drawn in a set is discharged by payment or otherwise, the whole bill is discharged.

Conflict of Laws.

72. Where a bill drawn in one country is negotiated, accepted, or payable in another, the rights, duties, and liabilities of the parties thereto are determined as follows:

(1.) The validity of a bill as regards requisites in form is determined by the law of the place of issue, and the validity as regards requisites in form of the supervening contracts, such as acceptance, or indorsement, or acceptance supra protest, is determined by the law of the place where such contract was made.

Provided that-
(a.) Where a bill is issued out of the United Kingdom it is not invalid by reason only that it is not stamped in accordance with the law of the place of issue:
(b.) Where a bill, issued out of the United Kingdom, conforms, as regards requisites in form, to the law of the United Kingdom, it may, for the purpose of enforcing payment thereof, be treated as valid as between all persons who negotiate, hold, or become parties to it in the United Kingdom.

(2.) Subject to the provisions of this Act, the interpretation of the drawing, indorsement, acceptance, or acceptance supra protest of a bill, is determined by the law of the place where such contract is made.

Provided that where an inland bill is indorsed in a foreign country the indorsement shall as regards the payer be interpreted according to the law of the United Kingdom.

(3.) The duties of the holder with respect to presentment for acceptance or payment and the necessity for or sufficiency of a protest or notice of dishonour, or otherwise, are determined by the law of the place where the act is done or the bill is dishonoured.

(4.) Where a bill is drawn out of but payable in the United Kingdom and the sum payable is not expressed in the currency of the United Kingdom, the amount shall, in the absence of some express stipulation, be calculated according to the rate of exchange for sight drafts at the place of payment on the day the bill is payable.

(5.) Where a bill is drawn in one country and is payable in another, the due date thereof is determined according to the law of the place where it is payable.

73. A cheque is a bill of exchange drawn on a banker payable on demand. Except as otherwise provided in this Part, the provisions of this Act applicable to a bill of exchange payable on demand apply to a cheque.

74. Subject to the provisions of this Act-

(1.) Where a cheque is not presented for payment within a reasonable time of its issue, and the drawer or the person on whose account it is drawn had the right at the time of such presentment as between him and the banker to have the cheque paid and suffers actual damage through the delay, he is discharged to the extent of such damage, that is to say, to the extent to which such drawer or person is a creditor of such banker to a larger amount than he would have been had such cheque been paid.

(2.) In determining what is a reasonable time regard shall be had to the nature of the instrument, the usage of trade and of bankers, and the facts of the particular case.

(3.) The holder of such cheque as to which such drawer or person is discharged shall be a creditor, in lieu of such drawer or person, of such banker to the extent of such discharge, and entitled to recover the amount from him.

75. The duty and authority of a banker to pay a cheque drawn on him by his customer are determined by-

(1.) Countermand of payment:

(2.) Notice of the customer's death.

Crossed Cheques.

76. (1.) Where a cheque bears across its face an addition of-

(a.) The words " and company " or any abbreviation thereof between two parallel transverse lines, either with or without the words " not negotiable "; or

(b.) Two parallel transverse lines simply, either with or without the words " not negotiable ";

that addition constitutes a crossing, and the cheque is crossed generally.

(2.) Where a cheque bears across its face an addition of the name of a banker, either with or without the words " not negotiable " that addition constitutes a crossing, and the cheque is crossed specially and to that banker.

77. (1.) A cheque may be crossed generally or specially by the drawer.

(2.) Where a cheque is uncrossed, the holder may cross it generally or specially.

(3.) Where a cheque is crossed generally the holder may cross it specially.

(4.) Where a cheque is crossed generally or specially, the holder may add the words " not negotiable ".

(5.) Where a cheque is crossed specially, the banker to whom it is crossed may again cross it specially to another banker for collection.

(6.) Where an uncrossed cheque, or a cheque crossed generally, is sent to a banker for collection, he may cross it specially to himself.

78. A crossing authorised by this Act is a material part of the cheque; it shall not be lawful for any person to obliterate or, except as authorised by this Act, to add to or alter the crossing.

79. (1.) Where a cheque is crossed specially to more than one banker except when crossed to an agent for collection being a banker, the banker on whom it is drawn shall refuse payment thereof.

(2.) Where the banker on whom a cheque is drawn which is so crossed nevertheless pays the same, or pays a cheque crossed generally otherwise than to a banker, or if crossed specially otherwise than to the banker to whom it is crossed, or his agent for collection being a banker, he is liable to the true owner of the cheque for any loss he may sustain owing to the cheque having been so paid.

Provided that where a cheque is presented for payment which does not at the time of presentment appear to be crossed, or to have had a crossing which has been obliterated, or to have been added to or altered otherwise than as authorised by this Act, the banker paying the cheque in good faith and without negligence shall not be responsible or incur any liability, nor shall the payment be questioned by reason of the cheque having being crossed, or of the crossing having been obliterated or having been added to or altered otherwise than as authorised by this Act, and of payment having been made otherwise than to a banker or to the banker to whom the cheque is or was crossed, or to his agent for collection being a banker, as the case may be.

80. Where the banker, on whom a crossed cheque is drawn, in good faith and without negligence pays it, if crossed generally, to a banker, and if crossed specially, to the banker to whom it is crossed, or his agent for collection being a banker, the banker paying the cheque, and, if the cheque has come

into the hands of the payee, the drawer, shall respectively be entitled to the same rights and be placed in the same position as if payment of the cheque had been made to the true owner thereof.

81.   Where a person takes a crossed cheque which bears on it the words " not negotiable " he shall not have and shall not be capable of giving a better title to the cheque than that which the person from whom he took it had.

82.   Where a banker in good faith and without negligence receives payment for a customer of a cheque crossed generally specially to himself, and the customer has no title or a defective title thereto, the banker shall not incur any liability to the true owner of the cheque by reason only of having received such payment.

PART IV.
PROMISSORY NOTES.

83.   (1.)   A promissory note is an unconditional promise in writing made by one person to another signed by the maker, engaging to pay, on demand or at a fixed or determinable future time, a sum certain in money, to, or to the order of, a specified person or to bearer.

          (2.)   An instrument in the form of a note payable to maker's order is not a note within the meaning of this section unless and until it is indorsed by the maker.

          (3.)   A note is not invalid by reason only that it contains also a pledge of collateral security with authority to sell or dispose thereof.

          (4.)   A note which is, or on the face of it purports to be, both made and payable within the British Islands is an inland note. Any other note is a foreign note.

84.   A promissory note is inchoate and incomplete until delivery thereof to the payee or bearer.

85.   (1.)   A promissory note may be made by two or more makers, and they may be liable thereon jointly, or jointly and severally according to its tenour.

          (2.)   Where a note runs " I promise to pay " and is signed by two or more persons it is deemed to be their joint and several note.

86.   (1.)   Where a note payable on demand has been indorsed, it must be presented for payment within a reasonable time of the indorsement. If it be not so presented the indorser is discharged.

          (2.)   In determining what is a reasonable time, regard shall be had to the nature of the instrument, the usage of trade, and the facts of the particular case.

(3.)   Where a note payable on demand is negotiated, it is not deemed to be overdue, for the purpose of affecting the holder with defects of title of which he had no notice, by reason that it appears that a reasonable time for presenting it for payment has elapsed since its issue.

87.   (1.)   Where a promissory note is in the body of it made payable at a particular place, it must be presented for payment at that place in order to render the maker liable. In any other case, presentment for payment is not necessary in order to render the maker liable.

          (2.)   Presentment for payment is necessary in order to render the indorser of a note liable.

          (3.)   Where a note is in the body of it made payable at a particular place, presentment at that place is necessary in order to render an indorser liable; but when a place of payment is indicated by way of memorandum only, presentment at that place is sufficient to render the indorser liable, but a presentment to the maker elsewhere, if sufficient in other respects, shall also suffice.

88.   The maker of a promissory note by making it-
          (1.)   Engages that he will pay it according to its tenour;
          (2.)   Is precluded from denying to a holder in due course the existence of the payee and his then capacity to indorse.

89.   (1.)   Subject to the provisions in this part and, except as by this section provided, the provisions of this Act relating to bills of exchange apply, with the necessary modifications, to promissory notes.

          (2.)   In applying those provisions the maker of a note shall be deemed to correspond with the acceptor of a bill, and the first indorser of a note shall be deemed to correspond with the drawer of an accepted bill payable to drawer's order.

          (3.)   The following provisions as to bills do not apply to notes;

               namely, provisions relating to-
               (a.)   Presentment for acceptance;
               (b.)   Acceptance;
               (c.)   Acceptance supra protest;
               (d.)   Bills in a set.

          (4.)   Where a foreign note is dishonoured, protest thereof is unnecessary.

PART V.
SUPPLEMENTARY.

90. A thing is deemed to be done in good faith, within the meaning of this Act, where it is in fact done honestly, whether it is done negligently or not.

91. (1.) Where, by this Act, any instrument or writing is required to be signed by any person, it is not necessary that he should sign it with his own hand, but it is sufficient if his signature is written thereon by some other person by or under his authority.

    (2.) In the case of a corporation, where, by this Act, any instrument or writing is required to be signed, it is sufficient if the instrument or writing be sealed with the corporate seal.

    But nothing in this section shall be construed as requiring the bill or note of a corporation to be under seal.

92. Where, by this Act, the time limited for doing any act or thing is less than three days, in reckoning time, non-business days are excluded.

" Non-business days " for the purposes of this Act mean-
(a.) Sunday, Good Friday, Christmas Day:
(b.) A bank holiday under the Bank Holidays Act, 1871, or Acts amending it:
(c.) A day appointed by Royal proclamation as a public fast or Thanksgiving Day.
Any other day is a business day.

93. For the purposes of this Act, where a bill or note is required to be protested within a specified time or before some further proceeding is taken, it is sufficient that the bill has been noted for protest before the expiration of the specified time or the taking of the proceeding; and the formal protest may be extended at any time thereafter as of the date of the noting.

94. Where a dishonoured bill or note is authorised or required to be protested, and the services of a notary cannot be obtained at the place where the bill is dishonoured, any householder or substantial resident of the place may, in the presence of two witnesses, give a certificate, signed by them, attesting the dishonour of the bill, and the certificate shall in all respects operate as if it were a formal protest of the bill.

The form given in Schedule 1 to this Act may be used with necessary modifications, and if used shall be sufficient.

95. The provisions of this Act as to crossed cheques shall apply to a warrant for payment of dividend.

96.   The enactments mentioned in the second schedule to this Act are hereby repealed as from the commencement of this Act to the extent in that schedule mentioned.

Provided that such repeal shall not affect anything done or suffered, or any right, title, or interest acquired or accrued before the commencement of this Act, or any legal proceeding or remedy in respect of any such thing, right, title, or interest.

97.   (1.)   The rules in bankruptcy relating to bills of exchange, promissory notes, and cheques, shall continue to apply thereto notwithstanding anything in this Act contained.

(2.)   The rules of common law including the law merchant, save in so far as they are inconsistent with the express provisions of this Act, shall continue to apply to bills of exchange, promissory notes, and cheques.

(3.)   Nothing in this Act or in any repeal effected thereby shall affect-

(a.)   The provisions of the Stamp Act, 1870, or Acts amending it, or any law or enactment for the time being in force relating to the revenue:

(b.)   The provisions of the Companies Act, 1862, or Acts amending it, or any Act relating to joint stock banks or companies:

(c.)   The provisions of any Act relating to or confirming the privileges of the Bank of England or the Bank of Ireland respectively:

(d.)   The validity of any usage relating to dividend warrants, or the indorsements thereof.

98.   Nothing in this Act or in any repeal effected thereby shall extend or restrict, or in any way alter or affect the law and practice in Scotland in regard to summary diligence.

99.   Where any Act or document refers to any enactment repealed by this Act, the Act or document shall be construed, and shall operate, as if it referred to the corresponding provisions of this Act.

100.   In any judicial proceeding in Scotland, any fact relating to a bill of exchange, bank cheque, or promissory note, which is relevant to any question of liability thereon, may be proved by parole evidence: Provided that this enactment shall not in any way affect the existing law and practice whereby the party who is, according to the tenor of any bill of exchange, bank cheque, or promissory note, debtor to the holder in the

amount thereof, may be required, as a condition of obtaining a sist of diligence, or suspension of a charge, or threatened charge, to make such consignation, or to find such caution as the court or judge before whom the cause is depending may require.

This section shall not apply to any case where the bill of exchange, bank cheque, or promissory note has undergone the essential prescription.

SCHEDULES
FIRST SCHEDULE

Form of protest which may be used when the services of a notary cannot be obtained.

Know all men that I, *A.B.* [householder], of   in the county of

in the United Kingdom, at the request of *C.D.*, there being no notary public available, did on the
        Day of   188   at   demand   payment [*or* acceptance] of the bill of exchange hereunder written, from *E.F.,* to which demand he made answer [state answer, if any] wherefore I now, in the presence of *G.H.* and *J.K.* do protest the said bill of exchange.

             (Signed)   A.B.

                        G.H. (Witness)
                        J.K. (Witness)

NB.   The Bill itself should be annexed, or a copy of the bill and all that is written thereon should be underwritten.

SECOND SCHEDULE
ENACTMENTS REPEALED

Session and Chapter.	Title of Act and extent of Repeal
9 Will. 3. c. 17.	An Act for the better payment of Inland Bills of Exchange.
3 & 4 Anne, c. 8.	An Act for giving like remedy upon Promissory Notes as is now used upon Bills of Exchange, and for the better payment of Inland Bills of Exchange.
17 Geo. 3. c. 30.	An Act for further restraining the negotiation of promissory notes and inland bills of exchange under a limited sum within that part of Great Britain called England.
39 & 40 Geo. 3. c. 42.	An Act for the better observance of Good Friday in certain cases therein mentioned.
48 Geo. 3. c. 88.	An Act to restrain the Negotiation of Promissory Notes and Inland Bills of Exchange under a Limited sum in England.
1 & 2 Geo. 4. c. 78.	An Act to regulate Acceptances of Bills of Exchange.
7 & 8 Geo. 4. c. 15.	An Act for declaring the law in relation to Bills of Exchange and Promissory Notes becoming payable on Good Friday or Christmas Day.
9 Geo. 4. c. 24.	An Act to repeal certain Acts, and to consolidate and amend the laws relating to bills of exchange and promissory notes in Ireland. in part; that is to say, Section two, four, seven, eight, nine, ten, eleven.
2 & 3 Will. 4. c. 98.	An Act for regulating the protesting for non-payment of Bills of Exchange drawn payable at a place not being the place of the residence of the drawee or drawees of the same.

6 & 7 Will. 4. c. 58.	An Act for declaring the law as to the day on which it is requisite to present for payment to Acceptor, or Acceptors supra protest for honour, or to the Referee or Referees, in case of need, Bills of Exchange which have been dishonoured.
8 & 9 Vict. c. 37. in part.	An Act to regulate the issue of bank notes in Ireland, and to regulate the repayment of certain sums advanced by the Governor and Company of the Bank of Ireland for the public service, in part; that is to say, Section twenty-four.
19 & 20 Vict. c. 97. in part.	The Mercantile Law Amendment Act, 1856, in part; that is to say, Sections six and seven.
23 & 24 Vict. c. 111. in part.	An Act for granting to Her Majesty certain duties of stamps, and to amend the laws relating to the stamp duties, in part; that is to say, Section nineteen.
34 & 35 Vict. c. 74.	An Act to abolish days of grace in the case of bills of exchange and promissory notes payable at sight or on presentation.
39 & 40 Vict. c. 81.	The Crossed Cheques Act, 1876.
41 & 42 Vict. c. 13.	The Bills of Exchange Act, 1878.

ENACTMENT REPEALED AS TO SCOTLAND

19 & 20 Vict. c. 60. in part.	The Mercantile Law (Scotland) Amendment Act, 1856, in part; that is to say, Sections ten, eleven, twelve, thirteen, fourteen, fifteen, and sixteen.

Mental Capacity Act 2005
(Sections 1, 2, 3, 4, 9, 10, 11, 12, 13 &14)

SECTION 1

Persons who lack mental capacity

The principles
1. **The principles**
- (1)   The following principles apply for the purposes of this Act.
- (2)   A person must be assumed to have capacity unless it is established that he lacks capacity.
- (3)   A person is not to be treated as unable to make a decision unless all practicable steps to help him to do so have been taken without success.
- (4)   A person is not to be treated as unable to make a decision merely because he makes an unwise decision.
- (5)   An act done, or decision made, under this Act for or on behalf of a person who lacks capacity must be done, or made, in his best interests.
- (6)   Before the act is done, or the decision is made, regard must be had to whether the purpose for which it is needed can be as effectively achieved in a way that is less restrictive of the person's rights and freedom of action.

Preliminary
2. **People who lack capacity**
- (1)   For the purposes of this Act, a person lacks capacity in relation to a matter if at the material time he is unable to make a decision for himself in relation to the matter because of an impairment of, or a disturbance in the functioning of, the mind or brain.

- (2)   It does not matter whether the impairment or disturbance is permanent or temporary.

- (3)   A lack of capacity cannot be established merely by reference to—
  - (a)   a person's age or appearance, or
  - (b)   a condition of his, or an aspect of his behaviour, which might lead others to make unjustified assumptions about his capacity.

- (4)   In proceedings under this Act or any other enactment, any question whether a person lacks capacity within the meaning of this Act must be decided on the balance of probabilities.

- (5)   No power which a person ("D") may exercise under this Act—
  - (a)   in relation to a person who lacks capacity, or

(b) where D reasonably thinks that a person lacks capacity, is exercisable in relation to a person under 16.

(6) Subsection (5) is subject to section 18(3).

3. Inability to make decisions

(1) For the purposes of section 2, a person is unable to make a decision for himself if he is unable—

(a) to understand the information relevant to the decision,

(b) to retain that information,

(c) to use or weigh that information as part of the process of making the decision, or

(d) to communicate his decision (whether by talking, using sign language or any other means).

(2) A person is not to be regarded as unable to understand the information relevant to a decision if he is able to understand an explanation of it given to him in a way that is appropriate to his circumstances (using simple language, visual aids or any other means).

(3) The fact that a person is able to retain the information relevant to a decision for a short period only does not prevent him from being regarded as able to make the decision.

(4) The information relevant to a decision includes information about the reasonably foreseeable consequences of—

(a) deciding one way or another, or

(b) failing to make the decision.

4. Best interests

(1) In determining for the purposes of this Act what is in a person's best interests, the person making the determination must not make it merely on the basis of—

(a) the person's age or appearance, or

(b) a condition of his, or an aspect of his behaviour, which might lead others to make unjustified assumptions about what might be in his best interests.

(2) The person making the determination must consider all the relevant circumstances and, in particular, take the following steps.

(3) He must consider—

(a) whether it is likely that the person will at some time have capacity in relation to the matter in question, and

(b) if it appears likely that he will when that is likely to be.

(4) He must, so far as reasonably practicable, permit and encourage the person to participate, or to improve his ability to participate, as

fully as possible in any act done for him and any decision affecting him.

(5) Where the determination relates to life-sustaining treatment he must not, in considering whether the treatment is in the best interests of the person concerned, be motivated by a desire to bring about his death.

(6) He must consider, so far as is reasonably ascertainable—
  (a) the person's past and present wishes and feelings (and, in particular, any relevant written statement made by him when he had capacity),
  (b) the beliefs and values that would be likely to influence his decision if he had capacity, and
  (c) the other factors that he would be likely to consider if he were able to do so.

(7) He must take into account, if it is practicable and appropriate to consult them, the views of—
  (a) anyone named by the person as someone to be consulted on the matter in question or on matters of that kind,
  (b) anyone engaged in caring for the person or interested in his welfare,
  (c) any donee of a lasting power of attorney granted by the person, and
  (d) any deputy appointed for the person by the court,

  as to what would be in the person's best interests and, in particular, as to the matters mentioned in subsection (6).

(8) The duties imposed by subsections (1) to (7) also apply in relation to the exercise of any powers which—
  (a) are exercisable under a lasting power of attorney, or
  (b) are exercisable by a person under this Act where he reasonably believes that another person lacks capacity.

(9) In the case of an act done, or a decision made, by a person other than the court, there is sufficient compliance with this section if (having complied with the requirements of subsections (1) to (7)) he reasonably believes that what he does or decides is in the best interests of the person concerned.

Lasting powers of attorney
9. Lasting powers of attorney
(1) A lasting power of attorney is a power of attorney under which the donor ("P") confers on the donee (or donees) authority to make decisions about all or any of the following—
  (a) P's personal welfare or specified matters concerning P's personal welfare, and

(b)   P's property and affairs or specified matters concerning P's property and affairs, and which includes authority to make such decisions in circumstances where P no longer has capacity.

(2)   A lasting power of attorney is not created unless—
(a)   section 10 is complied with,
(b)   an instrument conferring authority of the kind mentioned in subsection (1) is made and registered in accordance with Schedule 1, and
(c)   at the time when P executes the instrument, P has reached 18 and has capacity to execute it.

(3)   An instrument which—
(a)   purports to create a lasting power of attorney, but
(b)   does not comply with this section, section 10 or Schedule 1, confers no authority.

(4)   The authority conferred by a lasting power of attorney is subject to—
(a)   the provisions of this Act and, in particular, sections 1 (the principles) and 4 (best interests), and
(b)   any conditions or restrictions specified in the instrument.

10.   Appointment of donees
(1)   A donee of a lasting power of attorney must be—
(a)   an individual who has reached 18, or
(b)   if the power relates only to P's property and affairs, either such an individual or a trust corporation.

(2)   An individual who is bankrupt may not be appointed as donee of a lasting power of attorney in relation to P's property and affairs.

(3)   Subsections (4) to (7) apply in relation to an instrument under which two or more persons are to act as donees of a lasting power of attorney.

(4)   The instrument may appoint them to act—
(a)   jointly,
(b)   jointly and severally, or
(c)   jointly in respect of some matters and jointly and severally in respect of others.

(5)   To the extent to which it does not specify whether they are to act jointly or jointly and severally, the instrument is to be assumed to appoint them to act jointly.

(6)   If they are to act jointly, a failure, as respects one of them, to

comply with the requirements of subsection (1) or (2) or Part 1 or 2 of Schedule 1 prevents a lasting power of attorney from being created.

(7)   If they are to act jointly and severally, a failure, as respects one of them, to comply with the requirements of subsection (1) or (2) or Part 1 or 2 of Schedule 1—

(a)   prevents the appointment taking effect in his case, but

(b)   does not prevent a lasting power of attorney from being created in the case of the other or others.

(8)   An instrument used to create a lasting power of attorney—

(a)   cannot give the donee (or, if more than one, any of them) power to appoint a substitute or successor, but

(b)   may itself appoint a person to replace the donee (or, if more than one, any of them) on the occurrence of an event mentioned in section 13(6)(a) to (d) which has the effect of terminating the donee's appointment.

11.   Lasting powers of attorney: restrictions

(1)   A lasting power of attorney does not authorise the donee (or, if more than one, any of them) to do an act that is intended to restrain P, unless three conditions are satisfied.

(2)   The first condition is that P lacks, or the donee reasonably believes that P lacks, capacity in relation to the matter in question.

(3)   The second is that the donee reasonably believes that it is necessary to do the act in order to prevent harm to P.

(4)   The third is that the act is a proportionate response to—

(a)   the likelihood of P's suffering harm, and

(b)   the seriousness of that harm.

(5)   For the purposes of this section, the donee restrains P if he—

(a)   uses, or threatens to use, force to secure the doing of an act which P resists, or

(b)   restricts P's liberty of movement, whether or not P resists, or if he authorises another person to do any of those things.

(6)   But the donee does more than merely restrain P if he deprives P of his liberty within the meaning of Article 5(1) of the Human Rights Convention.

(7)   Where a lasting power of attorney authorises the donee (or, if more than one, any of them) to make decisions about P's personal welfare, the authority—

(a)   does not extend to making such decisions in circumstances other than those where P lacks, or the donee reasonably believes that P lacks, capacity,

(b)   is subject to sections 24 to 26 (advance decisions to refuse treatment), and

(c)   extends to giving or refusing consent to the carrying out or continuation of a treatment by a person providing health care for P.

(8)   But subsection (7)(c)—
(a)   does not authorise the giving or refusing of consent to the carrying out or continuation of life-sustaining treatment, unless the instrument contains express provision to that effect, and
(b)   is subject to any conditions or restrictions in the instrument.

12.   Scope of lasting powers of attorney: gifts

(1)   Where a lasting power of attorney confers authority to make decisions about P's property and affairs, it does not authorise a donee (or, if more than one, any of them) to dispose of the donor's property by making gifts except to the extent permitted by subsection (2).

(2)   The donee may make gifts—
(a)   on customary occasions to persons (including himself) who are related to or connected with the donor, or
(b)   to any charity to whom the donor made or might have been expected to make gifts,
if the value of each such gift is not unreasonable having regard to all the circumstances and, in particular, the size of the donor's estate.

(3)   "Customary occasion" means—
(a)   the occasion or anniversary of a birth, a marriage or the formation of a civil partnership, or
(b)   any other occasion on which presents are customarily given within families or among friends or associates.

(4)   Subsection (2) is subject to any conditions or restrictions in the instrument

13.   Revocation of lasting powers of attorney etc.

(1)   This section applies if—
(a)   P has executed an instrument with a view to creating a lasting power of attorney, or
(b)   a lasting power of attorney is registered as having been conferred by P,
and in this section references to revoking the power include revoking the instrument.

(2)   P may, at any time when he has capacity to do so, revoke the power.

(3)   P's bankruptcy revokes the power so far as it relates to P's property and affairs.

(4)   But where P is bankrupt merely because an interim bankruptcy restrictions order has effect in respect of him, the power is suspended, so far as it relates to P's property and affairs, for so long as the order has effect.

(5)   The occurrence in relation to a donee of an event mentioned in subsection (6)—
(a)   terminates his appointment, and
(b)   except in the cases given in subsection (7), revokes the power.

(6)   The events are—
(a)   the disclaimer of the appointment by the donee in accordance with such requirements as may be prescribed for the purposes of this section in regulations made by the Lord Chancellor,
(b)   subject to subsections (8) and (9), the death or bankruptcy of the donee or, if the donee is a trust corporation, its winding-up or dissolution,
(c)   subject to subsection (11), the dissolution or annulment of a marriage or civil partnership between the donor and the donee,
(d)   the lack of capacity of the donee.

(7)   The cases are—
(a)   the donee is replaced under the terms of the instrument,
(b)   he is one of two or more persons appointed to act as donees jointly and severally in respect of any matter and, after the event, there is at least one remaining donee.

(8)   The bankruptcy of a donee does not terminate his appointment, or revoke the power, in so far as his authority relates to P's personal welfare.

(9)   Where the donee is bankrupt merely because an interim bankruptcy restrictions order has effect in respect of him, his appointment and the power are suspended, so far as they relate to P's property and affairs, for so long as the order has effect.

(10)   Where the donee is one of two or more appointed to act jointly and severally under the power in respect of any matter, the reference in subsection (9) to the suspension of the power is to its suspension in so far as it relates to that donee.

(11)   The dissolution or annulment of a marriage or civil partnership does not terminate the appointment of a donee, or revoke the power, if the instrument provided that it was not to do so.

14.   **Protection of donee and others if no power created or power revoked**

(1)   Subsections (2) and (3) apply if—

    (a)   an instrument has been registered under Schedule 1 as a lasting power of attorney, but

    (b)   a lasting power of attorney was not created, whether or not the registration has been cancelled at the time of the act or transaction in question.

(2)   A donee who acts in purported exercise of the power does not incur any liability (to P or any other person) because of the non-existence of the power unless at the time of acting he—

    (a)   knows that a lasting power of attorney was not created, or

    (b)   is aware of circumstances which, if a lasting power of attorney had been created, would have terminated his authority to act as a donee.

(3)   Any transaction between the donee and another person is, in favour of that person, as valid as if the power had been in existence, unless at the time of the transaction that person has knowledge of a matter referred to in subsection (2).

(4)   If the interest of a purchaser depends on whether a transaction between the donee and the other person was valid by virtue of subsection (3), it is conclusively presumed in favour of the purchaser that the transaction was valid if—

    (a)   the transaction was completed within 12 months of the date on which the instrument was registered, or

    (b)   the other person makes a statutory declaration, before or within 3 months after the completion of the purchase, that he had no reason at the time of the transaction to doubt that the donee had authority to dispose of the property which was the subject of the transaction.

(5)   In its application to a lasting power of attorney which relates to matters in addition to P's property and affairs, section 5 of the Powers of Attorney Act 1971 (c. 27) (protection where power is revoked) has effect as if references to revocation included the cessation of the power in relation to P's property and affairs.

(6)   Where two or more donees are appointed under a lasting power of attorney, this section applies as if references to the donee were to all or any of them.

Oaths Act 1978

An Act to consolidate the Oaths Act 1838 and the Oaths Acts 1888 to 1977, and to repeal, as obsolete, section 13 of the Circuit Courts (Scotland) Act 1828. [30th June 1978]

BE IT ENACTED by the Queen's most Excellent Majesty, by and with the advice and consent of the Lords Spiritual and Temporal, and Commons, in this present Parliament assembled, and by the authority of the same, as follows:-

PART I
ENGLAND, WALES AND NORTHERN IRELAND

1.- (1) Any oath may be administered and taken in England, Wales or Northern Ireland in the following form and manner:-

The person taking the oath shall hold the New Testament, or, in the case of a Jew, the Old Testament, in his uplifted hand, and shall say or repeat after the officer administering the oath the words " I swear by Almighty God that ...... ", followed by the words of the oath prescribed by law.

(2) The officer shall (unless the person about to take the oath voluntarily objects thereto or is physically incapable of so taking the oath) administer the oath in the form and manner aforesaid without question.

(3) In the case of a person who is neither a Christian nor a Jew, the oath shall be administered in any lawful manner.

(4) In this section "officer" means any person duly authorised to administer oaths.

2.- In the following provisions, namely-

(a) section 28(1) of the Children and Young Persons Act 1963; and

(b) section 56(1) of the Children and Young Persons Act (Northern Ireland) 1968

(each of which prescribes the form of oath for use in juvenile courts and by children and young persons in other courts) for the words " section 2 of the Oaths Act 1909 " there shall be substituted the words "section 1 of the Oaths Act 1978".

PART II
UNITED KINGDOM

Oaths

3.- If any person to whom an oath is administered desires to swear with uplifted hand, in the form and manner in which an oath is usually administered in Scotland, he shall be permitted so to do, and the oath shall be administered to him in such form and manner without further question.

4.- (1) In any case in which an oath may lawfully be and has been administered to any person, if it has been administered in a form and manner other than that prescribed by law, he is bound by it if it has been administered in such form and with such ceremonies as he may have declared to be binding.

(2) Where an oath has been duly administered and taken, the fact that the person to whom it was administered had, at the time of taking it, no religious belief, shall not for any purpose affect the validity of the oath.

Solemn affirmations

5.- (1) Any person who objects to being sworn shall be permitted to make his solemn affirmation instead of taking an oath.

(2) Subsection (1) above shall apply in relation to a person to whom it is not reasonably practicable without inconvenience or delay to administer an oath in the manner appropriate to his religious belief as it applies in relation to a person objecting to be sworn.

(3) A person who may be permitted under subsection (2) above to make his solemn affirmation may also be required to do so.

(4) A solemn affirmation shall be of the same force and effect as an oath.

6.- (1) Subject to subsection (2) below, every affirmation shall be as follows: -

" I   do solemnly, sincerely and truly declare and affirm,"

and then proceed with the words of the oath prescribed by law, omitting any words of imprecation or calling to witness.

(2) Every affirmation in writing shall commence: -

" I,   of , do solemnly and sincerely affirm,"
and the form in lieu of jurat shall be "Affirmed at this day of 19 , Before me."

Supplementary

7.- (1) The enactments specified in Part I of the Schedule to this Act (consequential repeals) and Part II of that Schedule (enactment obsolete since the Oaths Act 1888) are hereby repealed to the extent specified in the third column of that Schedule.

(2) In so far as anything done under an enactment repealed by this Act could have been done under a corresponding provision of this Act, it shall not be invalidated by the repeal but shall have effect as if done under that provision.

(3) Where any instrument or document refers, either expressly or by implication, to an enactment repealed by this Act, the reference shall, except where the context otherwise requires, be construed as, or as including, a reference to the corresponding provision of this Act.

(4) The court-martial enactments (which make provision in relation to the use of affirmations at courts-martial corresponding to that made by subsection (2) of section 1 of the Oaths Act 1961) shall not be affected by the repeal of subsection (3) of that section (by virtue of which each of them was inserted in the section in which it appears).

(5) In this Act "the court-martial enactments" means
section 102(2) of the Army Act 1955;
section 102(2) of the Air Force Act 1955;
section 60(6) of the Naval Discipline Act 1957.

(6) Nothing in this Act shall be taken as prejudicing the operation of section 38 of the Interpretation Act 1889 (which relates to the effect of repeals).

8.- (1) This Act may be cited as the Oaths Act 1978.

(2) Part I of this Act does not extend to Scotland.

(3) It is hereby declared that this Act extends to Northern Ireland.

(4) In their application to each of the court-martial enactments subsections (4) and (5) of section 7 above extend to any territory to which that enactment extends.

(5) This Act shall come into force on the expiration of the period of one month from the date on which it is passed.

Repeals

Part I
Consequential Repeals

Chapter	Short Title	Extent of Repeal
1 & 2 Vict. c. 105.	Oaths Act 1838.	The whole Act.
51 & 52 Vict. c. 46.	Oaths Act 1888.	The whole Act.
9 Edw. 7 c. 39.	Oaths Act 1909.	The whole Act.
9 & 10 Eliz. 2 c. 21.	Oaths Act 1961.	The whole Act.
1977 c. 38.	Administration of Justice Act 1977.	Section 8. Section 32(2)

Part II
Repeal of an Obsolete Enactment

Chapter	Short Title	Extent of Repeal
1 & 2 Vict. c. 105.	Oaths Act 1838.	The whole Act.
51 & 52 Vict. c. 46.	Oaths Act 1888.	The whole Act.
9 Edw. 7 c. 39.	Oaths Act 1909.	The whole Act.
9 & 10 Eliz. 2 c. 21.	Oaths Act 1961.	The whole Act.
1977 c. 38.	Administration of Justice Act 1977.	Section 8. Section 32(2)

Commissioner for Oaths Act 1889

An Act for amending and consolidating enactments relating to the administration of Oaths.

[31st May 1889.]

BE it enacted by the Queen's most Excellent Majesty, by and with the advice and consent of the Lords Spiritual and Temporal, and Commons, in this present Parliament assembled, and by the authority of the same, as follows:

1.   (1.)   The Lord Chancellor may from time to time, by commission signed by him, appoint persons being practising solicitors or other fit and proper persons to be commissioners for oaths, and may revoke any such appointment.

       (2.)   A commissioner for oaths may, by virtue of his commission, in England or elsewhere, administer any oath or take any affidavit for the purposes of any court or matter in England, including any of the ecclesiastical courts or jurisdictions, matters ecclesiastical, matters relating to applications for notarial faculties, and matters relating to the registration of any instrument, whether under an Act of Parliament or otherwise, and take any bail or recognizance in or for the purpose of any civil proceeding in the Supreme Court, including all proceedings on the revenue side of the Queen's Bench Division.

       (3.)   Provided that a commissioner for oaths shall not exercise any of the powers given by this section in any proceeding in which he is solicitor to any of the parties to the proceeding, or clerk to any such solicitor, or in which he is interested.

2.   Every person who, being an officer of or performing duties in relation to any court, is for the time being so authorised by a judge of the court, or by or in pursuance of any rules or orders regulating the procedure of the court, and every person directed to take an examination in any cause or matter in the Supreme Court, shall have authority to administer any oath or take any affidavit required for any purpose connected with his duties.

3.   (1.)   Any oath or affidavit required for the purpose of any court or matter in England, or for the purpose of the registration of any instrument in any part of the United Kingdom, may be taken or made in any place out of England before any person having authority to administer an oath in that place.

       (2.)   In the case of a person having such authority otherwise than by the law of a foreign country, judicial and official notice shall be taken of his seal or signature affixed, impressed, or subscribed to or on any such oath or affidavit.

4.   The Lord Chancellor may, whenever it appears to him necessary to do so, authorise any person to administer oaths and take oaths for affidavits for any purpose relating to prize proceedings in the Supreme Court, whilst that person is on the high seas or out of Her Majesty's dominions, and it shall not be necessary to affix any stamp to the document by which he is so authorised.

5.   Every commissioner before whom any oath or affidavit is taken or made under this Act shall state truly in the jurat or attestation at what place and on what date the oath or affidavit is taken or made.

6.   (1.)   Every British ambassador, envoy, minister, chargé d'affaires, and secretary of embassy or legation exercising his functions in any foreign country, and every British consul-general, consul, vice-consul, acting- consul, pro-consul, and consular agent exercising his functions in any foreign place may, in that country or place, administer any oath and take any affidavit, and also do any notarial act which any notary public can do within the United Kingdom; and every oath, affidavit, and notarial act administered, sworn, or done by or before any such person shall be as effectual as if duly administered, sworn, or done by or before any lawful authority in any part of the United Kingdom.

        (2.)   Any document purporting to have affixed, impressed, or subscribed thereon or thereto the seal and signature of any person authorised by this section to administer an oath in testimony of any oath, affidavit, or act being administered, taken, or done by or before him, shall be admitted in evidence without proof of the seal or signature being the seal or signature of that person, or of the official character of that person.

7.   Whoever wilfully and corruptly swears falsely in any oath or affidavit taken or made in accordance with the provisions of this Act, shall be guilty of perjury in every case where if he had so sworn in a judicial proceeding before a court of competent jurisdiction he would be guilty of perjury.

8.   Whoever forges, counterfeits, or fraudulently alters the seal or signature of any person authorised by or under this Act to administer an oath, or tenders in evidence, or otherwise uses, any affidavit having any seal or signature so forged or counterfeited or fraudulently altered, knowing the same to be forged, counterfeited, or fraudulently altered, shall be guilty of felony, and liable on conviction to penal servitude for any term not exceeding seven years and not less than five years, or to imprisonment with or without hard labour for any term not exceeding two years.

9.   Any offence under this Act, whether committed within or without Her Majesty's dominions, may be inquired of, dealt with, tried, and punished in any county or place in the United Kingdom in which the person charged with the offence was apprehended or is in custody, and for all purposes

incidental to or consequential on the trial or punishment the offence shall be deemed to have been committed in that county or place.

10.   Where any offence under this Act is alleged to have been committed with respect to any affidavit, a judge of any court before which the affidavit is produced may order the affidavit to be impounded and kept in such custody and for such time and on such conditions as he thinks fit.

11.   In this Act, unless the context otherwise requires,-
" Oath " includes affirmation and declaration

" Affidavit " includes affirmation, statutory or other declaration, acknowledgment, examination, and attestation or protestation of honour

" Swear " includes affirm, declare, and protest

" Supreme Court " means the Supreme Court of Judicature in England.

12.   The enactments specified in the schedule to this Act are hereby repealed to the extent specified in that schedule.

Provided that this repeal shall not affect-
(a.)   anything done or suffered under any enactment repealed by this Act; nor
(b.)   any appointment made under or authority given by or in pursuance of any enactment so repealed; nor
(c.)   any punishment incurred or to be incurred in respect of any offence committed before the commencement of this Act against any enactment so repealed; nor
(d.)   any legal proceeding for enforcing any such punishment;

and any such legal proceeding may be instituted or continued and any such punishment may be imposed as if this Act had not been passed.

13.   A commissioner authorised before the commencement of this Act to administer oaths in the Supreme Court shall be deemed to be a commissioner for oaths within the meaning of this Act.

14.   This Act shall commence and come into operation on the first day of January one thousand eight hundred and ninety.

15.   This Act may be cited as the Commissioners for Oaths Act, 1889.

SCHEDULE

A description or citation of a portion of an Act is inclusive of the words, sections, or other parts, first and last mentioned, or otherwise referred to as forming the beginning, or as forming the end respectively, of the portion comprised in the description or citation.

Session and Chapter.	Title of Act and extent of Repeal	Extent of Repeal.
16 & 17 Chas. 2. c. 9.	An Act to empower the Chancellor of the duchy to grant commissions for taking affidavits within the duchy liberty.	The whole Act.
17 Geo. 2. c. 7.	An Act for taking and swearing affidavits to be made use of in any of the courts of the county palatine of Lancaster.	The whole Act.
4 Geo. 3. c. 21.	An Act for taking and swearing affidavits to be made use of in any of the courts of the county palatine of Durham.	The whole Act.
6 Geo. 4. c. 87.	An Act to regulate the payment of salaries and allowances to British consuls at foreign ports, and the disbursements at such ports for certain public purposes.	Section twenty.
3 & 4 Will. 4. c. 42.	An Act for the further amendment of the law and the better advancement of justice.	Section forty-two.
4 & 5 Will. 4. c. 42.	An Act to facilitate the taking of affidavits and affirmations in the court of the Vice Warden of the Stannaries of Cornwall.	The whole Act.
2 & 3 Vict. c. 58.	An Act to make further provision for the administration of justice and for improving the	Section six from "and that any "commissioner".

	practice and proceedings in the courts of the Stannaries of Cornwall.	
5 & 6 Vict. c. 103.	An Act for abolishing certain offices of the High Court of Chancery in England.	Sections seven and eight.
6 & 7 Vict. c. 82.	An Act the title of which begins with the words "An Act for extending," and ends with the words "examination of witnesses."	Sections one to four.
11 & 12 Vict. c. 10.	An Act for empowering certain officers of the High Court of Chancery to administer oaths and take declarations and affirmations.	The whole Act.
15 & 16 Vict. c. 76.	The Common Law Procedure Act, 1852.	Section twenty-three.
15 & 16 Vict. c. 86.	An Act to amend the practice and course of proceeding in the High Court of Chancery.	Sections twenty-two, twenty-three, and twenty-four.
16 & 17 Vict. c. 70.	The Lunacy Regulation Act, 1853.	Section fifty-seven.
16 & 17 Vict. c. 78.	An Act relating to the appointment of persons to administer oaths in Chancery, and to affidavits made for purposes connected with registration.	The whole Act.
17 & 18 Vict. c. 78.	The Admiralty Court Act, 1854.	Section six from "and any examiner" to the end of the section. Sections seven to eleven.
18 & 19 Vict. c. 42.	An act to enable British diplomatic and consular agents abroad to	The whole Act.

	administer oaths and do notarial acts.	
18 & 19 Vict. c. 134.	An Act the title of which begins with the words "An Act to make "further provision," and ends with the words "leasing and "sale therefore".	Section fifteen.
20 & 21 Vict. c. 77.	An Act to amend the law relating to probates and letters of administration in England.	Section twenty-seven to "Provided that" and from "any person who" to end of section.
21 & 22 Vict. c. 95.	An Act to amend the Act of the twentieth and twenty-first Victoria, chapter seventy-seven.	Sections thirty to thirty-four.
21 & 22 Vict. c. 108.	An Act to amend the Act of the twentieth and twenty-first Victoria, chapter eighty-five.	Sections twenty to twenty-three.
22 Vict. c. 16.	An Act the title of which begins with the words "An Act to enable," and ends with the words "of the Exchequer."	The whole Act except section five.
28 & 29 Vict. c. 104.	The Crown Suits,&c. Act, 1865.	Sections eighteen, nineteen, forty-three, and forty-four.
32 & 33 Vict. c. 38.	The Bails Act, 1869	The whole Act.
40 & 41 Vict. c. 25.	The Solicitors Act, 1877	Section eighteen.

FORMALITIES OF DOING BUSINESS

Formalities of doing business under the law of England and Wales or Northern Ireland

4.   Sections 43 to 47 apply to LLPs, modified so that they read as follows—

"LLP contracts

43.— (1)   Under the law of England and Wales or Northern Ireland a contract may be made—
  (a)   by an LLP, by writing under its common seal, or
  (b)   on behalf of an LLP, by a person acting under its authority, express or implied.

(2)   This is without prejudice to section 6 of the Limited Liability Partnerships Act 2000 (c. 12) (members as agents).

(3)   Any formalities required by law in the case of a contract made by an individual also apply, unless a contrary intention appears, to a contract made by or on behalf of an LLP.

Execution of documents

44.— (1)   Under the law of England and Wales or Northern Ireland a document is executed by an LLP—
  (a)   by the affixing of its common seal, or
  (b)   by signature in accordance with the following provisions.

(2)   A document is validly executed by an LLP if it is signed on behalf of the LLP—
  (a)   by two members, or
  (b)   by a member of the LLP in the presence of a witness who attests the signature.

(3)   A document signed in accordance with subsection (2) and expressed, in whatever words, to be executed by the LLP has the same effect as if executed under the common seal of the LLP.

(4)   In favour of a purchaser a document is deemed to have been duly executed by an LLP if it purports to be signed in accordance with subsection (2).

A "purchaser" means a purchaser in good faith for valuable consideration and includes a lessee, mortgagee or other person who for valuable consideration acquires an interest in property.

(5)   Where a document is to be signed by a person on behalf of more than one LLP, or on behalf of an LLP and a company, it is not duly signed by that person for the purposes of this section unless he signs it separately in each capacity.

(6)   References in this section to a document being (or purporting to be) signed by a member are to be read, in a case where that member is a firm, as references to its being (or purporting to be) signed by an individual authorised by the firm to sign on its behalf.

(7)   This section applies to a document that is (or purports to be) executed by an LLP in the name of or on behalf of another person whether or not that person is also an LLP.

Common seal

45.— (1)   An LLP may have a common seal, but need not have one.

(2)   An LLP which has a common seal shall have its name engraved in legible characters on the seal.

(3)   If an LLP fails to comply with subsection (2) an offence is committed by—
(a)   the LLP, and
(b)   every member of the LLP who is in default.

(4)   A member of an LLP, or a person acting on behalf of an LLP, commits an offence if he uses, or authorises the use of, a seal purporting to be a seal of the LLP on which its name is not engraved as required by subsection (2).

(5)   A person guilty of an offence under this section is liable on summary conviction to a fine not exceeding level 3 on the standard scale.

(6)   This section does not form part of the law of Scotland.

Execution of deeds

46.— (1)   A document is validly executed by an LLP as a deed for the purposes of section 1(2)(b) of the Law of Property (Miscellaneous Provisions) Act 1989 (c. 34) and for the purposes of the law of Northern Ireland if, and only if—
(a)   it is duly executed by the LLP, and
(b)   it is delivered as a deed.

(2)   For the purposes of subsection (1)(b) a document is presumed to be delivered upon its being executed unless a contrary intention is proved.

Execution of deeds or other documents by attorney

47.— (1)   Under the law of England and Wales or Northern Ireland an LLP may, by instrument executed as a deed, empower a person, either generally or in respect of specified matters, as its attorney to execute deeds or other documents on its behalf.

(2)   A deed or other document so executed, whether in the United Kingdom or elsewhere, has effect as if executed by the LLP.".

Companies Act 2006
(Sections 43, 44, 45, 46, 47, 48 & 49)

Formalities of doing business under the law of England and Wales or Northern Ireland

43.   Company contracts

(1)   Under the law of England and Wales or Northern Ireland a contract may be made—

(a)   by a company, by writing under its common seal, or

(b)   on behalf of a company, by a person acting under its authority, express or implied.

(2)   Any formalities required by law in the case of a contract made by an individual also apply, unless a contrary intention appears, to a contract made by or on behalf of a company.

44.   Execution of documents

(1)   Under the law of England and Wales or Northern Ireland a document is executed by a company—

(a)   by the affixing of its common seal, or

(b)   by signature in accordance with the following provisions.

(2)   A document is validly executed by a company if it is signed on behalf of the company—

(a)   by two authorised signatories, or

(b)   by a director of the company in the presence of a witness who attests the signature.

(3)   The following are "authorised signatories" for the purposes of subsection (2)—

(a)   every director of the company, and

(b)   in the case of a private company with a secretary or a public company, the secretary or any joint secretary) of the company.

(4)   A document signed in accordance with subsection (2) and expressed, in whatever words, to be executed by the company has the same effect as if executed under the common seal of the company.

(5)   In favour of a purchaser a document is deemed to have been duly executed by a company if it purports to be signed in accordance with subsection (2). A "purchaser" means a purchaser in good faith for valuable consideration and includes a lessee, mortgagee or other person who for valuable consideration acquires an interest in property.

(6)   Where a document is to be signed by a person on behalf of more than one company, it is not duly signed by that person for the purposes of this section unless he signs it separately in each capacity.

(7)   References in this section to a document being (or purporting to be) signed by a director or secretary are to be read, in a case where that office is held by a firm, as references to its being (or purporting to be) signed by an individual authorised by the firm to sign on its behalf.

(8)   This section applies to a document that is (or purports to be) executed by a company in the name of or on behalf of another person whether or not that person is also a company.

45.   Common seal
(1)   A company may have a common seal but need not have one.

(2)   A company which has a common seal shall have its name engraved in legible characters on the seal.

(3)   If a company fails to comply with subsection (2) an offence is committed by—
(a)   the company, and
(b)   every officer of the company who is in default.

(4)   An officer of a company, or a person acting on behalf of a company, commits an offence if he uses, or authorises the use of, a seal purporting to be a seal of the company on which its name is not engraved as required by subsection (2).

(5)   A person guilty of an offence under this section is liable on summary conviction to a fine not exceeding level 3 on the standard scale.

(6)   This section does not form part of the law of Scotland.

46.   Execution of deeds
(1)   A document is validly executed by a company as a deed for the purposes of section 1(2)(b) of the Law of Property (Miscellaneous Provisions) Act 1989 (c. 34) and for the purposes of the law of Northern Ireland if, and only if—
(a)   it is duly executed by the company, and
(b)   it is delivered as a deed.

(2)   For the purposes of subsection (1)(b) a document is presumed to be delivered upon its being executed, unless a contrary intention is proved.

47. **Execution of deeds or other documents by attorney**

(1) Under the law of England and Wales or Northern Ireland a company may, by instrument executed as a deed, empower a person, either generally or in respect of specified matters, as its attorney to execute deeds or other documents on its behalf.

(2) A deed or other document so executed, whether in the United Kingdom or elsewhere, has effect as if executed by the company.

Formalities of doing business under the law of Scotland

48. **Execution of documents by companies**

(1) The following provisions form part of the law of Scotland only.

(2) Notwithstanding the provisions of any enactment, a company need not have a company seal.

(3) For the purposes of any enactment—
    (a) providing for a document to be executed by a company by affixing its common seal, or
    (b) referring (in whatever terms) to a document so executed,

a document signed or subscribed by or on behalf of the company in accordance with the provisions of the Requirements of Writing (Scotland) Act 1995 (c. 7) has effect as if so executed.

Other matters

49. **Official seal for use abroad**

(1) A company that has a common seal may have an official seal for use outside the United Kingdom.

(2) The official seal must be a facsimile of the company's common seal, with the addition on its face of the place or places where it is to be used.

(3) The official seal when duly affixed to a document has the same effect as the company's common seal.

This subsection does not extend to Scotland.

(4) A company having an official seal for use outside the United Kingdom may—
    (a) by writing under its common seal, or
    (b) as respects Scotland, by writing subscribed in accordance with the Requirements of Writing (Scotland) Act 1995, authorise any person appointed for the purpose to affix the official seal to any deed or other document to which the company is party.

(5)   As between the company and a person dealing with such an agent, the agent's authority continues—

  (a)   during the period mentioned in the instrument conferring the authority, or

  (b)   if no period is mentioned, until notice of the revocation or termination of the agent's authority has been given to the person dealing with him.

(6)   The person affixing the official seal must certify in writing on the deed or other document to which the seal is affixed the date on which, and place at which, it is affixed.

Consular Relations Act 1968
(Section 10)

10.- (1) A diplomatic agent or consular officer of any State may, if authorised to do so under the laws of that State, administer oaths, take affidavits and do notarial acts-

    (a) required by a person for use in that State or under the laws thereof; or

    (b) otherwise required by a national of that State but not for use in the United Kingdom except under the laws of some other country.

(2) Her Majesty may by Order in Council exclude or restrict the provisions of the preceding subsection in relation to the diplomatic agents or consular officers of any State if it appears to Her that in any territory of that State diplomatic agents or consular officers of the United Kingdom are not permitted to perform functions corresponding in nature and extent to those authorised by that subsection.

(3) Her Majesty may by Order in Council make provision for applying section 6 of the Commissioners for Oaths Act 1889 (powers as to oaths and notarial acts abroad) to countries within the Commonwealth or the Republic of Ireland by requiring the section to be construed as if-

    (a) the references therein to a foreign country or place included such country or place as may be specified in the Order; and

    (b) the diplomatic ranks specified in that section included such ranks of any United Kingdom mission in a country specified in the Order as may be so specified in relation to that country.

(4) In this section "diplomatic agent" has the same meaning as in the Diplomatic Privileges Act 1964.

Access to Justice Act 1999
(Section 53)

Public notaries

Abolition of scriveners' monopoly

53.   A public notary may practise as a notary in, or within three miles of, the
City of London whether or not he is a member of the Incorporated
Company of Scriveners of London (even if he is admitted to practise only
outside that area).

Courts and Legal Services Act 1990
(Sections 57 and 66)

Notaries

57.— (1)   Public notaries shall no longer be appointed to practise only within particular districts in England, or particular districts in Wales.

(2)   It shall no longer be necessary to serve a period of apprenticeship before being admitted as a public notary.

(3)   Accordingly, the following enactments relating to public notaries shall cease to have effect—

     (a)   section 2 of the Public Notaries Act 1801 (which provides that no person shall be admitted as a public notary unless he has served as an apprentice for seven years);

     (b)   section 1 of the Public Notaries Act 1833 (which restricts the requirement to serve an apprenticeship to London and an area of ten miles from the Royal Exchange);

     (c)   section 2 of the Public Notaries Act 1833 (appointment of public notaries to practise within particular districts in England);

     (d)   section 3 of the Public Notaries Act 1843 (which reduced the period of apprenticeship to five years);

     (e)   section 37 of the Welsh Church Act 1914 (appointment of public notaries to practise within particular districts in Wales); and

     (f)   section 29 of the Administration of Justice Act 1969 (which reduced the period of apprenticeship for public notaries in London).

(4)   The Master may by rules make provision—

     (a)   as to the educational and training qualifications which must be satisfied before a person may be granted a faculty to practise as a public notary;

     (b)   as to further training which public notaries are to be required to undergo;

     (c)   for regulating the practice, conduct and discipline of public notaries;

     (d)   supplementing the provision made by subsections (8) and (9);

     (e)   as to the keeping by public notaries of records and accounts;

     (f)   as to the handling by public notaries of clients' money;

     (g)   as to the indemnification of public notaries against losses arising from claims in respect of civil liability incurred by them;

(h)   as to compensation payable for losses suffered by persons in respect of dishonesty on the part of public notaries or their employees; and

(i)   requiring the payment, in such circumstances as may be prescribed, of such reasonable fees as may be prescribed, including in particular fees for—

(i)   the grant of a faculty;

(ii)   the issue of a practising certificate by the Court of Faculties of the Archbishop of Canterbury; or

(iii) the entering in that court of a practising certificate issued under the Solicitors Act 1974.

(5)   The repeal of section 2 of the Act of 1833 and section 37 of the Act of 1914 by this Act shall not affect any appointment made under either of those sections; but the Master may by rules make such provision as he considers necessary or expedient in consequence of either, or both, of those repeals.

(6)   Rules made under subsection (5) may, in particular, provide for the grant by the Master of a new faculty for any person to whom the Notary Public (Welsh Districts) Rules 1924 applied immediately before the commencement of this section, in place of the faculty granted to him by the Clerk of the Crown in Chancery.

(7)   Subsections (4) to (6) shall not be taken to prejudice—

(a)   any other power of the Master to make rules; or

(b)   any rules made by him under any such power.

(8)   With effect from the operative date, any restriction placed on a qualifying district notary, in terms of the district within which he may practise as a public notary, shall cease to apply.

(9)   In this section—
"Master" means the Master of the Faculties;

"the operative date" means the date on which subsection (1) comes into force or, if on that date the notary concerned is not a qualifying district notary (having held his faculty for less than five years)—

(a)   the date on which he becomes a qualifying district notary; or

(b)   such earlier date, after the commencement of subsection (1), as the Master may by rules prescribe for the purpose of this subsection;

"prescribed" means prescribed by rules made under this section; and

"qualifying district notary" means a person who—

(a)   holds a faculty as a notary appointed under section 2 of the Act of 1833 or section 37 of the Act of 1914; and

(b)   has held it for a continuous period of at least five years.

(10)   Section 5 of the Ecclesiastical Licences Act 1533 (which amongst other things now has the effect of requiring faculties to be registered by the Clerk of the Crown in Chancery) shall not apply in relation to any faculty granted to a public notary.

(11)   Nothing in this section shall be taken—
  (a)   to authorise any public notary to practise as a notary or to perform or certify any notarial act within the jurisdiction of the Incorporated Company of Scriveners of London or to affect the jurisdiction or powers of the Company; or
  (b)   to restrict the power of the Company to require a person seeking to become a public notary within its jurisdiction to serve a period of apprenticeship.

66.— (1)   Section 39 of the Solicitors Act 1974 (which, in effect, prevents Multi-disciplinary solicitors entering into partnership with persons who are not solicitors) and multi-national shall cease to have effect. practices.

(2)   Nothing in subsection (1) prevents the Law Society making rules which prohibit solicitors from entering into any unincorporated association with persons who are not solicitors or restrict the circumstances in which they may do so.

(3)   Section 10 of the Public Notaries Act 1801 (which, in effect, prevents notaries entering into partnership with persons who are not notaries) shall cease to have effect.

(4)   Nothing in subsection (3) prevents the Master of the Faculties making rules which prohibit notaries from entering into any unincorporated association with persons who are not notaries, or restrict the circumstances in which they may do so.

(5)   It is hereby declared that no rule of common law prevents barristers from entering into any unincorporated association with persons who are not barristers.

(6)   Nothing in subsection (5) prevents the General Council of the Bar from making rules which prohibit barristers from entering into any such unincorporated association or restrict the circumstances in which they may do so.

Banking and Financial Dealings Act 1971
(Sections 1, 3 and 4 and Schedule 1)

Bank Holidays

1. - (1)   Subject to subsection (2) below, the days specified in Schedule 1 to this Act shall be bank holidays in England and Wales, in Scotland and Northern Ireland as indicated in the Schedule.

Bills of Exchange and promissory notes

3.- (1)   Section 92 of the Bills of Exchange Act 1882 (which, in a case in which the time limited by that Act for doing any act or thing is less than three days, excludes non-business days from the reckoning of that time, and defines such days for the purposes of the Act) shall have the effect as if, in paragraph (a) of the definition of non-business days, "Saturday" were inserted immediately before "Sunday".

This subsection shall not operate to extend to any period expiring at or before the time it comes into force.

(2)   For section 14(1) of the Bills of Exchange Act 1882 (under or by virtue of which the date of maturity of a bill or promissory note that does not say otherwise is arrived at by adding three days of grace to the time of payment as fixed by the bill or note, but is advanced or postponed if the last day of grace is a non-business day) there shall be substituted, except in its application to bills drawn and notes made before this subsection comes into force, the following paragraph –

"(1)   The bill is due and payable in all cases on the last day of the time of payment as fixed by the bill or, if that is a non-business day, on the succeeding business day."

4.   (4)   Accordingly in section 92 of the Bills of Exchange Act 1882, in the definition of "non-business days," for the words "the Bank Holidays Act 1871 or Acts amending it" in paragraph (b) there shall be substituted the words "the Banking and Financial Dealings Act 1971," and there shall be added as a new paragraph (d):-

"(d)   a day declared by an order under section 2 of the Banking and Financial Dealings Act 1971 to be a non-business day."

SCHEDULE 1

Bank Holidays

A1-127 1. The following are to be bank holidays in England and Wales:

Easter Monday.
The last Monday in May.
The last Monday in August.
26th December, if it be not a Sunday.
27th December in a year in which 25th or 26th December is a Sunday.

Statutory Declarations Act 1835

An Act to repeal an Act for the present Session of Parliament, intituled An Act for the more effectual Abolition of Oaths and Affirmations taken and made in various Departments of the State, and to substitute Declarations in lieu thereof, and for the more entire Suppression of voluntary and extra-judicial oaths and Affidavits; and to make other Provisions for the Abolition of unnecessary Oaths.

[9th September 1833.]

WHEREAS an Act was passed in the present Session of Parliament, intituled An Act for the more effectual Abolition of Oaths and Affirmations taken and made in various Departments of the State, and to substitute Declarations in lieu thereof; and for the more entire Suppression of voluntary and extra-judicial Oaths and Affidavits; and it was thereby enacted that the said Act should commence and take effect from and after the First Day of June in this present Year, the Year of our Lord One thousand eight hundred and thirty-five, it not being intended that the said recited Act should take effect before the same received the Royal Assent: And whereas the said recited Act did not receive the Royal Assent till after the said First Day of June One thousand eight hundred and thirty-five: And where it was enacted by the said recited Act, that from and after the First Day of June next ensuing it should not be lawful for any Justice of the Peace to ad minister or receive such voluntary Oaths as are therein mentioned, it being intended that the said Prohibition should talk effect from the Time of the Commencement of the said recited Act: And whereas it is expedient to amend the said Act, and to make some further Provisions for the better effecting the Object thereof, and to consolidate all the Provisions relating thereto into One Act: Be it therefore enacted by the King's most Excellent Majesty, by and with the Advice and Consent of the Lords Spiritual and Temporal, and Commons, in this present Parliament assembled, and by the Authority of the same, That from and after the passing of this Act the said recited Act shall be and the same is hereby repealed.

II.   And be it further enacted, That in any Case where, by any Act or Acts made or to be made relating to the Revenues of Customs or Excise, the Post Office, the Office of Stamps and Taxes, the Office of Woods and Forests, Land Revenues, Works, and Buildings, the War Office, the Army Pay Office, the Office of the Treasurer of the Navy, the Accountant General of the Navy, or the Ordnance, His Majesty's Treasury, Chelsea Hospital, Greenwich Hospital, the Board of Trade, or any of the Offices of His Majesty's Principal Secretaries of State, the India Board, the Office for auditing the Public Accounts, the National Debt Office, or any Office under the Control, Direction, or Superintendence of the Lords Commissioners of His Majesty's Treasury, or by any official Regulation in any Department, any Oath, solemn Affirmation, or Affidavit might, but for the passing of this Act, be required to be taken or made by any Person on the doing of any Act, Matter, or Thing, or for the Purpose of verifying any Book, Entry, or Return, or for any other Purpose whatsoever, it shall be lawful for the Lords Commissioners of, His Majesty's Treasury or any Three of them, if they shall so think fit, by Writing under their Hands and Seals, to substitute a

Declaration to the same Effect as the Oath, solemn Affirmation, or Affidavit which might but for the passing of this Act be required to be taken or made; and the Person who might under the Act or Acts imposing the same be required to take or make such Oath, solemn Affirmation, or Affidavit shall, in Presence of the Commissioners, Collector, other Officer or Person empowered by such Act or Acts to administer such Oath, solemn Affirmation, or Affidavit, make and subscribe such Declaration, and every such Commissioner, Collector, other Officer or Person is hereby empowered and required to administer the same accordingly.

III.   And be it enacted, That when the said Lords Commissioners of His Majesty's Treasury or any Three of them shall, in any such Case as herein-before mentioned, have substituted, in Writing under their Hands and Seals, a Declaration in lieu of an Oath, solemn Affirmation, or Affidavit, such Lords Commissioners shall, so soon as conveniently may be, cause a Copy of the Instrument substituting such Declaration to be inserted and published in the London Gazette; and from and after the Expiration of Twenty-one Days next following the Day of the Date of the Gazette wherein the Copy of such Instrument shall have been published, the Provisions of this Act shall extend and apply to each and every Case specified in such Instrument, as well and in the same Manner as if the same were specified and named in this Act.

IV.   And be it enacted, That after the Expiration of the said Twenty-one Days it shall not be lawful for any Commissioner, Collector, Officer, or other Person to administer or cause to be administered, or receive or cause to be received, any Oath, solemn Affirmation, or Affidavit, in the lieu of which such Declaration as aforesaid shall have been directed by the Lords Commissioners of His Majesty's Treasury to be substituted.

V.   And be it enacted, That if any Person, shall make and subscribe any such Declaration as herein-before mentioned in lieu of any Oath, solemn Affirmation, or Affidavit by any Act or Acts relating to the Revenues of Customs or Excise, Stamps and Taxes, or Post Office, required to be made on the doing of any Act, Matter, or Thing, or for verifying any Book, Account, Entry, or Return, or for any Purpose whatsoever, and shall wilfully make therein any false Statements as to any material Particular, the Person making the same shall be deemed guilty of a Misdemeanor.

VI.   Provided always, and be it enacted, That nothing in this Act contained shall extend or apply to the Oath of Allegiance in any Case in which the same now is or may be required to be taken by any Person who may be appointed to any Office, but that such Oath of Allegiance shall continue to be required, and shall be administered and taken, as well and in the same Manner as if this Act had not been passed.

VII.   Provided also, and be it enacted, That nothing in this Act contained shall extend or apply to any Oath, solemn Affirmation, or Affidavit which now is or hereafter may be made or taken, or be required to be made or taken, in any Judicial Proceeding in any Court of Justice, or in any Proceeding for or by way of summary Conviction before any Justice or Justices of the Peace, but all such Oaths, Affirmations, and Affidavits shall continue to be required, and to be administered, taken, and made, as well and in the same Manner as if this Act had not been passed.

VIII.   And be it enacted, That it shall be lawful for the Universities of Oxford and Cambridge, and for all other Bodies Corporate and Politic, and for all Bodies now by Law or Statute, or by any valid Usage, authorized to administer or receive any Oath, solemn Affirmation, or Affidavit, to make Statutes, Bye Laws, or Orders authorizing and directing the Substitution of a Declaration in lieu of any Oath, solemn Affirmation, or Affidavit now required to be taken or made: Provided always, that such Statutes, Bye Laws, or Orders be otherwise duly made and passed according to the Charter, Laws, or Regulations of the particular University, other Body Corporate and Politic, or other Body so authorized as aforesaid.

IX.   And whereas Persons serving the Offices of Churchwarden and Sidesman are at present required to take an Oath of Office before entering upon the Execution thereof, and also an Oath on quitting such Office, and it is expedient that a Declaration shall be substituted for such Oath of Office, and that the Oath on quitting the same shall be abolished; be it enacted, That in future every Person entering upon the Office of Churchwarden or Sidesman, before beginning to discharge the Duties thereof, shall, in lieu of such Oath of Office, make and subscribe, in the Presence of the Ordinary or other Person before whom he would, but for the passing of this Act, be required to take such Oath, a Declaration that he will faithfully and diligently perform the Duties of his Office, and such Ordinary or other Person is hereby empowered and required to administer the same accordingly: Provided always, that no Churchwarden or Sidesman shall in future be required to take any Oath on quitting Office, as has heretofore been practised.

X.   And be it enacted, That in any Case where, under any Act or Acts for making, maintaining, or regulating any Highway, or any Road, or any Turnpike Road, or for paving, lighting, watching, or improving any City, Town, or Place, or touching any Trust relating thereto, any Oath, solemn Affirmation, or Affidavit might, but for the passing of this Act, be required to be taken or made by any Person whomsoever, no such Oath, solemn Affirmation, or Affidavit shall in future be required to be or be taken or made, but the Person who might under the Act or Acts imposing the same be required to take or make such Oath, solemn Affirmation, or Affidavit shall, in lieu thereof, in the Presence of the Trustee, Commissioner, or other Person before whom he might under such Act or facts be required to take or make the same, make and subscribe a Declaration to the same Effect as such Oath, solemn Affirmation, or Affidavit, and such Trustee, Commissioner, or other Person is hereby empowered and required to administer and receive the same.

XI.   And be it enacted, That whenever any Person or Persons shall seek to obtain any Patent under the Great Seal for any Discovery or Invention, such

Person or Persons shall, in lieu of any Oath, Affirmation, or Affidavit which heretofore has or might be required to be, taken or made upon or before obtaining any such Patent, make and subscribe, in the Presence of the Person before whom he might, but for the passing of this Act, be required to take or make such Oath, Affirmation, or Affidavit, a Declaration to the same Effect as such Oath, Affirmation, or Affidavit; and such Declaration, when duly made and subscribed, shall be to all Intents and Purposes as valid and effectual as the Oath, Affirmation, or Affidavit in lieu whereof it shall have been so made and subscribed.

XII.   And be it enacted, That where by any Act or Acts at the Time in force for regulating the Business of Pawnbrokers any Oath, Affirmation, or Affidavit might, but for the passing of this Act, be required to be taken or made, the Person who by or under such Act or Acts might be required to take or make such Oath, Affirmation, or Affidavit shall in lieu thereof make and subscribe a Declaration to the same Effect; and such Declaration shall be made and subscribed at the same Time, and on the same Occasion, and in the Presence of the same Person or Persons, as the Oath, Affirmation, or Affidavit in lieu whereof it shall be made and subscribed would by the Act or Acts directing or requiring the same be directed or required to be taken or made; and all and every the Enactments, Provisions, and Penalties contained in or imposed by any such Act to such or Acts, as to any Oath, Affirmation, or Affidavit thereby directed or required to be taken or made, shall extend and apply to any Declaration in lieu thereof, as well and in the same Manner as if the same were herein expressly enacted with reference thereto.

XIII.   And whereas a Practice has prevailed of administering and receiving Oaths and Affidavits voluntarily taken and made in Matters not the Subject of any Judicial Inquiry, nor in anywise pending or at issue before the Justice of the Peace or other Person by whom such Oaths or Affidavits have been administered or received: And whereas Doubts have arisen whether or not such Proceeding is illegal; for the more effectual Suppression of such Practice and removing such Doubts, be it enacted, That from and after the Commencement of this Act it shall not be lawful for any Justice of the Peace or other Person to administer, or cause or allow to be administered, or to receive, or cause or allow to be received, any Oath, Affidavit, or solemn Affirmation touching any Matter or Thing whereof such Justice or other Person hath not Jurisdiction or Cognizance by some Statute in force at the Time being: Provided always, that nothing herein contained shall be construed to extend to any Oath, Affidavit, or solemn Affirmation before any Justice in any Matter or Thing touching the Preservation of the Peace, or the Prosecution, Trial, or Punishment of Offences, or touching any Proceedings before either of the Houses of Parliament or any Committee thereof respectively, nor to any Oath, Affidavit, or Affirmation which may be required by the Laws of any Foreign Country to give Validity to Instruments in Writing designed to be used in such Foreign Countries respectively.

XIV.   And be it further enacted, That in any Case in which it has been the usual Practice of the Bank of England to receive Affidavits on Oath to prove the Death of any Proprietor of any Stocks or Funds transferrable there, or to identify the

Person of any such Proprietor, or to remove any other Impediment to the Transfer of any such Stocks or Funds, or relating to the Loss, Mutilation, or Defacement of any Bank Note or Bank Post Bill, no such Oath or Affidavit shall in future be required to be taken or made, but in lieu thereof the Person who might have been required to take or make such Oath or Affidavit shall make and subscribe a Declaration to the same Effect as such Oath or Affidavit.

XV.   And whereas an Act was passed in the Fifth Year of the Reign of His late Majesty King George the Second, intituled An Act for the more easy Recovery of Debts in His Majesty's Plantations and Colonies in America: And whereas another Act was passed in the Fifty-fourth Year of the Reign of His late Majesty King George the Third, intituled An Act for the more easy Recovery of Debts in His Majesty's Colony of New South Wales: And whereas it is expedient that in future a Declaration should be substituted in lieu of the Affidavit on Oath authorised and required by the said recited Acts; be it therefore enacted, That from and after the Commencement of this Act, in any Action or Suit then depending or thereafter to be brought or intended to be brought in any Court of Law or Equity within any of the Territories, Plantations, Colonies, or Dependencies Abroad, being within and Part of His Majesty's Dominions, for or relating to any Debt or Account wherein any Person residing in Great Britain and Ireland shall be a Party, or for or relating to any Lands, Tenements, or Hereditaments or other Property situate, lying, and being in the said Places respectively, it shall and may be lawful to and for the Plaintiff or Defendant, and also to and for any Witness to be examined or made use of in such Action or Suit, to verify or prove any Matter or Thing relating thereto by solemn Declaration or Declarations in Writing in the Form in the Schedule hereunto annexed, made before any Justice of the Peace, Notary Public, or other Officer now by Law authorized to administer an Oath, and certified and transmitted under the Signature and Seal of any such Justice, Notary Public duly admitted and practising, or other Officer, which Declaration, and every Declaration relative to such Matter or Thing as aforesaid, in any Foreign Kingdom or State, or to the Voyage of any Ship or Vessel, every such Justice of the Peace, Notary Public, or other Officer shall be and he is hereby authorized and empowered to administer or receive; and every Declaration so made, certified, and transmitted shall in all such Actions and Suits be allowed to be of the same Force and Effect as if the Person or Persons making the same had appeared and sworn or affirmed the Matters contained in such Declaration viva voce in open Court , or upon a commission issued for the Examination of Witnesses or of any Party in such Action or Suit respectively; provided that in every such Declaration there shall be expressed the Addition of the Party making such Declaration, and the particular Place of his or her Abode.

XVI.   And be it further enacted, That it shall and may be lawful to and for any attesting Witness to the Execution of any Will or Codicil, Deed or Instrument in Writing, and to and for any other competent Person, to verify and prove the signing, sealing, Publication, or Delivery of any such Will, Codicil, Deed, or Instrument in Writing, made as aforesaid, and every such Justice, Notary, or other Officer shall be and is hereby authorized and empowered to administer or receive such Declaration.

XVII. And be it further enacted, That in all Suits now depending or hereafter to be brought in any Court of Law or Equity by or on behalf of His Majesty, His Heirs and Successors, in any of His said Majesty 's Territories, Plantations, Colonies, Possessions or Dependencies, for or relating to any Debt or Account, that His Majesty, His Heirs and Successors, shall and may prove His and their Debts and Accounts and examine His or their Witness or Witnesses by Declaration, in like Manner as any Subject or Subjects is or are impowered or may do by this present Act.

XVIII. And whereas it may be necessary and proper in many Cases not herein specified to require Confirmation of written Instruments or Allegations, or Proof of Debts, or of the Execution of Deeds or other Matters; be it therefore further enacted, That it shall and may be lawful for any Justice of the Peace, Notary Public, or other Officer now by Law authorized to administer an Oath, to take and receive the Declaration of any Person voluntarily making the same before him in the Form in the Schedule to this Act annexed; and if any Declaration so made shall be false or untrue in any material Particular the Person wilfully making such false Declaration shall be deemed guilty of a Misdemeanor.

XIX. And be it enacted, That whenever any Declaration shall be made and subscribed by any Person or Persons under or in pursuance of the Provisions of this Act, or any of them, all and every such Fees or Fee as would have been due and payable on the taking or making any legal Oath, solemn Affirmation, or Affidavit shall be in like Manner due and payable upon making and subscribing such Declaration.

XX. And be it further enacted, That in all Cases where a Declaration in lieu of an Oath shall have been substituted by this Act, or by virtue of any Power or Authority hereby given, or where a Declaration is directed or authorized to be made and subscribed under the Authority of this Act, or of any Power hereby given, although the same be not substituted in lieu of an Oath heretofore legally taken, such Declaration unless otherwise directed under the Powers hereby given, shall be in the Form prescribed in the Schedule hereunto annexed.

XXI. And be it further enacted, That in any Case where a Declaration is substituted for an Oath under the Authority of this Act, or by virtue of any Power or Authority hereby given, or is directed and authorized to be made and subscribed under the Authority of this Act, or by virtue of any Power hereby given, any Person who shall wilfully and corruptly make and subscribe any such Declaration, knowing the same to be untrue in any material Particular, shall be deemed guilty of a Misdemeanor.

XXII. And be it enacted, That this Act shall commence and take effect from and after the First Day of October in this present Year, the Year of our Lord One thousand eight hundred and thirty-five.

XXIII. And be it further enacted, That this Act may be amended, altered, or repealed by any Act to be passed in this present Session of Parliament.

SCHEDULE referred to by the foregoing Act.

I, A. B. do solemnly and sincerely declare, That
and I make this solemn Declaration conscientiously believing the same to be true,
and by virtue of the Provisions of an Act made and passed in the Year of the
Reign of His present Majesty, intituled An Act [here insert the Title of this Act].

Courts and Legal Services Act 1990
(Section 113)

113.- (1)   In this section—
"authorised person" means—

     (a)   any authorised advocate or authorised litigator, other than one who is a solicitor (in relation to whom provision similar to that made by this section is made by section 81 of the Solicitors Act 1974); or

     (b)   any person who is a member of a professional or other body prescribed by the Lord Chancellor for the purposes of this section; and

"general notary" means any public notary other than—

     (a)   an ecclesiastical notary; or

     (b)   one who is a member of the Incorporated Company of Scriveners (in relation to whom provision similar to that made by this section is made by section 65 of the Administration of Justice Act 1985).

(2)   Section 1(1) of the Commissioners for Oaths Act 1889 (appointment of commissioners by Lord Chancellor) shall cease to have effect.

(3)   Subject to the provisions of this section, every authorised person shall have the powers conferred on a commissioner for oaths by the Commissioners for Oaths Acts 1889 and 1891 and section 24 of the Stamp Duties Management Act 1891; and any reference to such a commissioner in an enactment or instrument (including an enactment passed or instrument made after the commencement of this Act) shall include a reference to an authorised person unless the context otherwise requires.

(4)   Subject to the provisions of this section, every general notary shall have the powers conferred on a commissioner for oaths by the Commissioners for Oaths Acts 1889 and 1891; and any reference to such a commissioner in an enactment or instrument (including an enactment passed or instrument made after the commencement of this Act) shall include a reference to a general notary unless the context otherwise requires.

(5)   No person shall exercise the powers conferred by this section in any proceedings in which he is interested.

(6)   A person exercising such powers and before whom any oath or affidavit is taken or made shall state in the jurat or attestation at which place and on what date the oath or affidavit is taken or made.

(7) A document containing such a statement and purporting to be sealed or signed by an authorised person or general notary shall be admitted in evidence without proof of the seal or signature, and without proof that he is an authorised person or general notary.

(8) The Lord Chancellor may, with the concurrence of the Lord Chief Justice and the Master of the Rolls, by order prescribe the fees to be charged by authorised persons exercising the powers of commissioners for oaths by virtue of this section in respect of the administration of an oath or the taking of an affidavit.

(9) In this section "affidavit" has the same meaning as in the Commissioners for Oaths Act 1889.

(10) Every—
  (a) solicitor who holds a practising certificate which is in force;
  (b) authorised person;
  (c) general notary; and
  (d) member of the Incorporated Company of Scriveners ("the Company") who has been admitted to practise as a public notary within the jurisdiction of the Company, shall have the right to use the title "Commissioner for Oaths".

Legal Services Act 2007
(Sections 12, 13, 14, 18 and 20, Schedules 2 and 4)

Reserved legal activities

12.   Meaning of "reserved legal activity" and "legal activity"

(1)   In this Act "reserved legal activity" means—

(a)   the exercise of a right of audience;

(b)   the conduct of litigation;

(c)   reserved instrument activities;

(d)   probate activities;

(e)   notarial activities;

(f)   the administration of oaths.

(2)   Schedule 2 makes provision about what constitutes each of those activities.

(3)   In this Act "legal activity" means—

(a)   an activity which is a reserved legal activity within the meaning of this Act as originally enacted, and

(b)   any other activity which consists of one or both of the following—

(i)   the provision of legal advice or assistance in connection with the application of the law or with any form of resolution of legal disputes;

(ii)   the provision of representation in connection with any matter concerning the application of the law or any form of resolution of legal disputes.

(4)   But "legal activity" does not include any activity of a judicial or quasi-judicial nature (including acting as a mediator).

(5)   For the purposes of subsection (3) "legal dispute" includes a dispute as to any matter of fact the resolution of which is relevant to determining the nature of any person's legal rights or liabilities.

(6)   Section 24 makes provision for adding legal activities to the reserved legal activities.

Carrying on the activities

13.   Entitlement to carry on a reserved legal activity

(1)   The question whether a person is entitled to carry on an activity which a reserved legal activity is to be determined solely in accordance with the provisions of this Act.

(2)   A person is entitled to carry on an activity ("the relevant activity") which is a reserved legal activity where—

(a)   the person is an authorised person in relation to the relevant activity, or

(b)   the person is an exempt person in relation to that activity.

(3)   Subsection (2) is subject to section 23 (transitional protection for non-commercial bodies).

(4)   Nothing in this section or section 23 affects section 84 of the Immigration and Asylum Act 1999 (c. 33) (which prohibits the provision of immigration advice and immigration services except by certain persons).

Offences

14.   Offence to carry on a reserved legal activity if not entitled

(1)   It is an offence for a person to carry on an activity ("the relevant activity") which is a reserved legal activity unless that person is entitled to carry on the relevant activity.

(2)   In proceedings for an offence under subsection (1), it is a defence for the accused to show that the accused did not know, and could not reasonably have been expected to know, that the offence was being committed.

(3)   A person who is guilty of an offence under subsection (1) is liable—
(a)   on summary conviction, to imprisonment for a term not exceeding 12 months or a fine not exceeding the statutory maximum (or both), and
(b)   on conviction on indictment, to imprisonment for a term not exceeding 2 years or a fine (or both).

(4)   A person who is guilty of an offence under subsection (1) by reason of an act done in the purported exercise of a right of audience, or a right to conduct litigation, in relation to any proceedings or contemplated proceedings is also guilty of contempt of the court concerned and may be punished accordingly.

(5)   In relation to an offence under subsection (1) committed before the commencement of section 154(1) of the Criminal Justice Act 2003 (c. 44), the reference in subsection (3)(a) to 12 months is to be read as a reference to 6 months.

Interpretation

18.   Authorised persons

(1)   For the purposes of this Act "authorised person", in relation to an activity ("the relevant activity") which is a reserved legal activity, means —
(a)   a person who is authorised to carry on the relevant activity by a relevant approved regulator in relation to the relevant activity (other than by virtue of a licence under Part 5), or

288

    (b)   a licensable body which, by virtue of such a licence, is authorised to carry on the relevant activity by a licensing authority in relation to the reserved legal activity.

(2)   A licensable body may not be authorised to carry on the relevant activity as mentioned in subsection (1)(a).

(3)   But where a body ("A") which is authorised as mentioned in subsection (1)(a) becomes a licensable body, the body is deemed by virtue of this subsection to continue to be so authorised from that time until the earliest of the following events—

    (a)   the end of the period of 90 days beginning with the day on which that time falls;

    (b)   the time from which the relevant approved regulator determines this subsection is to cease to apply to A;

    (c)   the time when A ceases to be a licensable body.

(4)   Subsection (2) is subject to Part 2 of Schedule 5 (by virtue of which licensable bodies may be deemed to be authorised as mentioned in subsection (1)(a) in relation to certain activities during a transitional period).

(5)   A person other than a licensable body may not be authorised to carry on the relevant activity as mentioned in subsection (1)(b).

(6)   But where a body ("L") which is authorised as mentioned in subsection (1)(b) ceases to be a licensable body, the body is deemed by virtue of this subsection to continue to be so authorised from that time until the earliest of the following events—

    (a)   the end of the period of 90 days beginning with the day on which that time falls;

    (b)   the time from which the relevant licensing authority determines this subsection is to cease to apply to L;

    (c)   the time when L becomes a licensable body.

20.   **Approved regulators and relevant approved regulators**

(1)   In this Act, the following expressions have the meaning given by this section—

"approved regulator";

"relevant approved regulator".

(2)   "Approved regulator" means—

    (a)   a body which is designated as an approved regulator by Part 1 of Schedule 4 or under Part 2 of that Schedule (or both) and whose regulatory arrangements are approved for the purposes of this Act, and

    (b)   if an order under section 62(1)(a) has effect, the Board.

(3)   An approved regulator is a "relevant approved regulator" in relation to an activity which is a reserved legal activity if—

        (a)   the approved regulator is designated by Part 1, or under Part 2, of Schedule 4 in relation to that reserved legal activity, or

        (b)   where the approved regulator is the Board, it is designated in relation to that reserved legal activity by an order under section 62(1)(a).

(4)   An approved regulator is a "relevant approved regulator" in relation to a person if the person is authorised by the approved regulator to carry on an activity which is a reserved legal activity.

(5)   Schedule 4 makes provision with respect to approved regulators other than the Board. In that Schedule—

        (a)   Part 1 designates certain bodies as approved regulators in relation to certain reserved legal activities,

        (b)   Part 2 makes provision for bodies to be designated by order as approved regulators in relation to one or more reserved legal activities, and

        (c)   Part 3 makes provision relating to the approval of changes to an approved regulator's regulatory arrangements.

(6)   An approved regulator may authorise persons to carry on any activity which is a reserved legal activity in respect of which it is a relevant approved regulator.

SCHEDULE 2

THE RESERVED LEGAL ACTIVITIES

Introduction

1   This Schedule makes provision about the reserved legal activities.

2   In this Schedule "the appointed day" means the day appointed for the coming into force of section 13 (entitlement to carry on reserved legal activities).

Rights of audience

3   (1)   A "right of audience" means the right to appear before and address a court, including the right to call and examine witnesses.

        (2)   But a "right of audience" does not include a right to appear before or address a court, or to call or examine witnesses, in relation to any particular court or in relation to particular proceedings, if immediately before the appointed day no restriction was placed on the persons entitled to exercise that right.

Conduct of litigation

4   (1)   The "conduct of litigation" means—

        (a)   the issuing of proceedings before any court in England and Wales,

        (b)   the commencement, prosecution and defence of such proceedings, and

        (c)   the performance of any ancillary functions in relation to such proceedings (such as entering appearances to actions).

    (2)   But the "conduct of litigation" does not include any activity within paragraphs (a) to (c) of sub-paragraph (1), in relation to any particular court or in relation to any particular proceedings, if immediately before the appointed day no restriction was placed on the persons entitled to carry on that activity.

Reserved instrument activities

5   (1)   "Reserved instrument activities" means—

        (a)   preparing any instrument of transfer or charge for the purposes of the Land Registration Act 2002 (c. 9);

        (b)   making an application or lodging a document for registration under that Act;

        (c)   preparing any other instrument relating to real or personal estate for the purposes of the law of England and Wales or instrument relating to court proceedings in England and Wales.

    (2)   But "reserved instrument activities" does not include the preparation of an instrument relating to any particular court proceedings if, immediately before the appointed day, no restriction was placed on the persons entitled to carry on that activity.

    (3)   In this paragraph "instrument" includes a contract for the sale or other disposition of land (except a contract to grant a short lease), but does not include—

        (a)   a will or other testamentary instrument,

        (b)   an agreement not intended to be executed as a deed, other than a contract that is included by virtue of the preceding provisions of this sub-paragraph,

        (c)   a letter or power of attorney, or

        (d)   a transfer of stock containing no trust or limitation of the transfer.

    (4)   In this paragraph a "short lease" means a lease such as is referred to in section 54(2) of the Law of Property Act 1925 (c. 20) (short leases).

Probate activities

6   (1)   "Probate activities" means preparing any probate papers for the purposes of the law of England and Wales or in relation to any proceedings in England and Wales.

    (2)   In this paragraph "probate papers" means papers on which to found or oppose—
        (a)   a grant of probate, or
        (b)   a grant of letters of administration.

Notarial activities

7   (1)   "Notarial activities" means activities which, immediately before the appointed day, were customarily carried on by virtue of enrolment as a notary in accordance with section 1 of the Public Notaries Act 1801 (c. 79).

    (2)   Sub-paragraph (1) does not include activities carried on—
        (a)   by virtue of section 22 or 23 of the Solicitors Act 1974 (c. 47) (reserved instrument activities and probate activities), or
        (b)   by virtue of section 113 of the Courts and Legal Services Act 1990 (c. 41)(administration of oaths).

Administration of oaths

8   The "administration of oaths" means the exercise of the powers conferred on a commissioner for oaths by—
        (a)   the Commissioners for Oaths Act 1889 (c. 10);
        (b)   the Commissioners for Oaths Act 1891 (c. 50);
        (c)   section 24 of the Stamp Duties Management Act 1891 (c. 38).

SCHEDULE 4
APPROVED REGULATORS

PART 1
EXISTING REGULATORS

1   (1)   Each body listed in the first column of the Table in this paragraph is an approved regulator.

       (2)   Each body so listed is an approved regulator in relation to the reserved legal activities listed in relation to it in the second column of the Table.

Table

Approved regulator	Reserved legal activities
The Law Society	The exercise of a right of audience. The conduct of litigation. Reserved instrument activities. Probate activities. The administration of oaths.
The General Council of the Bar	The exercise of a right of audience. The conduct of litigation. Reserved instrument activities. Probate activities. The administration of oaths.
The Master of the Faculties	Reserved instrument activities. Probate activities. Notarial activities. The administration of oaths.
The Institute of Legal Executives	The exercise of a right of audience. The administration of oaths.
The Council for Licensed Conveyancers	Reserved instrument activities. The administration of oaths.
The Chartered Institute of Patent Attorneys	The exercise of a right of audience. The conduct of litigation. Reserved instrument activities. The administration of oaths.
The Institute of Trade Mark Attorneys	The exercise of a right of audience. The conduct of litigation. Reserved instrument activities. The administration of oaths.
The Association of Law Costs Draftsmen	The exercise of a right of audience. The conduct of litigation. The administration of oaths.

2   (1)   The regulatory arrangements of a listed body, as they have effect immediately before paragraph 1 comes into force, are to be treated as having been approved by the Board for the purposes of this Act at the time that paragraph comes into force.

(2)   "Listed body" means a body listed in the first column of the Table in paragraph 1 as that Table has effect at the time that paragraph comes into force.

(3)   Sub-paragraph (1) is without prejudice to the Board's power to give Directions under section 32 (powers to direct an approved regulator to take steps in certain circumstances, including steps to amend its regulatory arrangements).

Law of Property (Miscellaneous Provisions) Act 1989
(Sections 1, 2, 3, 4, 5 and 6)

Chapter 34

An Act to make new provision with respect to deeds and their execution and contracts for the sale or other disposition of interests in land; and to abolish the rule of law known as the rule in Bain v. Fothergill. [27th July 1989]

BE IT ENACTED by the Queen's most Excellent Majesty, by and with the advice and consent of the Lords Spiritual and Temporal, and Commons, in this present Parliament assembled, and by the authority of the same, as follows:-

1.   (1)   Any rule of law which-

        (a)   restricts the substances on which a deed may be written; execution.

        (b)   requires a seal for the valid execution of an instrument as a deed by an individual; or

        (c)   requires authority by one person to another to deliver an instrument as a deed on his behalf to be given by deed, is abolished.

  (2)   An instrument shall not be a deed unless-

        (a)   it makes it clear on its face that it is intended to be a deed by the person making it or, as the case may be, by the parties to it (whether by describing itself as a deed or expressing itself to be executed or signed as a deed or otherwise); and

        (b)   it is validly executed as a deed by that person or, as the case may be, one or more of those parties.

  (3)   An instrument is validly executed as a deed by an individual if, and only if-

        (a)   it is signed-

            (i)   by him in the presence of a witness who attests the signature; or

            (ii)   at his direction and in his presence and the presence of two witnesses who each attest the signature; and

        (b)   it is delivered as a deed by him or a person authorised to do so on his behalf.

  (4)   In subsections (2) and (3) above "sign", in relation to an instrument, includes making one's mark on the instrument and

"signature" is to be construed accordingly.

  (5)   Where a solicitor or licensed conveyancer, or an agent or employee of a solicitor or licensed conveyancer, in the course of or in connection with a transaction involving the disposition or creation

of an interest in land, purports to deliver an instrument as a deed on behalf of a party to the instrument, it shall be conclusively presumed in favour of a purchaser that he is authorised so to deliver the instrument.

(6)   In subsection (5) above-
"disposition" and "purchaser" have the same meanings as in the Law of Property Act 1925; and

"interest in land" means any estate, interest or charge in or over land or in or over the proceeds of sale of land.

(7)   Where an instrument under seal that constitutes a deed is required for the purposes of an Act passed before this section comes into force, this section shall have effect as to signing, sealing or delivery of an instrument by an individual in place of any provision of that Act as to signing, sealing or delivery.

(8)   The enactments mentioned in Schedule 1 to this Act (which in consequence of this section require amendments other than those provided by subsection (7) above) shall have effect with the amendments specified in that Schedule.

(9)   Nothing in subsection (1)(b), (2), (3), (7) or (8) above applies in relation to deeds required or authorised to be made under-
(a)   the seal of the county palatine of Lancaster;
(b)   the seal of the Duchy of Lancaster; or
(c)   the seal of the Duchy of Cornwall.

(10)   The references in this section to the execution of a deed by an individual do not include execution by a corporation sole and the reference in subsection (7) above to signing, sealing or delivery by an individual does not include signing, sealing or delivery by such a corporation.

(11)   Nothing in this section applies in relation to instruments delivered as deeds before this section comes into force.

2.   (1)   A contract for the sale or other disposition of an interest in land can only be made in writing and only by incorporating all the terms which the parties have expressly agreed in one document or, where contracts are exchanged, in each.

(2)   The terms may be incorporated in a document either by being set out in it or by reference to some other document.

(3)   The document incorporating the terms or, where contracts are exchanged, one of the documents incorporating them (but not

necessarily the same one) must be signed by or on behalf of each party to the contract.

(4)   Where a contract for the sale or other disposition of an interest in land satisfies the conditions of this section by reason only of the rectification of one or more documents in pursuance of an order of a court, the contract shall come into being, or be deemed to have come into being, at such time as may be specified in the order.

(5)   This section does not apply in relation to-
(a)   a contract to grant such a lease as is mentioned in section 54(2) of the Law of Property Act 1925 (short leases);
(b)   a contract made in the course of a public auction; or
(c)   a contract regulated under the Financial Services Act 1986;

and nothing in this section affects the creation or operation of resulting, implied or constructive trusts.

(6)   In this section-
"disposition" has the same meaning as in the Law of Property Act 1925;

"interest in land" means any estate, interest or charge in or over land or in or over the proceeds of sale of land.

(7)   Nothing in this section shall apply in relation to contracts made before this section comes into force.

(8)   Section 40 of the Law of Property Act 1925 (which is superseded by this section) shall cease to have effect.

3.   The rule of law known as the rule in Sam v. Fothergill is abolished in relation to contracts made after this section comes into force.

4.   The enactments mentioned in Schedule 2 to this Act are repealed to the extent specified in the third column of that Schedule.

5.   (1)   The provisions of this Act to which this subsection applies shall come into force on such day as the Lord Chancellor may by order made by statutory instrument appoint.

(2)   The provisions to which subsection (1) above applies are-
(a)   section 1 above; and
(b)   section 4 above, except so far as it relates to section 40 of the Law of Property Act 1925.

(3)   The provisions of this Act to which this subsection applies shall come-into force at the end of the period of two months beginning with the day on which this Act is passed.

(4)   The provisions of this Act to which subsection (3) above applies are-

(a)   sections 2 and 3 above; and

(b)   section 4 above, so far as it relates to section 40 of the Law of Property Act 1925.

6.— (1)   This Act may be cited as the Law of Property (Miscellaneous Provisions) Act 1989.

(2)   This Act extends to England and Wales only.

Law of Property Act 1925
(Sections 74 and 74A)

Part II Contracts, Conveyances and Other Instruments

Conveyances and other Instruments

Execution of instruments by or on behalf of corporations

74.- [(1)   In favour of a purchaser an instrument shall be deemed to have been duly executed by a corporation aggregate if a seal purporting to be the corporation's seal purports to be affixed to the instrument in the presence of and attested by –
    (a)   two members of the board of directors, council or other governing body of the corporation, or
    (b)   one such member and the clerk, secretary or other permanent officer of the corporation or his deputy.]

[(1A) Subsection (1) of this section applies in the case of an instrument purporting to have been executed by a corporation aggregate in the name or on behalf of another person whether or not that person is also a corporation aggregate.]

[(1B) For the purposes of subsection (1) of this section, a seal purports to be affixed in the presence of and attested by an officer of the corporation, in the case of an officer which is not an individual, if it is affixed in the presence of and attested by an individual authorised by the officer to attest on its behalf.]

(2)   The board of directors, council or other governing body of a corporation aggregate may, by resolution or otherwise, appoint an agent either generally or in any particular case, to execute on behalf of the corporation any agreement or other instrument which is not a deed in relation to any matter within the powers of the corporation.

(3)   Where a person is authorised under a power of attorney or under any statutory or other power to convey any interest in property in the name or on behalf of a corporation sole or aggregate, he may as attorney execute the conveyance by signing the name of the corporation in the presence of at least one witness [who attests the signature], [ ] and such execution shall take effect and be valid in like manner as if the corporation had executed the conveyance.

(4)   Where a corporation aggregate is authorised under a power of attorney or under any statutory or other power to convey any interest in property in the name or on behalf of any other person (including any corporation), an officer appointed for that purpose by the board of directors, council or other governing body of the corporation by resolution or otherwise, may execute the [instrument

by signing it] in the name of such other person [or, if the instrument is to be a deed, by so signing it in the presence of a witness who attests the signature], and where an instrument appears to be executed by an officer so appointed, then in favour of a purchaser the instrument shall be deemed to have been executed by an officer duly authorised.

(5)   The foregoing provisions of this section apply to transactions wherever effected, but only to deeds an instruments executed after the commencement of this Act, except that, in the case of powers or appointments of an agent or officer, they apply whether the power was conferred or the appointment was made before or after the commencement of this Act or by this Act.

(6)   Notwithstanding anything contained in this section, any mode of execution or attestation authorised by law or by practice or by the statute, charter, memorandum or articles, deed of settlement or other instrument constituting the corporation or regulating the affairs thereof, shall (in addition to the modes authorised by this section) be as effectual as if this section had not been passed.

Execution of instrument as a deed
A1-355   [**74A.** (1)   An instrument is validly executed by a corporation aggregate as a deed for the purposes of section 1(2)(b) of the Law of Property (Miscellaneous Provisions) Act 1989, if and only if –
(a)   it is duly executed by the corporation, and
(b)   it is delivered as a deed.

(2)   An instrument shall be presumed to be delivered for the purposes of subsection (1)(b) of this section upon its being executed unless a contrary intention is proved.]

General definitions
A1-356   **205.**-(1)   In this Act unless the context otherwise requires, the following expressions have the meanings hereby assigned to them respectively, that is to say:-

[...]

(ii)   "Conveyance" includes a mortgage, charge, lease, assent, vesting declaration, vesting instrument, disclaimer, release and every other assurance of property or of an interest therein by any instrument, except a will; "convey" has a corresponding meaning; and "disposition" includes a conveyance and also a devise, bequest, or an appointment of property contained in a will; and "dispose of" has a corresponding meaning;

[...]

(xx)   "Property" includes any thing in action and any interest in real or personal property;

(xxi) "Purchaser" means a purchaser in good faith for valuable consideration and includes a lessee, mortgagee or other person who for valuable consideration acquires an interest in property except that in Part I of this Act and elsewhere where so expressly provided "purchaser" only means a person who acquires an interest in or charge on property for money or money's worth; and in reference to a legal estate includes a charge by way of legal mortgage; and where the context so requires "purchaser" includes an intending purchaser; "purchase" has a meaning corresponding with that of " purchaser"; and "valuable consideration" includes marriage but does not include a nominal consideration in money.

Fraud Act 2006
(Sections 2, 3, 4, 11 and 12)

2.   Fraud by false representation

(1)   A person is in breach of this section if he—

    (a)   dishonestly makes a false representation, and

    (b)   intends, by making the representation—

        (i)   to make a gain for himself or another, or

        (ii)   to cause loss to another or to expose another to a risk of loss.

(2)   A representation is false if—

    (a)   it is untrue or misleading, and

    (b)   the person making it knows that it is, or might be, untrue or misleading.

(3)   "Representation" means any representation as to fact or law, including a representation as to the state of mind of—

    (a)   the person making the representation, or

    (b)   any other person.

(4)   A representation may be express or implied.

(5)   For the purposes of this section a representation may be regarded as made if it (or anything implying it) is submitted in any form to any system or device designed to receive, convey or respond to communications (with or without human intervention).

3.   Fraud by failing to disclose information

A person is in breach of this section if he—

(a)   dishonestly fails to disclose to another person information which he is under a legal duty to disclose, and

(b)   intends, by failing to disclose the information—

    (i)   to make a gain for himself or another, or

    (ii)   to cause loss to another or to expose another to a risk of loss.

4.   Fraud by abuse of position

(1)   A person is in breach of this section if he—

    (a)   occupies a position in which he is expected to safeguard, or not to act against, the financial interests of another person,

    (b)   dishonestly abuses that position, and

    (c)   intends, by means of the abuse of that position—

        (i) to make a gain for himself or another, or

        (ii) to cause loss to another or to expose another to a risk of loss.

(2)   A person may be regarded as having abused his position even though his conduct consisted of an omission rather than an act.

Obtaining services dishonestly

11.   **Obtaining services dishonestly**

(1)   A person is guilty of an offence under this section if he obtains services for himself or another-

(a)   by a dishonest act, and

(b)   in breach of subsection (2).

(2)   A person obtains services in breach of this subsection if-

(a)   they are made available on the basis that payment has been, is being or will be made for or in respect of them,

(b)   he obtains them without any payment having been made for or in respect of them or without payment having been made in full, and

(c)   when he obtains them, he knows-

(i)   that they are being made available on the basis described in paragraph (a), or

(ii)   that they might be, but intends that payment will not be made, or will not be made in full.

(3)   A person guilty of an offence under this section is liable-

(a)   on summary conviction, to imprisonment for a term not exceeding 12 months or to a fine not exceeding the statutory maximum (or to both);

(b)   on conviction on indictment, to imprisonment for a term not exceeding 5 years or to a fine (or to both).

(4)   Subsection (3)(a) applies in relation to Northern Ireland as if the reference to 12 months were a reference to 6 months.

Supplementary

12.   **Liability of company officers for offences by company**

(1)   Subsection (2) applies if an offence under this Act is committed by a body corporate.

(2)   If the offence is proved to have been committed with the consent or connivance of-

(a)   a director, manager, secretary or other similar officer of the body corporate, or

(b)   a person who was purporting to act in any such capacity, he (as well as the body corporate) is guilty of the offence and liable to be proceeded against and punished accordingly.

(3)   If the affairs of a body corporate are managed by its members, subsection (2) applies in relation to the acts and defaults of a member in connection with his functions of management as if he were a director of the body corporate.

The Perjury Act 1911
(Sections 1, 2, 5, 7, 9, 15 & 16)

1.   (1)   If any person lawfully sworn as a witness or as an interpreter in a judicial proceeding wilfully makes a statement material in that proceeding, which he knows to be false or does not believe to be true, he shall be guilty of perjury, and shall, on conviction thereof on indictment, be liable to penal servitude for a term not exceeding seven years, or to imprisonment with or without hard labour for a term not exceeding two years, or to a fine or to both such penal servitude or imprisonment and fine.

    (2)   The expression "judicial proceeding" includes a proceeding before any court, tribunal, or person having by law power to hear, receive, and examine evidence on oath.

    (3)   Where a statement made for the purposes of a judicial proceeding is not made before the tribunal itself but is made on oath before a person authorised by law to administer an oath to the person who makes the statement, and to record or authenticate the statement, it shall, for the purposes of this section, be treated as having been made in a judicial proceeding.

    (4)   A statement made by a person lawfully sworn in England for the purposes of a judicial proceeding-
    (a)   in another part of His Majesty's dominions; or
    (b)   in a British tribunal lawfully constituted in any place by sea or land outside His Majesty's dominions; or
    (c)   in a tribunal of any foreign state, shall, for the purposes of this section, be treated as a statement made in a judicial proceeding in England.

    (5)   Where, for the purposes of a judicial proceeding in England, a person is lawfully sworn under the authority of an Act of Parliament-
    (a)   in any other part of His Majesty's dominions; or
    (b)   before a British tribunal or a British officer in a foreign country, or within the jurisdiction of the Admiralty of England;

    a statement made by such person so sworn as aforesaid (unless the Act of Parliament under which it was made otherwise specifically provides) shall be treated for the purposes of this section as having been made in the judicial proceeding in England for the purposes whereof it was made.

(6) The question whether a statement on which perjury is assigned was material is a question of law to be determined by the court of trial.

2. If any person –
    (1) being required or authorised by law to make any statement on oath for any purpose, and being lawfully sworn (otherwise than in a judicial proceeding) wilfully makes a statement which is material for that purpose and which he knows to be false or does not believe to be true; or

    (2) wilfully uses any false affidavit for the purposes of the Bills of Sale Act, 1878, as amended by any subsequent enactment, he shall be guilty of a misdemeanour, and, on conviction thereof on indictment, shall be liable to penal servitude for a term not exceeding seven years or to imprisonment, with or without hard labour, for a term not exceeding two years, or to a fine or to both such penal servitude or imprisonment and fine.

5. If any person knowingly and wilfully makes (otherwise than on oath) a statement false in a material particular, and the statement is made-
    (a) in a statutory declaration; or
    (b) in an abstract, account, balance sheet, book, certificate, declaration, entry, estimate, inventory, notice, report, return, or other document which he is authorised or required to make, attest, or verify, by any public general Act of Parliament for the time being in force; or
    (c) in any oral declaration or oral answer which he is required to make by, under, or in pursuance of any public general Act of Parliament for the time being in force, he shall be guilty of a misdemeanour and shall be liable on conviction thereof on indictment to imprisonment, with or without hard labour, for any term not exceeding two years, or to a fine or to both such imprisonment and fine.

7. (1) Every person who aids, abets, counsels, procures, or suborns another person to commit an offence against this Act shall be liable to be proceeded against, indicted, tried and punished as if he were a principal offender.

    (2) Every person who incites or attempts to procure or suborn another person to commit an offence against this Act shall be guilty of a misdemeanour, and, on conviction thereof on indictment, shall be liable to imprisonment, or to a fine, or to both such imprisonment and fine.

9. (1) Where any of the following authorities, namely, a judge of, or person presiding in, a court of record, or a petty sessional court, or any justice of the peace sitting in special sessions, or any sheriff or his lawful deputy before whom a writ of inquiry or a writ of trial is executed, is of opinion that any person has, in the course of a

proceeding before that authority, been guilty of perjury, the authority may order the prosecution of that person for such perjury, in case there shall appear to be reasonable cause for such prosecution, and may commit him, or admit him to bail, to take his trial at the proper court, and may require any person to enter into a recognizance to prosecute or give evidence against the person whose prosecution is so ordered, and may give the person so bound to prosecute a certificate of the making of the order for the prosecution, for which certificate no charge shall be made.

(2) An order made or a certificate given under this section shall not be given in evidence for the purpose or in the course of any trial of a prosecution resulting therefrom.

15. (1) For the purposes of this Act, the forms and ceremonies used in administering an oath are immaterial, if the court or person before whom the oath is taken has power to administer an oath for the purpose of verifying the statement in question, and if the oath has been administered in a form and with ceremonies which the person taking the oath has accepted without objection or has declared to be binding on him.

(2) In this Act-
The expression " oath " in the case of persons for the time being allowed by law to affirm or declare instead of swearing, includes " affirmation " and " declaration," and the expression " swear " in the like case includes It affirm " and " declare "; and

The expression " statutory declaration " means a declaration made by virtue of the Statutory Declarations Act, 1835, or of any Act, Order in Council, rule or regulation applying or extending the provisions thereof; and

The expression " indictment " includes " criminal information."

16. (1) Where the making of a false statement is not only an offence under this Act, but also by virtue of some other Act is a corrupt practice or subjects the offender to any forfeiture or disqualification or to any penalty other than penal servitude, or imprisonment, or fine, the liability of the offender under this Act shall be in addition to and not in substitution for his liability under such other Act.

(2) Nothing in this Act shall apply to a statement made without oath by a child under the provisions of the Prevention of Cruelty to Children Act, 1904, and the Children Act, 1908.

(3) Where the making of a false statement is by any other Act, whether passed before or after the commencement of this Act, made

punishable on summary conviction, proceedings may be taken either under such other Act or under this Act:

Provided that where such an offence is by any Act passed before the commencement of this Act, as originally enacted, made punishable only on summary conviction, it shall remain only so punishable.

327. Concealing etc.
(1) A person commits an offence if he-
    (a)   conceals criminal property;
    (b)   disguises criminal property;
    (c)   converts criminal property;
    (d)   transfers criminal property;
    (e)   removes criminal property from England and Wales or from Scotland or from Northern Ireland.
(2) But a person does not commit such an offence if-
    (a)   he makes an authorised disclosure under section 338 and (if the disclosure is made before he does the act mentioned in subsection (1)) he has the appropriate consent;
    (b)   he intended to make such a disclosure but had a reasonable excuse for not doing so;
    (c)   the act he does is done in carrying out a function he has relating to the enforcement of any provision of this Act or of any other enactment relating to criminal conduct or benefit from criminal conduct.
(3) Concealing or disguising criminal property includes concealing or disguising its nature, source, location, disposition, movement or ownership or any rights with respect to it.

328. Arrangements
(1) A person commits an offence if he enters into or becomes concerned in an arrangement which he knows or suspects facilitates (by whatever means) the acquisition, retention, use or control of criminal property by or on behalf of another person.
(2) But a person does not commit such an offence if-
    (a)   he makes an authorised disclosure under section 338 and (if the disclosure is made before he does the act mentioned in subsection (1)) he has the appropriate consent;
    (b)   he intended to make such a disclosure but had a reasonable excuse for not doing so;
    (c)   the act he does is done in carrying out a function he has relating to the enforcement of any provision of this Act or of any other enactment relating to criminal conduct or benefit from criminal conduct.

329. Acquisition, use and possession
(1) A person commits an offence if he-
    (a)   acquires criminal property;
    (b)   uses criminal property;
    (c)   has possession of criminal property.
(2) But a person does not commit such an offence if-
    (a)   he makes an authorised disclosure under section 338 and (if the disclosure is made before he does the act mentioned in subsection (1)) he has the appropriate consent;

(b)	he intended to make such a disclosure but had a reasonable excuse for not doing so;
(c)	he acquired or used or had possession of the property for adequate consideration;
(d)	the act he does is done in carrying out a function he has relating to the enforcement of any provision of this Act or of any other enactment relating to criminal conduct or benefit from criminal conduct.

(3)   For the purposes of this section-

(a)	a person acquires property for inadequate consideration if the value of the consideration is significantly less than the value of the property;
(b)	a person uses or has possession of property for inadequate consideration if the value of the consideration is significantly less than the value of the use or possession;
(c)	the provision by a person of goods or services which he knows or suspects may help another to carry out criminal conduct is not consideration.

330.   Failure to disclose: regulated sector

(1)   A person commits an offence if each of the following three conditions is satisfied.

(2)   The first condition is that he-

(a)	knows or suspects, or
(b)	has reasonable grounds for knowing or suspecting, that another person is engaged in money laundering.

(3)   The second condition is that the information or other matter-

(a)	on which his knowledge or suspicion is based, or
(b)	which gives reasonable grounds for such knowledge or suspicion, came to him in the course of a business in the regulated sector.

(4)   The third condition is that he does not make the required disclosure as soon as is practicable after the information or other matter comes to him.

(5)   The required disclosure is a disclosure of the information or other matter-

(a)	to a nominated officer or a person authorised for the purposes of this Part by the Director General of the National Criminal Intelligence Service;
(b)	in the form and manner (if any) prescribed for the purposes of this subsection by order under section 339.

(6)   But a person does not commit an offence under this section if-

(a)	he has a reasonable excuse for not disclosing the information or other matter;
(b)	he is a professional legal adviser and the information or other matter came to him in privileged circumstances;
(c)	subsection (7) applies to him.

(7)   This subsection applies to a person if-

(a)	he does not know or suspect that another person is engaged in money laundering, and
(b)	he has not been provided by his employer with such training as is specified by the Secretary of State by order for the purposes of this section.

(8) In deciding whether a person committed an offence under this section the court must consider whether he followed any relevant guidance which was at the time concerned-

    (a)   issued by a supervisory authority or any other appropriate body,

    (b)   approved by the Treasury, and

    (c)   published in a manner it approved as appropriate in its opinion to bring the guidance to the attention of persons likely to be affected by it.

(9) A disclosure to a nominated officer is a disclosure which-

    (a)   is made to a person nominated by the alleged offender's employer to receive disclosures under this section, and

    (b)   is made in the course of the alleged offender's employment and in accordance with the procedure established by the employer for the purpose.

(10) Information or other matter comes to a professional legal adviser in privileged circumstances if it is communicated or given to him-

    (a)   by (or by a representative of) a client of his in connection with the giving by the adviser of legal advice to the client,

    (b)   by (or by a representative of) a person seeking legal advice from the adviser, or

    (c)   by a person in connection with legal proceedings or contemplated legal proceedings.

(11) But subsection (10) does not apply to information or other matter which is communicated or given with the intention of furthering a criminal purpose.

(12) Schedule 9 has effect for the purpose of determining what is-

    (a)   a business in the regulated sector;

    (b)   a supervisory authority.

(13) An appropriate body is any body which regulates or is representative of any trade, profession, business or employment carried on by the alleged offender.

333. Tipping off

(1) A person commits an offence if-

    (a)   he knows or suspects that a disclosure falling within section 337 or 338 has been made, and

    (b)   he makes a disclosure which is likely to prejudice any investigation which might be conducted following the disclosure referred to in paragraph (a).

(2) But a person does not commit an offence under subsection (1) if-

    (a)   he did not know or suspect that the disclosure was likely to be prejudicial as mentioned in subsection (1);

    (b)   the disclosure is made in carrying out a function he has relating to the enforcement of any provision of this Act or of any other enactment relating to criminal conduct or benefit from criminal conduct;

    (c)   he is a professional legal adviser and the disclosure falls within subsection (3).

(3) A disclosure falls within this subsection if it is a disclosure-

    (a)   to (or to a representative of) a client of the professional legal adviser in connection with the giving by the adviser of legal advice to the client, or

(b) to any person in connection with legal proceedings or contemplated legal proceedings.

(4) But a disclosure does not fall within subsection (3) if it is made with the intention of furthering a criminal purpose.

340. Interpretation

(1) This section applies for the purposes of this Part.

(2) Criminal conduct is conduct which-
   (a) constitutes an offence in any part of the United Kingdom, or
   (b) would constitute an offence in any part of the United Kingdom if it occurred there.

(3) Property is criminal property if-
   (a) it constitutes a person's benefit from criminal conduct or it represents such a benefit (in whole or part and whether directly or indirectly), and
   (b) the alleged offender knows or suspects that it constitutes or represents such a benefit.

(4) It is immaterial-
   (a) who carried out the conduct;
   (b) who benefited from it;
   (c) whether the conduct occurred before or after the passing of this Act.

(5) A person benefits from conduct if he obtains property as a result of or in connection with the conduct.

(6) If a person obtains a pecuniary advantage as a result of or in connection with conduct, he is to be taken to obtain as a result of or in connection with the conduct a sum of money equal to the value of the pecuniary advantage.

(7) References to property or a pecuniary advantage obtained in connection with conduct include references to property or a pecuniary advantage obtained in both that connection and some other.

(8) If a person benefits from conduct his benefit is the property obtained as a result of or in connection with the conduct.

(9) Property is all property wherever situated and includes-
   (a) money;
   (b) all forms of property, real or personal, heritable or moveable;
   (c) things in action and other intangible or incorporeal property.

(10) The following rules apply in relation to property-
   (a) property is obtained by a person if he obtains an interest in it;
   (b) references to an interest, in relation to land in England and Wales or Northern Ireland, are to any legal estate or equitable interest or power;
   (c) references to an interest, in relation to land in Scotland, are to any estate, interest, servitude or other heritable right in or over land, including a heritable security;
   (d) references to an interest, in relation to property other than land, include references to a right (including a right to possession).

(11) Money laundering is an act which-
   (a) constitutes an offence under section 327, 328 or 329,
   (b) constitutes an attempt, conspiracy or incitement to commit an offence specified in paragraph (a),
   (c) constitutes aiding, abetting, counselling or procuring the commission of an offence specified in paragraph (a), or

311

(d)   would constitute an offence specified in paragraph (a), (b) or (c) if done in the United Kingdom.

(12)   For the purposes of a disclosure to a nominated officer-

(a)   references to a person's employer include any body, association or organisation (including a voluntary organisation) in connection with whose activities the person exercises a function (whether or not for gain or reward), and

(b)   references to employment must be construed accordingly.

(13)   References to a constable include references to a person authorised for the purposes of this Part by the Director General of the National Criminal Intelligence Service.

REQUIREMENTS FOR LEGALISATION OF DOCUMENTS

Please note that these pages should be used for guidance purposes only. The Author or publisher will not be liable for any errors or omissions.

In these pages FCO means Foreign & Commonwealth Office and ABCC means Arab British Chamber of Commerce.

Afghanistan
Apostille from FCO & Consular Legalisation

Albania
Apostille from FCO
No Consular legalisation required

Algeria
Apostille from FCO & Consular Legalisation
Also requires ABCC

Andora
Apostille from FCO
No Consular legalisation required

Angola
Apostille from FCO & Consular Legalisation
Embassy requires Portuguese translations
Commercial documents require backup

Antigua & Barmuda
Apostille from FCO
No Consular legalisation required

Argentina
Apostille from FCO
No Consular legalisation required

Armenia
Apostille from FCO
No Consular legalisation required

Australia
Apostille from FCO
No Consular legalisation required
Usually Notary Public is acceptable

Austria
Apostille from FCO
No Consular legalisation required

Azerbaijan
Apostille from FCO
No Consular legalisation required

Bahamas
Apostille from FCO
No Consular legalisation required

Bahrain
Apostille from FCO
No Consular legalisation required

Bangladesh
Apostille from FCO & Consular Legalisation

Barbados
Apostille from FCO
No Consular legalisation required

Belarus (Republic of)
Apostille from FCO
No Consular legalisation required

Belgium
Apostille from FCO
No Consular legalisation required

Belize
Apostille from FCO
No Consular legalisation required

Bolivia
Apostille from FCO
No Consular Legalisation required

Bosnia & Herzegovina
Apostille from FCO
No Consular legalisation required

Botswana
Apostille from FCO
No Consular legalisation required

Brazil
Apostille from FCO
No Consular legalisation required

Bulgaria
Apostille from FCO
No Consular legalisation required

Brunei
Apostille from FCO
No Consular legalisation required

Burma (Mynamar)
Apostille from FCO & Consular Legalisation

Cambodia (Royal government of)
Apostille from FCO
No Consular legalisation required

Canada
Apostille from FCO
No Consular legalisation required

Cape Verde
Apostille from FCO
No Consular legalisation required

Cayman Islands
Apostille from FCO
No Consular legalisation required

Chile
Apostille from FCO
No Consular legalisation required

China
Apostille from FCO & Consular Legalisation
Documents must be bound together and sealed.
Must not mention Hong Kong or Taiwan.

Colombia
Apostille from FCO
No Consular legalisation required

Costa Rica
Apostille from FCO
No Consular legalisation required

Croatia
Apostille from FCO
No Consular legalisation required

Cuba
Apostille from FCO & Consular Legalisation
Embassy requires Spanish translation

Cyprus
Apostille from FCO
No Consular legalisation required

Czech Republic
Apostille from FCO
No Consular legalisation required

Denmark
Apostille from FCO
No Consular legalisation required

Dominican Republic
Apostille from FCO
No Consular legalisation required

Ecuador
Apostille from FCO
No Consular legalisation required

Egypt
Apostille plus Consular Legalisation

El Salvador
Apostille from FCO
No Consular legalisation required

Ethiopia
Apostille from FCO & Consular Legalisation

Fiji
Apostille from FCO
No Consular legalisation required

Finland
Apostille from FCO
No Consular legalisation required

France
Apostille from FCO
No Consular legalisation required

Gambia
Apostille plus Consular Legalisation

Georgia
Apostille from FCO
No Consular legalisation required

Germany
Apostille from FCO
No Consular legalisation required

Ghana
Apostille from FCO & Consular Legalisation

Greece
Apostille from FCO
No Consular legalisation required

Grenada
Apostille from FCO
No Consular legalisation required

Guatemala
Apostille from FCO
No Consular legalisation required

Guyana
Apostille from FCO & Consular Legalisation

Haiti
Apostille from FCO
Nearest Consulate is in Brussels

Holland
Apostille from FCO
No Consular legalisation required

Honduras
Apostille from FCO
No Consular legalisation required

Hong Kong
Apostille from FCO
No Consular legalisation required

Hungary
Apostille from FCO
No Consular legalisation required

Iceland
Apostille from FCO.
No Consular legalisation required.

India
Apostille from FCO.
No Consular legalisation required.

Indonesia
Apostille from FCO & Consular Legalisation.
Back up documentation required at embassy.

Iran
Apostille from FCO & Consular Legalisation.
FCO and local chamber of commerce.

Iraq (Islamic Republic of)
Apostille plus Consular Legalisation.
Also requires ABCC for commercial documents.

Ireland
Apostille from FCO
No Consular legalisation required

Israel
Apostille from FCO
No Consular legalisation required

Italy
Apostille from FCO
No Consular legalisation required

Ivory Coast
Apostille from FCO & Consular Legalisation

Jamaica
Apostille from FCO & Consular Legalisation

Japan
Apostille from FCO
No Consular legalisation required

Jordan
Apostille from FCO & Consular Legalisation

Kazakhstan
Apostille from FCO
No Consular legalisation required

Kenya
Apostille from FCO & Consular Legalisation

Korea (Republic of)
Apostille from FCO
No Consular legalisation required

Kuwait
Apostille from FCO & Consular Legalisation
Commercial documents require ABCC.

Kyrghystan
Apostille from FCO
No Consular legalisation required

Latvia
Apostille from FCO
No Consular legalisation required

Lebanon
Apostille from FCO & Consular Legalisation

Lesotho
Apostille from FCO
No Consular legalisation required

Liberia
Apostille from FCO
No Consular legalisation required

Libya
Apostille from FCO & Consular legalisation
Arabic translation required

Luxemburg
Apostille from FCO
No Consular legalisation required

Madagascar (Republic of)
Apostille from FCO
No Consular legalisation required

Malavi
Apostille from FCO
No Consular legalisation required

Malaysia
Apostille from FCO & Consular Legalisation
Usually Notary Public is acceptable

Malta
Apostille from FCO
No Consular legalisation required

Mauritius
Apostille from FCO
No Consular legalisation required

Mexico
Apostille from FCO
No Consular legalisation required

Mongolia
Apostille from FCO
No Consular legalisation required

Morocco
Apostille from FCO
No Consular legalisation required

Namibia
Apostille from FCO
No Consular legalisation required

Nepal
Apostille from FCO & Consular Legalisation

Netherlands
Apostille from FCO
No Consular legalisation required

New Zealand
Apostille from FCO
No Consular legalisation required

Nicargua
Apostille from FCO
No Consular legalisation required

Nigeria
Apostille from FCO & Consular Legalisation

Niue
Apostille from FCO
No Consular Legalisation required

Norway
Apostille from FCO
No Consular legalisation required

Oman
Apostille from FCO
No Consular Legalisation required

Pakistan
Apostille from FCO & Consular Legalisation

Palestine
Apostille from FCO & Consular Legalisation

Panama
Apostille from FCO
No Consular legalisation required

Paraguay
Apostille from FCO
No Consular legalisation required

Peru
Apostille from FCO
No Consular legalisation required

Philippines
Apostille from FCO & Consular Legalisation

Poland
Apostille from FCO
No Consular legalisation required

Portugal
Apostille from FCO
No Consular legalisation required

Qatar (State of)
Apostille from FCO & Consular Legalisation

Ras Al-Khaimah
Apostille from FCO & Consular Legalisation (UAE)

Romania
Apostille from FCO
No Consular legalisation required

Russian Federation
Apostille from FCO
No Consular legalisation required

Rwanda
Apostille from FCO & Consular Legalisation

San Marino
Apostille from FCO
No Consular legalisation required

Sao Tome
Apostille from FCO
No Consular Legalisation required

Saudi Arabia
Apostille from FCO & Consular Legalisation.
Also requires ABCC for commercial documents.
Also requires a passport copy of the signatory.

Senegal
Apostille from FCO & Consular Legalisation

Serbia
Apostille from FCO
No Consular legalisation required

Seychelles
Apostille from FCO
No Consular legalisation required

Sharjah
Apostille from FCO & Consular Legalisation (UAE)

Sierra Leone
Apostille from FCO
No Consular legalisation required
Singapore
Apostille from FCO & Consular Legalisation

Slovak Republic
Apostille from FCO
No Consular legalisation required

Slovenia
Apostille from FCO
No Consular legalisation required

South Africa
Apostille from FCO
No Consular legalisation required

Spain
Apostille from FCO
No Consular legalisation required

Sri Lanka
Apostille from FCO & Consular Legalisation

Sudan
Apostille from FCO & Consular Legalisation

Sweden
Apostille from FCO
No Consular legalisation required

Switzerland
Apostille from FCO
No Consular legalisation required

Syria
Apostille from FCO & Consular Legalisation
Embassy is closed until further notice.
ABCC is all that can be done.

Tadjikstan
Apostille from FCO & Consular Legalisation (Russia)

Taiwan
Apostille from FCO & Consular Legalisation
Also requires notarised letter of authorisation.
Personal documents (Passport copy required)
Commercial documents (certification of incorporation required)

Tanzania
Apostille from FCO & Consular Legalisation

Thailand
Apostille from FCO & Consular Legalisation

Tonga
Apostille from FCO
No Consular legalisation required

Trinidad & Tobago
Apostille from FCO
No Consular legalisation required

Tunisia
Apostille from FCO
No Consular legalisation required

Turkey
Either notary & Apostille from FCO or
Chamber of Commerce & Consular Legalisation (Cannot be both)

Turkmenistan
Apostille from FCO & Consular Legalisation

Uganda
Apostille from FCO & Consular Legalisation

Ukraine
Apostille from FCO
No Consular legalisation required

Ummal-Qaiwan
Apostille from FCO & Consular Legalisation (UAE)

United Arab Emirates
Apostille from FCO & Consular Legalisation
Embassy will not accept bundled documents or foreign documents

United States of America
Apostille from FCO
No Consular legalisation required

Uruguay
Apostille from FCO
No Consular legalisation required

Uzbekistan
Apostille from FCO
No Consular legalisation required

Venezuela
Apostille from FCO
No Consular legalisation required

Vietnam
Apostille from FCO
Consular legalisation required

Yemen
Apostille from FCO & ABCC & Consular Legalisation

Zaire
Apostille from FCO & Consular Legalisation (Congo)

Zambia
Apostille from FCO & Consular Legalisation

Zimbabwe
Apostille from FCO & Consular Legalisation

The Hague Convention, 1961

THE HAGUE APOSTILLE CONVENTION, 1961

CONVENTION ABOLISHING THE REQUIREMENT OF LEGALISATION
FOR FOREIGN PUBLIC DOCUMENTS
(Concluded 5 October 1961)
(Entered into force 24 January 1965)

The States signatory to the present Convention,
Desiring to abolish the requirement of diplomatic or consular legalisation for foreign public documents,
Have resolved to conclude a Convention to this effect and have agreed upon the following provisions:

Article 1
The present Convention shall apply to public documents which have been executed in the territory of one Contracting State and which have to be produced in the territory of another Contracting State.
For the purposes of the present Convention, the following are deemed to be public documents:

a)   documents emanating from an authority or an official connected with the courts or tribunals of the State, including those emanating from a public prosecutor, a clerk of a court or a process-server ("huissier de justice");

b)   administrative documents;

c)   notarial acts;

d)   official certificates which are placed on documents signed by persons in their private capacity, such as official certificates recording the registration of a document or the fact that it was in existence on a certain date and official and notarial authentications of signatures.

However, the present Convention shall not apply:

a)   to documents executed by diplomatic or consular agents;

b   to administrative documents dealing directly with commercial or customs operations.

Article 2
Each Contracting State shall exempt from legalisation documents to which the present Convention applies and which have to be produced in its territory. For the purposes of the present Convention, legalisation means only the formality by which the diplomatic or consular agents of the country in which the document has to be produced certify the authenticity of the signature, the capacity in which the person signing the document has acted and, where appropriate, the identity of the seal or stamp which it bears.

Article 3

The only formality that may be required in order to certify the authenticity of the signature, the capacity in which the person signing the document has acted and, where appropriate, the identity of the seal or stamp which it bears, is the addition of the certificate described in Article 4, issued by the competent authority of the State from which the document emanates.

However, the formality mentioned in the preceding paragraph cannot be required when either the laws, regulations, or practice in force in the State where the document is produced or an agreement between two or more Contracting States have abolished or simplified it or exempt the document itself from legalisation.

Article 4

The certificate referred to in the first paragraph of Article 3 shall be placed on the document itself or on an "allonge", it shall be in the form of the model annexed to the present Convention.

It may, however, be drawn up in the official language of the authority which issues it. The standard terms appearing therein may be in a second language also. The title "Apostille (Convention de La Haye du 5 octobre 1961)" shall be in the French language.

Article 5

The certificate shall be issued at the request of the person who has signed the document or of any bearer.

When properly filled in, it will certify the authenticity of the signature, the capacity in which the person signing the document has acted and, where appropriate, the identity of the seal or stamp which the document bears.

The signature, seal and stamp on the certificate are exempt from all certification.

Article 6

Each Contracting State shall designate by reference to their official function, the authorities who are competent to issue the certificate referred to in the first paragraph of Article 3.

It shall give notice of such designation to the Ministry of Foreign Affairs of the Netherlands at the time it deposits its instrument of ratification or of accession or its declaration of extension. It shall also give notice of any change in the designated authorities.

Article 7

Each of the authorities designated in accordance with Article 6 shall keep a register or card index in which it shall record the certificates issued, specifying:

a)   the number and date of the certificate,

b)   the name of the person signing the public document and the capacity in which he has acted, or in the case of unsigned documents, the name of the authority which has affixed the seal or stamp.

At the request of any interested person, the authority which has issued the certificate shall verify whether the particulars in the certificate correspond with those in the register or card index.

Article 8

When a treaty, convention or agreement between two or more Contracting States contains provisions which subject the certification of a signature, seal or stamp to certain formalities, the present Convention will only override such provisions if those formalities are more rigorous than the formality referred to in Articles 3 and

Article 9

Each Contracting State shall take the necessary steps to prevent the performance of legalisation by its diplomatic or consular agents in cases where the present Convention provides for exemption.

Article 10

The present Convention shall be open for signature by the States represented at the Ninth Session of the Hague Conference on Private International Law and Iceland, Ireland, Liechtenstein and Turkey.

It shall be ratified, and the instruments of ratification shall be deposited with the Ministry of Foreign Affairs of the Netherlands.

Article 11

The present Convention shall enter into force on the sixtieth day after the deposit of the third instrument of ratification referred to in the second paragraph of Article 10.

The Convention shall enter into force for each signatory State which ratifies subsequently on the sixtieth day after the deposit of its instrument of ratification.

Article 12

Any State not referred to in Article 10 may accede to the present Convention after it has entered into force in accordance with the first paragraph of Article 11. The instrument of accession shall be deposited with the Ministry of Foreign Affairs of the Netherlands.

Such accession shall have effect only as regards the relations between the acceding State and those Contracting States which have not raised an objection to its accession in the six months after the receipt of the notification referred to in sub-paragraph *d)* of Article 15. Any such objection shall be notified to the Ministry of Foreign Affairs of the Netherlands.

The Convention shall enter into force as between the acceding State and the States which have raised no objection to its accession on the sixtieth day after the expiry of the period of six months mentioned in the preceding paragraph.

Article 13

Any State may, at the time of signature, ratification or accession, declare that the present Convention shall extend to all the territories for the international relations of which it is responsible, or to one or more of them. Such a declaration shall take effect on the date of entry into force of the Convention for the State concerned.

At any time thereafter, such extensions shall be notified to the Ministry of Foreign Affairs of the Netherlands.

When the declaration of extension is made by a State which has signed and ratified, the Convention shall enter into force for the territories concerned in accordance with Article 11. When the declaration of extension is made by a State which has acceded, the Convention shall enter into force for the territories concerned in accordance with Article 12.

Article 14
The present Convention shall remain in force for five years from the date of its entry into force in accordance with the first paragraph of Article 11, even for States, which have ratified it or acceded to it subsequently.

If there has been no denunciation, the Convention shall be renewed tacitly every five years.

Any denunciation shall be notified to the Ministry of Foreign Affairs of the Netherlands at least six months before the end of the five year period.

It may be limited to certain of the territories to which the Convention applies.

The denunciation will only have effect as regards the State which has notified it. The Convention shall remain in force for the other Contracting States.

Article 15
The Ministry of Foreign Affairs of the Netherlands shall give notice to the States referred to in Article 10, and to the States which have acceded in accordance with Article 12, of the following:

a)   the notifications referred to in the second paragraph of Article 6;

b)   the signatures and ratifications referred to in Article 10;

c)   the date on which the present Convention enters into force in accordance with the first paragraph of Article 11;

d)   the accessions and objections referred to in Article 12 and the date on which such accessions take effect;

e)   the extensions referred to in Article 13 and the date on which they take effect;

f)   the denunciations referred to in the third paragraph of Article 14.

In witness whereof the undersigned, being duly authorised thereto, have signed the present Convention.

Done at The Hague the 5th October 1961, in French and in English, the French text prevailing in case of divergence between the two texts, in a single copy which shall be deposited in the archives of the Government of the Netherlands, and of which a certified copy shall be sent, through the diplomatic channel, to each of the States represented at the Ninth Session of the Hague Conference on Private International Law and also to Iceland, Ireland, Liechtenstein and Turkey.

Appendix 2

Post Admission Requirements

Formal application to be admitted a General Notary – A qualified notary should complete those relevant parts and omit the remainder of the application on a good quality engrossment paper. If you are a solicitor, admitted in England and Wales you should give the date of your enrolment a solicitor, omit the rest of this section and pass on to the section covering completion of the qualification requirements. It would assist if you could let the Faculty Office have a copy of your current SRA Practising Certificate, as the Faculty Office will be taking up a reference. If you have an objection to the taking of such reference, you should advise the Faculty Office accordingly. Once received, the reference will be added to your formal papers and at that stage, the Faculty Office will be in a position to place the application before the Master of the Faculties for his consideration. You should also let the Faculty Office have either the originals or certified copies of your module/exam results and a note of the name of the notary who is to supervise you in your first two years of notarial practice.

Certificate of Fitness – must be completed by a notary who knows you and is able to give the certificate. It is appropriate for that person to be the same notary who is to supervise you under the requirements of the Notaries (Post-Admission) Rules 2009.

Certificate of Good Character – to be completed by a professional person to whom you are not related and who has known you for at least five years and who is not one of your professional partners, your employer or any employee. Please note that the two certificates cannot be given by the same person.

The fees in respect of the appointment amount to £575.00 and cheques should be made payable to "The Faculty Office". The fees will become due when the Master has formally approved the appointment.

TO: THE RIGHT WORSHIPFUL CHARLES RICHARD GEORGE
ONE OF HER MAJESTY'S COUNSEL
COMISSARY OR MASTER OF THE FACULITIES

APPLICATION AND DECLARATION

I, ...of ....:.........................in the County of
..........................…... hereby apply for appointment as a Public Notary in respect
of which I submit the following information:

{Complete and/or delete as appropriate}

1.   I hold a degree from the University of ....in
(subject) .... which was conferred on [Insert Date]

2.   I am a Solicitor of the Senior Courts of England and Wales and was
admitted and enrolled on [Insert Date].

I hold a current practising certificate which expires on [Insert Date]and I practise
at (address) ....

3.   I am a barrister at law and have been a practice at the Bar of England and
Wales for a period of ....years.

I hold a current practising certificate which expires on (date) ....….............…..
and I practise at (address) ....…..

4.   I formally practised with ....….. (name
of firm/chambers) of (address) ....but ceased to do
so   on   (date)   ....…..
because...

5.   I have been in practise as a Licensed Conveyancer/Associate/Fellow of the
Institute of Legal Executives for a period of ....…..….years

AND that I have satisfied the requirements of Part III of the Notaries
(Qualification) Rules 2013 and evidence thereof is attached hereto

I therefore petition of the Master to appoint and admit me a Notary Public to
practise to all places in England and Wales and I undertake, if so appointed, to
keep myself insured by suitable professional indemnity and fidelity insurance as
may be required, from time to time, buy the Master.

DECLARATION

I understand that a notary is required to be of a good character, honest and trustworthy and I make the following declaration:

1. I have not been convicted of any offence (other than a minor Road Traffic offence);

2. I have not been subject to any disciplinary proceedings, nor are any such proceedings pending against me in respect of my conduct as a member of a profession;

3. I am not aware of any complaint against me being investigated by the professional body of which I am currently a member.

I confirm that the contents of this application and declaration are true and complete.

I consent to enquires being made of any relevant professional or other body to which I belong to verify any matters contained in this application and declaration.

Signed ....

Date ....

SPECIMEN (Engross on good quality paper please)

CERTIFICATE OF FITNESS

TO: THE RIGHT WORSHIPFUL CHARLES RICHARD GEORGE
ONE OF HER MAJESTY'S COUNSEL
COMISSARY OR MASTER OF THE FACULITIES

I, [Full Name] the undersigned Notary Public do HEREBY CERTIFY THAT [name of Applicant] is a literate person now residing at [   ] in the County of [   ] aged [   ] years and upwards and is known to me and I further certify that having made due enquiry s/he is to the best of my knowledge and belief a fit and proper person to be created a Notary Public

Signed:

Notary Public

of

(Full address)

Date:

SPECIMEN (Engross on good quality paper please)

CERTIFICATE OF GOOD CHARACTER

TO: THE RIGHT WORSHIPFUL CHARLES RICHARD GEORGE
ONE OF HER MAJESTY'S COUNSEL
COMISSARY OR MASTER OF THE FACULITIES

I, [   ] of [   ] hereby certify as follows:-

1.   I am *[state occupation]* and a person of good standing and character.

2.   [Name of Applicant] of [place]) ("the Applicant") has been known to me for five years and upwards as (state capacity in which applicant is known) but is not related to me by blood, marriage or adoption. I am not a professional partner, employer or employee of the Applicant.

3.   I understand that the Applicant has applied to be created a Notary Public and that as a Notary Public s/he will hold money on behalf of his/her clients and will have access to confidential papers and documents and will be required to conduct his/her practice in an efficient, responsible and professional manner.

4.   To the best of my knowledge and belief the Applicant is of good character and is honest, reliable, diligent and trustworthy.

5.   I know of no reason why the Applicant should not be created a Notary Public.

Signed ....

Dated ....

Appendix 3

NOTARIES (CONDUCT & DISCIPLINE) RULES 2015
GUIDANCE FOR NOMINATED NOTARIES ISSUED BY THE MASTER OF
THE FACULTIES

Introduction

1) Under rule 8.2 of the Notaries (Conduct and Discipline) Rules 2015 ("the Rules"), where the Registrar receives evidence of or an allegation concerning the conduct or practice of a notary which appears to him to amount to an allegation of Notarial Misconduct he must refer it to a Nominated Notary to investigate the allegation pursuant to rule 8.

2) A Nominated Notary is defined in rule 2.1 as a notary appointed by the Registrar under rule 6 who must be a notary who holds a Notarial Practising Certificate and has held such a Certificate for not less than five years.

3) Under rules 8.2 and 8.3 a Nominated Notary may be appointed by the Registrar to investigate an allegation of Notarial Misconduct referred to him by the Registrar and, if he thinks fit, to prepare and prosecute disciplinary proceedings against a notary in the Court of Faculties ("the Court") and to carry out such other functions as may be provided by the rules. Rule 6.3 requires the Nominated Notary to be independent of, and not personally acquainted with, the notary who is the subject of the investigation.

4) Under rule 24.4 where it comes to the attention of the Registrar that a Relevant Body as defined in rule 24.1 and the Schedule has found a complaint against a notary to be substantiated, the Registrar must appoint a Nominated Notary to investigate it and if he thinks fit, prepare and prosecute disciplinary proceedings as if he were acting under rule 8.

5) Where a notary applies to the Court under rule 25.1 for a review of an Order made under the Rules (or the rules which they replaced) rule 25.4 requires the Registrar to appoint a Nominated Notary to act as respondent to the application. Although it is not so stated the requirement of independence imposed by rule 6.3 must apply equally to a Nominated Notary appointed under rule 25.4

6) Rules 11 to 18 lay down the detailed procedure governing the determination by the Court of complaints of Notarial Misconduct and rule 25 governs the determination of any application by the notary for review of an Order. However, they do not seek to prescribe the manner in which the Nominated Notary should exercise his functions.

7) Experience suggests that it would be helpful to provide Nominated Notaries with some guidance as to the manner in which they should investigate allegations of Notarial Misconduct which have been referred to them under rule 8.2 and the criteria governing their decision whether to institute disciplinary proceedings.

8) It must be emphasised that the guidance which follows is intended to be precisely that. It has no legal status and there may be cases where it is appropriate to depart from it to some extent. It is not intended to fetter the discretion of the Nominated Notary to perform his functions in whatever manner he considers to be fair and just in a particular case. It is not a Practice Direction issued by the Court under rule 18.3. It is believed, however, that it will provide helpful guidance in the large majority of cases. The status of the Nominated Notary.

9) His functions under rule 8.3 are (a) to investigate diligently and expeditiously the allegation of Notarial Misconduct which has been referred to him, (b) to decide whether to make a formal complaint of Notarial Misconduct to the Court, (c) if he decides to do so, to prepare and make such a complaint and (d) to prosecute any such complaint.

10) The role of the Nominated Notary is that of an independent investigator and prosecutor. The need for him to be independent of the notary who is the subject of the investigation is expressed in rule 6.3. He must equally, however, act independently of the Faculty Office. Once the Registrar has referred an allegation to him all decisions about its investigation, the making of a complaint and the manner of its prosecution are made by the Nominated Notary. He should not seek advice from, or consult with, the Faculty Office on these matters. He should not communicate with the Faculty Office except for the purpose of obtaining information or documents necessary for his functions or for purely administrative or procedural purposes. Copies of any such communications should be sent to the notary under investigation.

11) The Registrar is bound by rule 8.2 to refer to a Nominated Notary any evidence or allegation concerning the conduct or practice of a notary "which appears to him to amount to an allegation of Notarial Misconduct". The Registrar's role is limited to deciding on the apparent nature of the allegation. He is not concerned with the question whether it is well founded. The Nominated Notary should not, therefore, assume that, because the allegation has been referred to him, there is necessarily any substance in it. He must approach his investigation with an entirely open mind. Notarial Misconduct.

12) Since the first function of the Nominated Notary is to determine whether an allegation of Notarial Misconduct is well founded the definition of that phrase is obviously critical.

13) It is defined in rule 2.1 as meaning:- "(i) Fraudulent conduct, (ii) Practising as a notary without a valid Practising Certificate or in breach of a condition or limitation imposed on a Practising Certificate, or 3 (iii) Other serious misconduct which may inter alia include failure to observe requirements of these rules or of the Notaries Practice Rules 2014 or falling seriously below the standard of service reasonably to be expected of a notary or persistent failure to provide the standard of service reasonably to be expected of a notary."

335

14) The three specific examples of serious misconduct given in (iii) are not intended to be exhaustive. Any serious misconduct will constitute Notarial Misconduct. The meaning of "serious misconduct" in this context was considered by the Court of Faculties in the case of In the Matter of F (a notary) [2011]. The Court held at paragraph 35 of its decision that serious misconduct includes "conduct connected with the notary's profession in which the notary has fallen seriously short of the standards to be expected of notaries". The investigation

15) The investigation in many cases referred to the Nominated Notary the nature of the allegations will be clear and the facts will appear from the documents to be undisputed. In some cases, particularly where the allegations are made by clients of the notary or other members of the public, it may be less clear what the precise allegations are. Where this is so, it will be useful to try to agree with the complainant a summary of the issues before the notary is asked to address them. Where this has been done, the complainant should be asked to set out this agreed summary in a written statement.

16) There may also be cases where it is clear that other evidence supporting the allegations is likely to be available, either written evidence from witnesses other than the complainant or other documentary evidence. Where this is so, it may save time to try to obtain this evidence before writing to the notary so that he is aware of the full case which he has to address.

17) When he is in a position to do so the Nominated Notary should write to the notary setting out the nature of the allegations made and summarising the evidence on which they are based. Copies of any evidence, including not only formal statements, if any, but also letters from the complainant, and any other documents which may be relied on in support of the allegations, should be sent to the notary.

18) The notary should be required to respond to each allegation, making it clear which facts he admits and which he does not. If there are particular factual issues which the Nominated Notary considers as being of obvious importance he should specifically identify them. He should ordinarily require the notary to provide a copy of his file relating to any transaction giving rise to the allegations and copies of any other documents on which the notary may rely. If appropriate, the notary should be asked to supply any evidence from other witnesses on which he may rely. The time allowed for the notary to respond should be reasonable and realistic, having regard to the complexity of the case, but not unduly relaxed. It is suggested that 28 days should be 4 ample in most cases but it may be reasonable to accede to a request for a short extension of time if a good reason for it is shown.

19) The notary should be warned that, if he fails to respond within the stipulated time (including any extension allowed), the Nominated Notary will proceed to review the case on the evidence before him and reach a decision whether or not to make a formal complaint based on that evidence.

20) The Nominated Notary may wish to raise further queries with the notary arising out of his response or clarify it in some respects. In particular, if the notary has admitted facts which appear to constitute Notarial Misconduct, it may be appropriate to invite him to state any mitigating features or other reasons why a formal complaint should not be made.

21) If, following the notary's response, the basic facts are reasonably clear the Nominated Notary should be in a position to decide whether to make a formal complaint. If the response shows that there may be significant factual issues the Nominated Notary may wish to raise these with the complainant and obtain his comments on them.

22) It may happen that during the investigation evidence emerges which would support an additional or different allegation of Notarial Misconduct. If so, the notary must of course be given a full opportunity to deal with it before a decision is made to make a formal complaint which is based on it.

23) There is no obligation to send a proposed complaint in draft to the notary for his comments but there is no objection to this being done and it will be desirable to do this if the Nominated Notary feels any doubt whether the notary has had a full opportunity to deal with it. It is not appropriate to send the draft complaint to the original complainant or the Faculty Office.

24) In the vast majority of cases this process should be able to be conducted by letter or email but in exceptional cases the Nominated Notary may consider it necessary to interview the complainant, the notary or conceivably others either by telephone or in person. If he does, exceptionally, interview the complainant or other witnesses he should also offer an interview to the notary.

25) The Nominated Notary has power in the course of an investigation to inspect relevant documents of the notary, under rule 6.5, but subject to the restriction of the use of such documents set out in rule 6.6. The decision to make and prepare a complaint

26) Before deciding to make a complaint the Nominated Notary should be satisfied that (a) it is more probable than not that the court would make a finding of Notarial Misconduct, (b) it would be in the public interest for a complaint to be made and (c) there is nothing which would make it an abuse of process to make a complaint. The Nominated Notary should always have at the forefront of his mind the costs involved in 5 any investigation and any subsequent hearing before the Court of Faculties. He should consider not only the costs which he incurs as the Nominated Notary but the costs which may be incurred in defending the complaint. He has a duty to ensure that his investigation is at all times focussed and he should avoid being side-tracked into areas which may not add in any significant way either to the strength of the case or to the seriousness of the conduct complained of against the notary.

27) The standard of proof to be adopted by the Court is dealt with in rule 19. Where the allegation made against the notary involves directly or by implication a finding of fraud, dishonesty or criminal activity on the part of the notary, the Court applies the higher criminal standard of proof when adjudicating on a complaint. In all other cases the Court applies the lower civil, standard of proof.

28) There may be matters which suggest that the public interest, which in this context primarily means the interest in achieving the proper regulation of notaries, does not require a complaint to be made even though it appears more probable than not that the Court would find it proved. Examples of such matters, which are by no means exhaustive, are:- (a) the availability of other means of disposing satisfactorily of the dispute which gave rise to the allegations; (b) that the conduct in question resulted from a mistake or misunderstanding rather than any deliberate wrongdoing; (c) the age and state of health of the notary and any possible impact of the prosecution of a complaint on his health; (d) that the notary is no longer in practice and does not intend to practise again; and (e) that the notary has promptly put right any consequences of his misconduct.

29) Even if some of these factors are present they may of course be outweighed by the seriousness of the allegations. In deciding whether it is in the public interest for a complaint to be made the Nominated Notary may take into account any previous findings of Notarial Misconduct which have been made against the notary by the Court but not previous allegations or complaints which have not resulted in such findings.

30) In exceptional circumstances delay in making the allegations of misconduct may render it unfair and consequently an abuse of process to prosecute a complaint, particularly if the delay has made it more difficult for the notary to contest the allegations. In considering whether he should decide not to make a complaint on this ground the Nominated Notary should take into account the length of the delay, the reasons for it (including in particular the extent to which the notary is responsible for it) and the seriousness of the allegations.

31) If the Nominated Notary decides not to make a complaint to the Court he should give brief reasons for the decision. Such reasons should in particular indicate (a) which one 6 or more of the requirements set out in paragraph 26 above are not satisfied and, in each case, why they are considered not to be satisfied and (b) in cases falling within paragraphs 32 or 33 below, why a departure from the usual presumption that a complaint will be made is considered to be justified.

32) Where a Nominated Notary has been appointed to investigate a matter under rule 24 and the notary has been struck off or suspended from practice by the Relevant Body, a complaint to the Court shall be made unless there are wholly exceptional circumstances which justify not doing so. This is because such a penalty will ordinarily result from serious misconduct.

33) In other matters referred to a Nominated Notary under rule 24.4 a complaint should ordinarily be made to the Court unless there are special reasons for not doing so. The prosecution of the complaint

34) The form of the complaint is prescribed in Form 1 in the Appendix to the Rules. Only a very brief summary of the allegations of Notarial Misconduct should be set out in the complaint itself. The supporting evidence exhibiting all documents relied on should be contained in the witness statement in support.

35) In the conduct of the proceedings the Nominated Notary should not regard himself as representing a party and he should not press for a finding of Notarial Misconduct at all costs. His duty is to place before the Court fairly and impartially all the facts on which the complaint is based and ensure that all relevant evidence is either presented by him or made available to the notary.

36) The procedure adopted for the hearing of a complaint has some similarities to that of a criminal trial. The Nominated Notary should therefore be fully prepared to make an opening statement outlining the case against the notary, call any witness in support of the complaint (see paragraph 41 below) and re-examine the witness where necessary, to cross-examine the notary and any witnesses called on his behalf and to sum up the case after all the evidence has been heard.

37) The Nominated Notary should keep under constant review during the proceedings the question whether he should continue to prosecute the claim. In particular he should review the position when the notary has delivered an answer to the complaint and any witness statement in reply to it. If at any stage he considers that the probability of a finding of Notarial Misconduct has been reduced to below 50% or that it is no longer in the public interest to pursue the complaint he should seek the leave of the Court to withdraw it under rule 15.

38) Subject to obtaining leave of the Court, it is open to the Nominated Notary to amend the complaint at any stage, so long as it does not cause unfairness to the notary against whom the complaint has been made (see the Court of Faculties' ruling on abuse and privilege In the matter of Imison (a notary) [2014] at paragraph 6). 7 Evidence

39) Rule 14 enables the Nominated Notary to have "without prejudice" discussions with the notary with a view to reaching an agreement on facts and issues which can be placed before the Court in the form of an agreed statement. Once the notary has delivered an answer to the complaint and a witness statement in reply to it the Nominated Notary should always consider what scope there may be for reaching agreement on facts and issues. Rule 14 also enables the Nominated Notary and the notary to place before the Court an agreed statement which contains an admission by the notary of Notarial

Misconduct and a proposed sanction and/or offer of redress. When the evidence is complete the Nominated Notary should also consider, particularly in less serious cases where it appears unlikely that the notary would be struck off or suspended from practice, whether it would be appropriate to explore the possibility of proposing to the Court such an agreed disposal.

40) It is not appropriate for the Nominated Notary to express any view about the sanctions which should be imposed upon a notary who has been found guilty of Notarial Misconduct. However, it is not inappropriate for him if the Court requests it, to provide to the Court factual information, including information about possible practice conditions and training courses, which may assist the Court in its decision on sanctions.

41) Where evidence in support of the complaint is to be called, the Commissary is likely, save in exceptional cases, to direct that the written statement of the witness shall be taken as his evidence-in-chief and thereafter the witness can be cross-examined.

42) If the evidence is relevant and admissible, the Nominated Notary may seek to call evidence of previous complaints or prior conduct whether or not the complaint has been proved in disciplinary proceedings. Such evidence is likely to be admissible in, but not restricted to, the following circumstances:- if the parties to the proceedings agree to the evidence being admissible, or it is important explanatory evidence, or it is relevant to an important matter in issue in the instant complaint. For the general principles which will apply, see s.101 etc of the Criminal Justice Act 2003. See also the Court of Faculties' ruling in the matter of Robert JH Ward, a Notary [2015] at paras 4-9.

43) The prior conduct will ordinarily be proved by adducing evidence of the finding of the Court together with an agreed statement of facts. If the previous conduct has not been proved against the notary, then the Nominated Notary will have to call admissible evidence of the prior conduct (see R. v. Z (Prior Acquittal) [2000] 2 A.C.483).

44) In either case, if the Nominated Notary wishes to adduce such evidence he should proceed in the following way. He should inform the notary or his representative and the Court of his intention to adduce such evidence at the earliest opportunity and before the Commissary has given directions under rule 16. If the need for such evidence becomes apparent after directions have been given by the Commissary further directions should be requested. If the notary does not consent to the evidence being adduced, then the Nominated Notary should provide a skeleton argument setting out the 8 evidence and any arguments in favour of its admission and provide it to the notary or his representative and the Court. He should invite the notary to submit a skeleton argument if he wishes to do so. The Commissary will usually decide its admissibility by giving directions in advance of the hearing of the complaint and notify both sides of his decision. It should be understood that this till not

prevent the notary from addressing the Court on its admissibility at the hearing if the preliminary ruling went against him. Only in exceptional circumstances would it be right for the Nominated Notary to seek to re-open the issue of admissibility at the hearing.

45) It will not be competent for the Nominated Notary to make unspecific and/or unsupported allegations of previous misconduct at a hearing or to adduce evidence of prior misconduct which bears no relevance to the issues to be decided in the instant complaint.

46) Where a Nominated Notary is appointed as respondent following an application by a notary for a review of an Order his functions are described in rule 25.9 as being "…to ensure that the applicant is put to proof of his case and to bring to the attention of the Court all such facts and matters as the Respondent thinks should be before the court…". He need not lodge a written statement but, if he wishes to do so, under rule 25.9, he must do so at least 28 days before the hearing. He clearly should present a written statement if he intends to rely on facts not contained in the applicant's evidence.

47) What is said above about the general role of the Nominated Notary in relation to complaints applies equally to applications for a review. It is his function to ensure that any such application is scrutinised thoroughly and critically and to consider whether the notary has proved that there has been a relevant change in circumstances since the Order was made and it would not be contrary to the public interest for the Order to be reviewed, see rule 25.2. He needs to take into account in addition to evidence of changes of circumstances all the evidence which was before the Court which made the Order, see rule 25.10. If he considers at any stage that there is no ground for objecting to a review he should inform the Court of this.

48) Professional advice - In the great majority of cases the Nominated Notary will have the experience and expertise to perform all his functions without other professional assistance. There may, however, be rare cases where he needs help from a solicitor in interviewing witnesses or assembling the evidence. There may also be rare cases where he needs specialist advice from a solicitor or barrister on questions of law which have arisen during his consideration of the case.

49) The Rules permit any party to be represented at the hearing by a notary, a solicitor or counsel. There could be rare cases of sufficient complexity to justify the Nominated 9 Notary instructing a specialist advocate, whether a solicitor or counsel, to represent him at the hearing, but this requires leave of the Court.

50) The instruction by the Nominated Notary of other professionals to advise or represent him will have financial implications which are mentioned in the following paragraphs. Costs

51) Costs - Rule 23.3 provides that an order for costs will not be made against the Nominated Notary who is always entitled to an order for costs to be paid out of the Contingency Fund. The amount of such costs is prescribed in Part IV of the Notaries (Conduct and Discipline) Fees and Costs Order 2015 ('the Fees and Costs Order'). The Nominated Notary should provide the Court at the end of the hearing with a schedule of the costs claimed by him.

52) Where an investigation does not lead to the issue of a complaint, rule 23.5 provides that the Nominated Notary is entitled to be paid out of the Contingency Fund such fixed fee as has been previously authorised by the Registrar or such fee as the Registrar may determine should be paid for work properly done after considering a bill and other representations by the Nominated Notary.

53) Rule 4.2 of the Fees and Costs Order requires the Nominated Notary to obtain the leave of the Court before instructing a litigator or advocate to assist him in his functions or representing him at the hearing. If he incurs expenditure under rule 4.2 in instructing such persons without authority it will not be recoverable by him out of the Contingency Fund. If leave of the Court is given, rule 4.2 of the Fees and Costs Order provides that the fees of persons instructed are those prescribed in Part V.

CHARLES GEORGE QC Master of the Court of Faculties
14 January 2016

BIBLIOGRAPHY

1. The Faculty Office website

2. The Legal Ombudsman Website

3. The National Archives Website

4. Foreign and Commonwealth Office Website

5. Cheeswrights Website

6. The General Notary by Tony Dunford, The Notaries Society 1999

7. Brookes Notary by N P Ready, Sweet & Maxwell 13th Edition

8. The Notaries Society Website

9. The Scriveners Society Website

10. HCCH Website

11. The Civil Law Notary- Neutral Lawyer for the Situation, Peter Murray, Verlag C.H.Beck Munchen 2010

SPG Charity

Make the difference...

Helping one person might not change the world, but it could change the world for one person. SPG Charity supports various registered charities in the UK.

Get involved and make a big impact with a small contribution

You can make the difference. Please consider donating to SPG Charity.

Account Name: SPG Charity
Bank: HSBC
Account Number: 91586963
Sort Code: 40-28-03
or send a cheque payable to **SPG Charity** to
219 Bramcote Lane, Wollaton, Nottingham, NG8 2QL, UK

SPG Charity has supported UK Cancer Research, Macmillan Cancer Support, Great Ormond Street Hospital, Crohn's & Colitis UK and Hindu Temples in Nottingham & Leicester.